MW00531710

The Athlete

Greatness, Grace and the Unprecedented Life of Charlie Ward

Jon Finkel

Thanks for reading!

Published in the United States by JF Publishing.

Presented by:
The National Football Foundation & College Football
Hall of Fame

www.jonfinkel.com

ISBN: 978-0-9986273-2-8 (Hardcover)
978-0-9986273-3-5 (Paperback)

Book Design by: Clark Kenyon

Cover Design by: Kinsey Stewart

Florida State Football Photo: Ryals Lee

New York Knicks Photo: Dave Saffran/MSG Photos

First Edition

To Reese and Grant,

May you both live your own unprecedented and unparalleled lives.

Table of Contents

Prologue

Charlie Ward's 1993 Heisman Trophy isn't displayed in a glitzy case at Doak Campbell Stadium on the campus of Florida State University. It's also not in the school's hall of fame building like Gino Torretta's at the University of Miami, or at his parents' house like fellow Heisman winners Cam Newton, Mark Ingram, Tim Tebow and a slew of others. It's not even in his own house like Sam Bradford's or Matt Leinart's or Andre Ware's awards. And it's certainly not in a Buffalo Wild Wings restaurant like Ron Dayne's.

No, Charlie Ward's Heisman Trophy is in one of the most unlikely, unsuspecting places you would ever expect an award of its magnitude to be. If you're imagining a location like the Downtown Athletic Club in lower Manhattan, where the award originated, or the Broadway address in New York City where the award is currently presented, think again. Even if you think of the complete opposite type of venue, you probably still won't be getting warmer to his Heisman's permanent home.

Once you begin studying Charlie and the Ward family, however, and you get to know them and talk to them, you quickly understand that the chosen location of Charlie's Heisman is the most Charlie thing ever, or rather, the most 'Junior' thing ever. (In Ward's hometown of Thomasville, Georgia, the name *Charlie* refers to his father, Charlie Ward Sr., while the Charlie Ward of national championship, New York Knicks and Heisman Trophy fame, and the most famous resident in the town's 192-year history, simply goes by Junior.)

If you're now guessing that Charlie's Heisman is in Georgia, you're getting warmer.

• • •

Most of the 35-mile road from Tallahassee International Airport to Thomasville is lined with centuries-old oak trees standing guard along the highway, with thick, outstretched limbs flexing toward the sky. The branches themselves are the size of small trees, with bushy, white-green beards of Spanish moss tumbling toward the ground. Halfway through the trip you cross the state line from Florida to Georgia and are greeted by this sign:

WELCOME. WE'RE GLAD GEORGIA'S ON YOUR MIND.

It's a nice sentiment, but one that you can imagine a seventeen- or eighteen-year-old Charlie Ward viewing in 1989 as a subtle recruiting nudge from his home state.

The ratio of pick-up trucks to cars on this stretch of US-319 is easily two-to-one, and road signs tout a rotating selection of churches and plantations with names like Pebble Hill and Longpine. About fifteen minutes before you reach Thomasville, you pass Sinkola Plantation, where Charlie Ward Sr. was born on July 20th, 1939 in what's known as the Red Hills Region of Georgia. In contrast to the heavy, thick oaks on the highway, Sinkola is populated by thousands of pine trees that jut out of the ground and spike the sky.

The last stretch of 319 leads directly into the heart of Thomasville's downtown area, North Broad Street. Local, southern restaurants sit on either side of the red-brick road. Jonah's Fish & Grits. Savannah Moon Bakery and Café. Grassroots Coffee. Chophouse on the Bricks. The avenue is so perfectly Anytown, USA that it was actually honored by the National Trust Main Street Center as being an official *Great American Main Street.*

Past the independent bookstore and clothing store and drug store, Broad Street hits Jefferson and the municipal part of town. There's the Thomasville National Bank, the Thomas County Tax Collector's Office (with its own clock tower and bells), the First Baptist Church (which takes up a whole city block), and slightly to the southwest, the Thomas County Public Library.

Your search for the Heisman Trophy is warming up.

• • •

The entryway to the Thomas County Public Library holds no surprises and the design of the interior is standard-issue: beige floors, brown-paneled registration desk, wood-backed and cloth-cushioned reading chairs, metal book shelves, newspaper and magazine racks…it's all there as it should be, with no pedestals or spotlights showcasing the most prestigious award in college football.

Off to the right, beyond a small reading area, sits rows of fiction, non-fiction and reference book shelves lined up like dominos in the classic library layout. There's a fairly comprehensive sports book and sports reference section by the windows, including the hard-to-find 1984 classic, *The Heisman: A Symbol of Excellence* by John T. Brady, which documents the life of John W. Heisman (who the award is named after), the history of the award and its first fifty or so winners.

The book is filled with photos of Heisman winners sharing the spotlight with icons like John Wayne and presidents like John F. Kennedy. It features photos of ticket stubs, old programs and former emcees of the award presentation. It tells you everything you need to know, really, but a substitute for laying eyes on an actual Heisman Trophy it is not.

As you make your way back to the registration desk, you realize there's only one other room in the library you haven't been to, so that's where you head, toward the giant, multi-colored sign that reads in comic-sans font: CHILDREN.

The trophy can't be in there, can it? In the kids room?

This is the trophy of Bo Jackson and Barry Sanders; Herschel Walker and Archie Griffin (twice) and Roger Staubach and the Old Ball Coach, Steve Spurrier. Davey O'Brien and Danny Wuerffel won the award and now have their own awards named after them.

Is THE Heisman Trophy really in the children's reading room of a public library in a small Georgia town?

Yes, yes it is.

Just beyond a row of kids computer stations, a small play area, the story room and a round wooden table, and sitting right next to a windowsill of stuffed zoo animals, is a five-foot-tall display case featuring Charlie Ward's

Heisman Trophy, a framed picture of him holding the award, a jersey, and, if you look closely, a New York Knicks basketball card for good measure.

Far from the cottage industry of books written by Ward's coach at Florida State, Bobby Bowden, that reside across the library in the aforementioned sports section, Ward's display case sits three feet from well-read copies of *Giraffes Can't Dance, Hannah and the Seven Dresses* and books about a far more popular *Bobby* with this demographic, *Bob the Builder.*

A framed white piece of paper that lists all of Charlie's accomplishments in his final year at Florida State sits on top of the display case. It's printed in about 10-point type to fit everything on a single page: *Heisman Winner, AAU Sullivan Award Winner, Davey O'Brien Award Winner, Johnny Unitas Golden Arm Winner, Walter Camp Player of the Year, Chevrolet Offensive Player of the Year, Scripps Howard Player of the Year, ACC Player of the Year, Toyota Leader of the Year, The Sporting News Player of the Year, UPI Player of the Year, ACC Offensive Player of the Year and the Football News Offensive Player of the Year.*

Next to that frame is a quote from Ward on a piece of paper taped to the wall.

One way to get a quality education is to read what you don't want and do what you'd rather not.

In front of that sits a small vertical plaque making the same request that librarians have made of their patrons since the very first library opened its doors:

Speak Quietly Please.

This last sign is almost an inside joke among those who know Ward, because whether you talk to his NBA coach Jeff Van Gundy, his college football coaches Bobby Bowden and Mark Richt, his college basketball coach Pat Kennedy, or any of his teammates, friends or family, the number one word they use to describe Charlie is *quiet.* That his Heisman Trophy case has a sign asking others to speak quietly is beyond perfect.

It's also necessary.

The display, which showcases an award won twenty-five years ago, still draws handfuls of visitors almost every weekend, with most of them not carrying Thomas County Library cards.

"You can always tell when someone's looking for the trophy and they're not from here," says Melissa Denham, a Thomas County librarian who works in the children's section on the weekends. "It's usually an adult or two who wanders into the kids section wearing a Florida State shirt or hat. They come over to us and ask about the trophy and Charlie."

Essentially, it puts the library on the map, turning Charlie's Seminole moment into a seminal moment for traveling FSU fans.

But how did it end up here?

Longtime Thomasville resident Randy Young, who is the radio voice for Central High School football, where Charlie played, and was also coached by Charlie Sr. when he was in high school, says that the location of the trophy is vintage Ward.

"It fits him and his family perfectly," Young says. "They've always been such community-oriented people. I'm sure they looked at that award as the culmination of work put in by all his coaches, his high school teammates, his college teammates and everyone along the way who helped clear the path for Junior's success."

In southern Georgia, as in other parts of the country where football is the focal point of the community, when something as significant as the Heisman is bestowed on a hometown hero, it feels like it is bestowed on the entire town.

"We had a Heisman rally for Junior after he won," Young says. "Three thousand people crammed into his high school gym to see him. It validated everything we all believed about him. We knew he was special, and Charlie felt that connection. I'm sure that played into his decision to put the award in a public place in Thomasville where anyone can see it. Being the coach's son that he is, he sees the importance of an award like that and knows that it's bigger than him. I'm sure he was thinking about what he could do with it to help other people, and having it sit in the kids library will inspire other kids to chase their own dreams."

Later on, at Ward's parents' house on Heisman Way (we'll get into that later), about six minutes from the library, Ward smiles at the thought of his trophy on display next to *Dora the Explorer* books and plush farm animals. Yes, he put the trophy there for all the reasons Young described, including to inspire kids, but with Ward, there are always several other layers of thought that go into his decisions. In this case, practicality and a nod to family.

"When I got the trophy, my first thought was to give it to my parents," he says, standing in their living room. "But everyone knows them and I didn't want people showing up at their door at all hours to look at it. I also didn't want anyone to try to break in to get it, so I wanted a public place that was secure, where anyone could look at it. Add that to the fact that my mom was a librarian and my dad was a teacher and coach, the kids library is the perfect place to honor their careers and let everyone see it."

See, the most Junior thing ever.

Chapter 1

Meet the Wards

Florida A&M University • Introduction to Education 101 • September 1958

A sophomore girl is sitting with her friend in a large college classroom. With only a few minutes left in the period, her teacher, Reverend Cunningham, randomly selects her to be in charge of a committee to master one of the chapters in their textbook.

This presents a challenge because the girl is admittedly on the quiet side and chairing a committee isn't really her thing. Reverend Cunningham then selects other people to be in charge of other chapters and tells the remaining students to volunteer for the open spots in each group. The girl, Willard, is momentarily relieved when her friend Phyllis agrees to join her, but the joy is fleeting when, eyeing the two empty chairs in front of two cute girls, a football player and his friend saunter over to fill out their four-person committee. The football player is huge. The other guy is just over six feet tall but wouldn't weigh 170 pounds holding a cinder block.

"Ugh," Willard groans to Phyllis as they approach. "A football player. You know how football players are."

"Yeah, we're gonna have to do all the work," Phyllis says.

"Yup," Willard whispers as the boys get closer. "He isn't going to do a thing. Aren't we lucky."

"I think they're both on the football team," Phyllis says quickly.

"The shorter one can't be," Willard answers. "He's too scrawny."

The girls share a quick smirk as the boys finally sit down, leading to the usual awkward pause between just-met college coeds. Willard, taking her chairmanship seriously, breaks the silence by setting up the team's first out-of-class meeting for the following day in her dormitory. The guys agree to be there.

The next day, Willard is standing in the foyer of her dorm with Phyllis, looking at the clock on the wall. She's finding herself irritated already. They're supposed to meet in one minute and the guys aren't there.

"We should just start because you know they aren't coming," Willard says. "You sure the skinny one plays football? He's too little."

"I'm pretty sure," Phyllis says.

"Let's just get started," Willard says. "They aren't gonna show."

Practically before she can finish her sentence the big guy and the skinny guy walk in. A twinge of guilt creeps into the back of her head. *Was she wrong about them?*

"You're here," she says, trying not to act surprised.

"Of course," the skinny one says. "We said we would be."

She leads them to the study room in the basement, and when she points out the table they're going to work at both young men get there first and pull over chairs for the girls.

"Hmmm," she says to herself. *"They're polite. This is interesting."*

"We didn't have time to introduce ourselves at the end of class, so I thought we'd start with that," Willard says to the skinny guy sitting across from her. "Phyllis is from Key West and I went to private school in Jacksonville for four years, and then South Carolina for one before FAMU. All I know is that your name is Charlie."

"Yes, Charlie Ward from Thomasville, Georgia," the skinny guy says. "I play football here."

"Interesting," Willard says.

The study session goes along smoothly and the boys are willing and eager to divide up the work equally. As the minutes pass, Willard finds herself more and more impressed with the boys, particularly the shorter one. She's also itching for the meeting to end because one of her fellow sorority pledges is from Thomasville so she must be able to give Willard the skinny on Charlie.

When the meeting is finally over, Willard races to her friend's room to ask about him.

"Do you know Charlie Ward?" she asks.

"Oh, yes!" her friend says. "He's a great football player and basketball player, and he's a real nice boy."

• • •

Fifty-one years later, sitting on the couch of the trophy room dedicated to the accomplishments of Junior, their five other children and their many grandchildren, Willard Ward shakes her head looking at Charlie Ward Sr.

"He was so skinny," she says. "I truly didn't believe that he could play football for FAMU."

Charlie Sr. laughs.

"I was skinny," he says with a twinkle in his eye. "But I was good."

"After that first committee meeting, we didn't start seeing each other yet because at that time he had so many girlfriends. He was the ladies man on campus," Willard says.

Charlie Sr. shrugs and smiles.

"That one's true too," he says sheepishly, patting Willard on the knee.

Following that first study session Charlie Sr. and Willard continued to talk and very soon Charlie had no use for any other girls. Within a year, they were getting serious and Willard expected Charlie to bring her a ring signifying their relationship heading into their senior year.

"We were very involved at that time, and back then it was customary for a girl to get a ring from her boyfriend if things were serious," Willard explains. "Well, he came back from summer break after our junior year and he didn't give me a ring. So for a minute I thought he was just trying to string me along."

Turns out Charlie Sr. gave the money he had saved up for a ring to his mom and sister to help out with some bills around the house.

"And I wasn't sure if she was serious about me either," he says. "I didn't know if she had changed her mind about me or anything. I wasn't going to spend my money on a ring and come back to school and find out she changed her mind."

"But we got it sorted out," Willard says. "And he went back to his mom and sister and they gave him the money and we went together to pick out the ring. We got this really nice, cute little ring that I wore for fifty years."

With the ring situation squared away, the next step was the big one: marriage.

But for that to take place, Charlie Sr. would have to get Willard's father's blessing. Fortunately, he was a football fan.

"My dad loved sports," she says. "Football in particular. Once he got to know Charlie he loved watching him play ball. When he first met him he was very guarded, of course, because he was protecting his daughter. He even asked around about Charlie to find out what kind of person he was."

Charlie passed the initial test, but almost failed the second one.

Once he knew he wanted to marry Willard, he sat down to compose a letter to her father to ask his permission to propose. He drew upon every ounce of literary muscle he could muster and poured his heart into the letter. He rehearsed it, rewrote it and rewrote it again. When he was finally happy with it, he put it in the mail and… nothing.

One week passed. Then two. Then three. No phone call. No letter. No response.

"I didn't know what was going on," Charlie Sr. says. "But then I heard he was coming up for a football game so I figured I'd talk to him after that and get an answer one way or the other."

Gameday arrived, and not only did Charlie have a challenge ahead of him on the field that day, but he knew that off the field waiting was a nerve-wracking conversation with the man he hoped would be his future father-in-law.

"I got beat up good that game," Charlie Sr. says.

"He got his teeth knocked out," Willard says.

The scene sets up like this:

The game ends and Willard's father has to head home, which means if Charlie Sr. wants to talk to him—and he very badly does—he doesn't have time to change out of his uniform, let alone shower. He's also missing a bunch of teeth. And the only place they can get some privacy to talk is in Willard's dad's car.

Charlie Sr. doesn't want to let her father drive off without talking to him, so he takes off his pads, puts his jersey back on and gets in the back seat of the car. He's hot. He's hurt. He's sweaty.

"And he stunk from having just come off the field," Willard says.

"I sat there for a minute and finally said, 'Sir, I wrote you a letter asking about your daughter's hand in marriage,'" Charlie Sr. says. "Did you get it?"

"Then my dad told him, 'I don't give away my daughter's hand in marriage with no letter,'" Willard says, delighting in the moment. "You've got to ask me in person."

"And that's what I did right then and there," Charlie Sr. says. "Sweat-covered and all. He gave me permission."

"After Charlie left the car my dad told me, probably joking, that he didn't care if I graduated in the morning and walked down the aisle in the afternoon, as long as I didn't get married until after I had my degree," Willard says. "And I basically did that. We graduated on April 18th and got married on April 25th.

That's how the boy she assumed too skinny to play football, the boy who was dating too many other girls at the time to consider, and the boy who she didn't want to team with in fear of being stuck with all the work, became her husband less than three years after their first meeting.

Chapter 2

Senior

At 70, Charlie Ward Sr. hasn't put on a helmet and pads in five decades, but the former FAMU football star still moves through space cooler and more confidently than a man half his age. The athlete's glide, like his jump shot or punching power, is the last to go.

On this particular day, he's wearing a buttoned-up beige short-sleeve shirt with the Houston Rockets logo on it—a remnant of Junior's playing and coaching days with the team. He's lanky, with long limbs and long fingers and a long stride. His hair is white, and at certain moments he looks like a shorter version of Boston Celtics legend and NBA Hall of Famer Bill Russell. The conversation we're having is about the athletic genes that course through the Ward family tree.

"Junior's great grandmother on my side was a good little basketball player," Charlie Sr. says. "I remember being a kid watching her play on a dirt court growing up. That was a long time ago but I know she could play. My father was a great baseball player. He was a really strong pitcher; could throw in the 80s. Willard's dad was an excellent baseball player too. And Junior's maternal grandmother was a terrific tennis player. The whole family used to talk about it. She could beat anyone. There's no doubt about it, Junior has a good amount of athletic genes in him. There's no shortage of athletes in this family, that's for sure."

We're sitting on a couch in the center of the trophy room at the Wards' house in Thomasville, surrounded by some of Junior's most impressive hardware, including the Davey O'Brien Trophy, the Johnny Unitas Golden Arm Award, the ACC Player of the Year Award, signed New York Knicks basketball shoes, a National Championship Trophy and helmet, and too many other items to count. In all, there are five floor-to-ceiling shelving units jam-packed with awards; three of them are dedicated to Charlie Ward Jr. and the other two are shared by the rest of the family, which includes Junior's siblings and a host of grandkids. Those shelves are filled to the edges as well.

Sprinkled amongst the memorabilia on the shelving unit farthest to the right, and sitting between Knicks Eastern Conference Champions rally towels from 1999, an Orange Bowl trophy from 1993 and several encased footballs, are a host of items belonging to another athlete in the family, Charlie Sr. There is a reunion photo of his 1963 Florida A&M football team and, incredibly, a framed photo of him posing in uniform mimicking the famous trophy his son would win roughly thirty years later.

"The first Ward to think about the Heisman trophy was me," Charlie Sr. says, laughing. "I remember Ernie Davis from Syracuse won it when I was playing in college. You know, at first my dad wouldn't even let me play football. I had to beg and beg every year until he finally let me play when I got to high school. That's why I played so many other sports—and you know what, I was good at all of them. That's the truth."

When you ask him which sports he played, his eyes light up and a smile spreads across his face as if he's been waiting all day for the question.

"Pick one and I'll tell you," he says with a twinkle in his eye.

Basketball?

"I started varsity in the ninth grade," he says.

Track?

"Oooh, I couldn't be beat."

Swimming?

"If you swim against me I'll beat you, and if you're ahead of me I'll catch you. I was a lifeguard and I could save anyone," he says. "Swimming might have been my best sport."

Golf?

"I learned to play at age eleven. I caddied at a private country club here in Thomasville, and in my heyday I was a barely over-par shooter."

Diving?

"Oh yeah. I could do a two-and-a-half flip, no problem."

In the brief moment between thinking of another sport, Charlie Sr. chimes back in about football.

"Even in football I played several positions," he says. "I was the quarterback, punter, kickoff returner and safety in high school. The funny thing about it is I could have played golf and been on the swim team at a bunch of other colleges, but football paid for me to go to school so I went with that, and in 1959 I accepted a scholarship at Florida A&M."

Examining the weight and signifigance of that scholarship in the context of the modern college football landscape is impossible. To understand the gravity of the offer, and the tumultuous times in which Senior accepted it, we must revisit the Deep South in the middle of the twentieth century, when segregation was rampant and options for blue chip African-American athletes were severely limited.

• • •

"Imagine the African-American talent in the Deep South not being able to attend the Alabamas, the Floridas, the Florida States or the Georgias of the world," Alvin Hollins Jr., the Assistant Sports Information Director for Florida A&M wrote me in one of our e-mail exchanges about Charlie Sr.'s time at FAMU. "It was an embarrassment of riches in a sense in that era for Historically Black Colleges and Universities like Florida A&M. Most of the better teams overwhelmed you with their quality and depth, much like a modern day Florida or Ohio State. Remember the late, great 'Deacon' Jones? FAMU was so stocked with talent during the (coach) Jake Gaither Era (1945-1969) that Jones was turned away and ended up at South Carolina State."

Perhaps the year that best illustrates the level of talent at FAMU is the 1961 team, which won all ten of its games by an average score of 51-3. That team was so talented that "Bullet" Bob Hayes, an eventual Olympic champion, Super Bowl Champion and NFL Hall of Famer with the Dallas Cowboys, was a back-up.

"Gaither recruited the combined eventual talent pools of Miami, Florida State and Florida at one school," author and cultural critic Bijan C.

Bayne recalls. "They won their first six games in '61 by an average of 71-1. Not only did they have Hayes on the bench, but they had three sprinters on that one team who ran 9.3 seconds or faster in the 100-yard dash."

Essentially, Gaither had an Olympic-caliber 4x100 relay team in his backfield with the alternates as his wide receivers. Just as any team in Major League Baseball in the early '50s could have chosen to break the color barrier and stack their roster with Willie Mays, Ernie Banks, Jackie Robinson and Satchel Paige all at the same time, any of the major programs that now dominate the Southeastern Conference or Atlantic Coast Conference could have done the same thing in regards to recruiting African-American college athletes.

But they didn't.

The intended consequence of this, of course, was to keep African-Americans from attending state schools and to keep them segregated. One of the unintended consequences, however, was that the Historically Black Colleges and Universities in the south, like Eddie Robinson's Grambling State University in Louisiana and Gaither's Florida A&M, had a seemingly endless supply of what would be called modern five-star recruits to choose from with a limited number of roster spots to give out each year.

At Grambling, Hall of Fame Coach Eddie Robinson had African-American players begging to play for him. They wrote him letters. They sent him report cards. They sent him their stats and sprinting times. With no access to the major programs, they wanted to be a part of something great and to follow a great man. For many young African-American men in Louisiana and the surrounding states, Robinson was that man and gave them that chance.

On the heels of what Robinson was building, Gaither began laying the foundation for his own legacy at FAMU in Tallahassee.

The season before Gaither's arrival, the team had a record of 2-4-1 with a roster of small players who played on a small patch of grass in a small town. Twenty-four years later he'd leave with a career record of 203-36-4, three undefeated seasons, a bunch of championships and dozens of players in the National Football League.

In terms of his recruiting strategy, the Gaither Network is described perfectly in Samuel G. Freedman's excellent book, *Breaking the Line*, and it's worth quoting at length:

> Early in the football season of 1953, Jake Gaither composed a letter to a former player named Bradley Mitchell. After starting for several years at split end for Florida A&M, Mitchell had graduated with a degree in industrial education and taken a job teaching and coaching in West Palm Beach. "Here is what I want you to do," Gaither wrote. "Send me the drop on your best boys. I don't want any whom you are in doubt about. I only want your exceptional boys." Mindful of the recent armistice ending the Korean War, Gaither added, "Include any boys who might be coming back from the service." And then, in an apparent reference to divisive internal politics at Mitchell's high school, the coach offered some advice: "Take care of yourself. Be tactful in every respect. Keep your mouth shut. Do your work. Keep out of trouble."
>
> That letter served as a kind of Rosetta Stone, a decoding ring, for the man Jake Gaither was becoming in midcentury Florida A&M. Appointed head coach in 1945, he went 9-1 in his opening season, beginning the Rattlers' six-year reign as conference champions... More than establishing excellence—indeed, dominance—on the field, Gaither efficiently set himself at the hub of a wheel that extended the length and breadth of Florida. The Gaither network reached 750 miles from Pensacola to Jacksonville to Miami, wherever black people lived, worked, went to church, attended school, and, most important, coached or played football."

This is the backdrop into which Charlie Ward Sr. was recruited to Florida A&M. Not only did he have to possess the elite physical talent to make the roster, he had to have the traits of what Gaither called a 'hungry boy', explained in *Breaking the Line*:

> "I don't mean hungry for food in his stomach and clothes on his back," Gaither once said of such boys. "But hungry for recognition, hungry for satisfaction of ego, hungry to be recognized as 'I'm somebody.' I love to deal with the hungry boy."

In addition to the above desire, Gaither liked young men who were, in his now-famous phrase that has been stolen by every single high school football coach in America since: "agile, mobile and hostile."

Also, violent.

In an Associated Press story that ran in several papers on November 3 of 1969, on the eve of a game in which Gaither's team was playing Southern University for his two hundredth win, a reporter sat with him to discuss the kind of young men he recruited that enabled him to reach such a milestone. The piece was titled, appropriately, *Jake Gaither Loves Violence.*

Among his tremendous quotes in the piece are these:

"I like players with the desire to destroy. Don't give me these good-natured kids. I like fighters, hitters...winners."

"Just imagine you had a hunting dog. You tie him up Thursday and don't feed him all day. Then, when ready to go hunting on Friday, you lift his tail and squirt a little turpentine to make him mad. Point him in the right direction and let him go. That, my friend, is mobile."

"I like my players to have a mean streak. I don't want 'em knocking somebody down and then apologizing for it. They should knock an opponent down and stand over him saying, 'I'll eat you alive if you come this way again'. You've got to make that opponent wish he was never born."

"Football is a game of dangers. I want players to be the leather-popping daredevil types who ask no quarter and give none."

To top it off, each year Gaither had so much talent on his teams that he assembled a rotation of three starting line-ups and named them, appropriately, 'Blood', 'Sweat' and 'Tears'.

And not once did he apologize for running up a score on an inferior opponent.

"You kill a mosquito with an axe," he was famously quoted as saying when asked about that very topic.

All of this is to say that for Charlie Ward Sr. to be offered a scholarship to Florida A&M in 1959, we're talking about, relatively speaking, a school whose roster was as tough to crack as a modern-day Alabama or Michigan.

• • •

Charlie Sr. was recruited by Gaither to play quarterback, but he admits that at the time he was very raw and was mostly relying on his athleticism.

"You know Louisville's quarterback Lamar Jackson who won the Heisman Trophy in 2017?" he asks. "You're looking at him. I played just like him. When I saw him play Florida State and they couldn't tackle him and then were *afraid* to try to tackle him late in the game, that was me in high school. That's exactly how I played."

Unfortunately, Charlie Sr. never got to lace up as a quarterback for the Rattlers because he broke his leg before his freshman year. The team finished 9-1.

At the time, FAMU played single platoon football, meaning the starting groups played both ways and rotated between Gaither's Blood, Sweat and Tears units.

"When I got back after my injury I became a halfback," Charlie Sr. said. "But I started right away."

Due to the platoon system and shared playing time, the stats for many of Gaither's players were never as eye-popping as the team's records, and they weren't a great indication of the player's individual speed and ability on the field.

Point-in-fact, according to the media guides from the early 1960s: In 1961 Charlie Sr. rushed for 167 yards and three touchdowns on sixteen carries, had two receptions for 42 yards, three punt returns for 62 yards and one interception with a 22-yard return.

"I was a team player and I did whatever needed to be done out there," he said. "I was a quick learner and had the skills to play anywhere on the field, so I did everything coach asked of me."

Charlie Sr. wasn't alone.

That 1961 Florida A&M team has gone down in school and college football history as one of the most unstoppable, talented teams the game has ever seen.

In a special 30th anniversary feature celebrating the '61 team, called *"Gaither's Best"* for the *Tallahassee Democrat* on November 2 of 1991, the writer, David Lee Simmons, caught up with a then 88-year-old Gaither and some of the players from that team to reminisce.

"Florida A&M's 1961 team was indomitable and unbeatable," Simmons wrote to open the piece. "A gifted group of athletes lashed together by Jake Gaither and his staff, mental toughness and a togetherness born of the stormy racial climate of the time."

Over the course of that ten-game undefeated season, the Rattlers outscored their opponents 506-33.

"Certainly, it was the greatest team we ever had," Gaither said in the article. "They represented the type of team we wanted to present."

Charles Hobbs, a guard on the team and eventual Director of Housing for FAMU, was also interviewed in the piece and spoke particularly about that squad's unity.

"When you talk about the closeness of the team, this was at a period of time when the climate throughout America was not good, especially for black people," Hobbs said. "In those early 1960s, when racial hatred and animosity was so strong, Jake Gaither and the Rattlers offered black people a shining ray of hope. Everybody loves a winner."

And FAMU won. A lot.

Not only did the 1961 Rattlers go undefeated, score half a thousand points, beat their rival Jackson State in the Orange Blossom Classic and win a fifth conference championship, their team was filled with talent that would succeed at the next level.

"Roughly half of the starters on the '61 team went to the National Football League," Simmons wrote. "Bob Hayes starred for eleven seasons with the Dallas Cowboys. Fullback Hewritt Dixon played ten years with the Oakland Raiders. Alfred Denson played three different receiving positions for the Denver Broncos."

There were several others, including James Tullis, who played for the Chicago Bears and, if not for a leg injury his senior year, Charlie Ward Sr.

"I had really strong seasons after that '61 title year," Charlie Sr. said.

According to the FAMU media guides, in 1962 Ward rushed for 177 yards on 39 carries and three touchdowns, while also scoring on eight of nine two-point conversion attempts for a total of 34 points. He had one reception for ten yards, two kickoff returns for twenty-four yards and one pass interception.

In 1963, he rushed for 150 yards on 39 carries with two touchdowns, while scoring on five two-point conversions for twenty-two total points. He had one catch and one interception that year as well.

"Even the 'feature' backs in those days rarely ran for more than 500-600 yards," Hollins wrote me. "Despite all the NFL talent, there was only one 1,000-yard rusher from that era, Willie Galimore, who did it in 1953. FAMU didn't have another one until Ike Williams did it in 1978."

And yet, about fifty players from the Gaither years were drafted by NFL teams.

"Before I hurt my leg I was told that the Cowboys were seriously looking at me," Charlie Sr. says. "My injury was either an MCL or ACL tear, and nowadays I'd have been back on the field or at least back to 100% in less than a year. Back then, that was it. My career was over. It hurt because the injury happened in our last game. I remember after my injury the guys saw me in the whirlpool in the locker room at halftime and they said, 'We need you, man.' But when I got out I couldn't walk. That was the end for me as a player."

Without that injury, who knows? Maybe Charlie Sr. would have played for the Cowboys and the Wards would have raised their family in Texas, and Junior would have grown up a die-hard Texas Longhorns fan and become a Texas legend, and then maybe he doesn't bring Bobby Bowden and FSU to the promised land and they're still snake-bitten to this day when it comes to big games.

Or maybe if his dad played in the NFL he would have decided to play in the NFL like him and he'd have never played in the NBA.

Or Senior could have been traded to an NFL team in the Northeast like the Giants or Eagles and Junior would've been inclined to escape the cold weather inside the basketball gym and dropped football altogether.

And it's possible that if Senior had a long NFL career he may not have started coaching, and Junior wouldn't have spent his formative years in gyms and on football fields tagging along with his dad/coach and his players and maybe he wouldn't have had such a high sports IQ and he wouldn't have been as good.

It's all speculation, but you can't help but think how different the trajectory of the Wards' lives (and FSU's program) may have been if Charlie Sr. had success playing in the NFL. With so many of his teammates having had pro careers, it certainly wasn't out of the question.

• • •

As fate (and the Gaither network) would have it, football would still play an immediate role in Charlie Sr.'s life following graduation, when he accepted his first job as a teacher and head football coach at Monitor High School in 1964. The principal who hired him was a FAMU graduate.

"My first year as a young coach we played eight games," Charlie Sr. says. "We lost the first seven, but we won the game they most wanted us to win, against our rival who the school hadn't beaten in six years. Thankfully after we beat them, they forgot about the other seven losses."

While Charlie Sr. could have stayed at Monitor and capitalized on his lone, yet important victory, a coaching and teaching opportunity came up at Magnolia High School, the all African-American high school in his hometown of Thomasville, and he took it.

Yearbook photos from the Magnolia High School Buccaneer show a clean-shaven, short-haired Charlie Ward Sr. looking barely a day older than many of his graduating seniors.

Arriving in Thomasville too late to hold any spring practices, Charlie Sr. inherited a coaching staff of three and an underwhelming and undersized team. Even so, his first year with the Bucs was more successful than his first year as head coach at Monitor, leading Thomasville to a 4-4 record. A deeper dive on the season reveals another slow start by his squad.

"We lost the first four games," he says. "We didn't have enough practice and I was just playing the guys who started the year before, and they weren't very eager and were kind of stuck in their ways. After that fourth loss, I replaced most of the seniors with freshmen who I knew were young and excited to play and who listened to what I was coaching. They were raw, but we won the last four games in a row that year and got some momentum for the program."

It would also establish some momentum for the Wards, who decided to settle down in Thomasville for the long haul. They bought a house that was nestled under tall pine trees and oaks at the corner of Plum Street and South Street, in a neighborhood teeming with children—the perfect place to raise a family that would eventually have enough kids to field their own basketball team.

Over the next five years, Charlie Sr., along with Assistant Coach Robert Pritchett, would counsel, cajole, coax and coach the young men of Magnolia into a powerhouse team. Playing off their Buccaneer mascot, they developed the vaunted "Black Pearl" defense, which would soon become the bane of offenses throughout southern Georgia.

"We ran the famous Chicago Bears defense before they did," Charlie Sr. said. "We took our most aggressive guys, stuck them on defense and challenged them to go man-to-man for the most part. We built them up to the point they felt not one young man on the other team could stop them and we turned 'em loose. We didn't give them much to think about beyond that. Just hostile, agile and mobile."

Coach Gaither would have been proud.

In 1970, the Buccaneers went undefeated, capping off a remarkable five-year turnaround for Charlie Sr.'s program. They made the playoffs and participated in one of the coldest games in Georgia high school football history. Various reports put the game-time temperature at around twenty degrees, but Charlie Sr. says it was 18. Either way, pretty darn cold for a game anywhere outside of Green Bay.

Despite the chill, the shivering hands and the rock hard football helmets, the Black Pearl defense hung tough the entire game, not yielding a single point.

"It was one of those games where whoever scored first was going to win," Charlie Sr. says. "And nobody scored for a long time. Then, we made a mistake on offense."

The play was called 36 Lateral and it had worked well all year long. It was a timing play that involved a QB fake, a halfback fake and a timed pitch to break the back to the outside and to daylight, around the defensive line.

Whether it was the wind or numb hands or shivering bones, or a combination of all three, the play turned out to be a disaster. The QB pitched it to empty air and a defensive lineman scooped it up and ran it the other way for a touchdown.

Game over.

"I guess we had the wrong play or the wrong QB in at the time," Charlie Sr. said, still visibly irritated about the play almost fifty years later. "We lost 7-0."

Following that season, a seismic change was about to take place in the Thomasville school system in the form of integration, and Charlie Sr. found himself dead center in the middle of the social upheaval.

• • •

After an undefeated regular season, an unprecedented five-year run and the development of the Black Pearl defense, most of the students and faculty at Magnolia figured Charlie Sr. was a shoe-in for the head football coach position at the about-to-be-integrated Thomasville Central High School when Magnolia closed down at year's end.

They were wrong.

Charlie Sr. was caught up in a state-mandated desegregation system that, while integrating students, systematically removed many African-American teachers, coaches and administrators from their leadership positions in the new schools. In a paper on that subject, titled *Equalization Schools in Georgia's African-American Communities, 1951-1970,* author Steve Moffson explains:

Principal was the highest position that a black administrator could achieve during segregation. Some black principals were retained as assistant principals in integrated schools, some returned to the classroom, or some were forced out.

Some black coaches were forced out too.

"I knew nobody could outcoach me," Charlie Sr. says. "And we had just come off a big season… But I was told point blank that the town wasn't ready for a black head coach to be in charge of their newly integrated school."

The players were devastated. The ex-Magnolia high school parents were furious. There was nothing anybody could do.

Charlie Sr. had to watch as an inferior coach with an inferior record was brought in to run a team whose roster was stacked with boys he coached and he cared for and who, running his Black Pearl defense, were coming off a tough playoff loss they wanted to avenge.

Rather than be a distraction or cause problems for the new coach as an assistant, Charlie Sr. left the team and for the first time since he was in high school, spent a year away from football.

"I was so frustrated," he said. "I had to get out of football. I thought I should have had that job, and when I didn't get it I left the team. But I stayed in the classroom as a teacher and told my players to play as hard as they could for their new coach."

Following a brief boycott, most of the students listened, joined the integrated team and then proceeded to suffer through an awful season.

Remember the Titans, this was not.

The newly formed Thomasville Central High School Yellow Jackets muddled their way through a 1-9 season, and almost as soon as it was over the head coach left.

Once again Charlie Sr. thought he was the man to be the head coach, but this time the school brought in a man who was an assistant head coach for the Thomasville Bulldogs about five years before integration, Will Roy Cooley.

Cooley had been a head coach in Live Oak, Florida for four years before getting the call to return to the town he fell in love with a half-decade earlier. For him, the job in Thomasville was as much about coming home as it was being among the people that he loved.

"I drove into town and thought, *if these people will have me, this is where I want to live,*" Cooley said in an interview with the *Thomasville Times-Enterprise* in December 2005 . "It's a clean town and a good-looking town. Everybody was classy. I thought these were the kind of people I wanted to be involved with."

While Cooley was getting the call and making arrangements to move from Live Oak to Thomasville, Charlie Sr. was in heavy talks with his family about what he should do regarding football. His conundrum involved passion, pride and responsibility.

On the passion side, he loved football and he loved his students and athletes; he loved his teaching job and he loved the school and community. He and Willard had also decided to raise their family in Thomasville. On the pride side, he believed with all his heart that he should be the head coach and that it was an injustice he was being denied the spot due to social paradigms out of his control. But he also believed he was still responsible for his former athletes. Eventually, a long talk with his father-in-law helped him make his decision.

"My father-in-law told me that he understood why I felt the way I did, but some things are bigger than your own ego," Charlie Sr. said. "He told me that whether it was me or the new coach, someone was going to have to show these boys how to act and be men in this new school system and society, and I could either stand by and watch or I could get involved and help. I realized the kids and the community needed me, and so I talked to Coach Cooley about a position on his staff. He knew about me from his previous time in Thomasville and he knew I could coach, so he brought me on and I remained an assistant head coach for twenty years until 1991."

During those two decades, Charlie Sr. would be in charge of the running backs and the offense, which from 1985 to 1988 included Charlie Ward Jr. He'd also become the head basketball coach, with Junior as his point guard as well. But long before the Ward coach/player, father/son combination could take place, and long before Junior would spend a majority of his youth hanging out on the sidelines absorbing his dad's coaching lessons through osmosis, he was just child number three in the Ward household, barely a year old when his dad ended his one-year sabbatical from football.

Chapter 3

He Just Had "It"

Though Charlie Ward Jr. would grow up to become one of the greatest quarterbacks in the history of college football and play professionally in the National Basketball Association for twelve years, the inner circle of the Ward family unanimously agrees on the exact time and place that people noticed he was gifted athletically—and it wasn't on a field, court or blacktop.

It was on a shuffleboard.

He was two years old.

"We were members of a club called The Aquarius Club, and each summer we'd go on outings and picnics and such," Willard says. "When Junior was barely two we were at an event at one of the local plantations with members of our club. All the kids were playing and somehow Junior wandered over to the shuffleboard dribbling a small ball. Not just pushing it around or bouncing it, but really dribbling it. I hadn't seen anything like it. One of the members grabbed my arm and said, 'Look at your boy!' Look how he's handling that ball. You sure he's two?'"

Charlie Sr. remembers the event the exact same way.

"Soon all these women were gathering around Junior to watch him," he says. "He had the reflexes of a cat. He was so advanced. Nobody had ever seen a two-year-old with that kind of coordination. Everyone could tell he was special."

Then again, the very first toy Charlie had was a ball, and the first present Charlie Sr. bought Willard after his birth was a flower in a football vase. By the time of the shuffleboard incident, Charlie had already spent a vast majority of his young life either looking at a ball, learning to hold a ball, holding a ball or playing with a ball. Nearly every story involving him as a little kid includes the obligatory baseball or football or basketball or tennis ball or rolled up sock to be used as a ball.

The family photos reveal a similar pattern.

Here's Charlie, age three, sitting at a kids picnic table with a blue ball that barely fits in his lap.

There's Charlie, age four, holding an NFL-sized football teetering above his head.

And another one of him, age five, holding a regulation NBA basketball on his hip that's wider than his waist, trying to be cool, but barely able to stay on his own two feet.

His sister Leta, who is five years older, says their house on Plum Street echoed nonstop with the sounds of Charlie bouncing balls off walls and doors and floors.

"My dad got him one of those basketball goals you could hang on the door and he would shoot on it for hours," she says. "If we took the ball away he'd roll up a sock or ball up a shirt and shoot that. He eventually ruined the door. He was always getting into trouble by playing ball in the house."

He broke neighbors' windows.

He broke tree branches.

He broke lamps.

He even broke his grandparents' TV antenna.

"We were visiting Sebring, Florida and my parents had just put up a brand new television antenna," Willard explains. "Charlie has his ball outside and decides to see if he can throw it over the house. He tries it a few times and then boom, he knocks over the new antenna. He got in trouble, but the next time he was outside he was trying to throw the ball over the house again."

None of this should come as a surprise, considering the considerable hold that sports held over the Ward house in particular, and Charlie Sr. in general.

Not only was Senior an excellent football player and coach, but he was a die-hard fan of almost every sport. In addition to him coaching games on Friday nights, the family television would be on college football all day Saturday and whatever NFL games were showing on Sunday.

In Thomasville, nearly every Florida State Seminoles game aired along with a healthy dose of Georgia and Georgia Tech games. Bobby Bowden did a weekly television show every Sunday as well.

"We'd watch his show every Sunday morning before going to church," Charlie Jr. remembers.

From September to January, the Wards had a set Sunday schedule: Bowden on TV, followed by church, followed by the national NFL games playing in the family room, with Charlie Sr. and Junior lobbing a Nerf ball back and forth on the couch as they watched the action unfold on the screen.

In the 1970s, the national games typically featured Charlie Sr.'s one-time suitor, the Dallas Cowboys, and the iconic Pittsburgh Steelers teams with "Mean" Joe Greene, Franco Harris and Terry Bradshaw. Those teams would win six of ten Super Bowls starting in 1972, facing each other twice (the Steelers won both times).

Unfortunately for young Charlie, he latched on to the Cowboys while his sister Leta hitched her wagon to the Steelers.

"He would be so disappointed when my Steelers won," she said. "He was a sore loser back when he was little, and I'd just pick at him and tell him my Steelers were better and sometimes he would literally cry."

On the positive side, Charlie became a fan of two men he'd eventually have a lot in common with, Dallas Cowboys quarterbacks Roger Staubach and Danny White. Staubach won the Heisman Trophy along with a slew of other college football awards that Charlie would one day win, and they'd both become members of the College Football Hall of Fame. White had a powerful leg and would first join the Cowboys as a back-up quarterback and starting punter, the same roles Ward had when he joined Florida State.

Charlie was also a fan of Tony Dorsett, Walter Payton, O.J. Simpson and a host of other running backs. He looked up to the guys who made defenders miss the most. Elusiveness was something young Charlie Ward was already fond of.

Yet for all of the game watching and ball throwing and trash talking about their favorite teams, Charlie Sr. wouldn't let Junior play any organized sports until he was in fifth grade. Instead, he chose to let his son explore his natural talents on the street and in the backyard, without coaches or structure or anything else that might hinder the joy of playing for the love of the game and nothing else. As evidenced by his son's eventual dominance in two sports at a very high level, Charlie Sr. was an early opponent of kids specializing in only one sport, believing it hindered overall athletic growth and development.

"Kids need to learn how to be coordinated across a lot of sports and a lot of physical activities," he said. "I wanted Charlie to have a chance to play everything." So he played everything.

Literally.

CHAPTER 4

Neighborhood Legend

The house where Charlie Ward Jr. grew up at the corner of Plum and South streets is almost indistinguishable from the others in the neighborhood, save for one feature. While it's relatively the same size as the others and is shaded by oaks and pine trees like the others and even has a similarly shaped front lawn, driveway and lot as the others, there's one glaring difference: in front of the Wards' old house there is a roughly thirty-by-twenty-five-foot paved blacktop basketball court that butts up against the house and runs halfway to the street.

Today, the original hoop is long gone and the once-even blacktop is weathered with grass pushing through certain parts of it, but throughout the 1980s the court and the Wards' house might as well have been declared a public park by the city of Thomasville. Every evening after homework and practically every afternoon and weekend in the summer, the court was filled with neighborhood kids hanging out, playing ball and competing.

"Before Charlie's dad laid down the blacktop for us to play on the Wards used to have plum trees in front of their house," Aloysius Henderson, a childhood friend of Charlie's said. "When they weren't home, people would always be stealing plums. He thought when he put the court up people would stop coming by, but then they came by to play basketball. Charlie's yard was the neighborhood playground. If you were a boy in our neighborhood, that's where you went to play. We'd even have kids from other towns show up to challenge us in pick-up games. Football. Basketball. Baseball. We'd play everything."

The nickname for the neighborhood was Fruit City (in addition to Plum Street there was Pear Street, Peach Street, Orange Street and Persimmon Street) and the Wards' house was its capitol. Henderson remembers the exact route he used to take from his grandmother's house, through a few backyards, to get to the basketball court. Almost every other kid in the neighborhood has the same story. To this day, Willard Ward is stopped by grown men at Target, the grocery store and even while getting gas with a thank you for letting them play at her house when they were kids, though she can hardly remember all the faces of the dozens of boys who called her driveway their 'home court' decades ago.

In addition to the draw of an open court and hanging out with friends, there was an added bonus for the neighborhood kids who made their way to the heart of Fruit City to hoop or play football in the street: playing with Charlie Ward Jr., or, more to the point, being lucky enough to have Junior on your team so you could win.

When a group of boys would shoot for captains, they either wanted Charlie to be a captain and get picked on his team or they wanted to be a captain and grab him as their first pick—didn't matter the age or the sport. Charlie was picked first by kids two and three years older than him all the time.

"Back then Charlie was a great shooter," Henderson says. "He was quick and he didn't miss. We never worried when kids would come from other towns to challenge us. Man, if we had Charlie out there playing we always knew we could beat any kids who showed up."

Tommy Rainge, who would one day transfer to Central High School and play football with Charlie as one of the most prolific quarterback-to-wide receiver combinations Georgia High School football had ever seen, first saw him on the basketball court when they were eight or nine years old.

"I'll never forget when I first saw him," Rainge said. "The dude was just so smooth and so natural at whatever he did with a basketball. He had such confidence in himself."

He especially thrived against older kids, begging to play against his sister and her guy friends who were five years older than him.

"They'd tell him he was too small to play," she said. "But he was competitive and he'd play, and once he hit about ten years old he'd win all the time. No matter what he was playing, but especially in football."

• • •

Magnolia Junior High School (no longer attached to its long-closed senior high counterpart)lies roughly 400 yards east of the house Ward grew up in. It's a series of old brick building with large, white rectangular shutters around the windows. Behind it lies a beat up, mostly dirt football field where a young Charlie Ward Jr. dropped his first jaws playing quarterback. Never receiver. Never running back. Always quarterback.

Why?

Because every single person remembers two things about Charlie back then: He had an absolute rifle for an arm, and nobody could touch him or catch him when he scrambled.

Once Charlie hit third and fourth grade, he became part of a regular group of boys and fathers who would head down to the field behind Magnolia every Saturday morning to play pick-up football, including another boy who would one day become an ACC quarterback, Georgia Tech's Shawn Jones.

Charlie and Shawn were always separated and the teams were built around the two young talents. But even against someone else who would eventually break records under center at an ACC school, Charlie managed to play at a higher level. Such a high level, in fact, that some kids were even a little freaked out by it.

"Nobody could do what he was doing at our age," Tommy Rainge said. "It was like Charlie was three steps ahead. We were playing a game, but he was playing games with all of us."

Ask any group of Thomasville dads who used to watch the Saturday pick-up games at Magnolia and they'll all use the same phrase to describe watching Charlie: "I had never seen anything like it."

Before he was ten years old, Charlie Ward Jr. had an arsenal of jukes, fakes, spin moves, stutter steps, slides, glides and bursts of speed the likes of which grown men, now in their 70s and 80s, can still barely describe.

And what about the kids who played with and against him?

They still sound like teenagers, describing his ability in video game terms, about how his attributes like speed, quickness, arm strength and intelligence would all be turned up to 100.

"He would run around and run around on that field and nobody would touch him," his sister Leta said. "Then he'd throw it a mile to whoever was open. People still talk about what he did on that field as a kid. It was like he could see what was gonna happen before it happened."

This is a different version of another common phrase people use to describe Charlie, often saying he had a sixth sense when it came to moving around the football field. He had a knack for changing direction a split second before it even seemed necessary, or spinning left a moment before a defender even committed to his right side. The tales of "this one move he did" all have as their major plot point a common theme that goes something like this: "and right before X happened, Charlie did Y and escaped and nobody laid a finger on him!"

It's almost like they're describing a Marvel character in *The Avengers* or *The Defenders.*

The simple answer for his preternatural ability to evade defenders is that he was born with a talent to do so. That's part of it. Having his father's genes and athletic ability certainly didn't hurt.

One man who knows Charlie and the Wards very well has another theory that veers more toward common sense than the supernatural. His name is Randy Young, and as mentioned in the prologue, Charlie Sr. was his coach in high school and he became the radio voice for Thomasville football and called games when Charlie played.

"Part of being a coach's son is that he was always around the game and he was constantly hearing instructions," Young said. "I distinctly remember him always being on the sidelines paying attention to whatever his dad was talking about. He wasn't bored. He was listening and absorbing everything his father was saying to us. And I know after Senior did his coaching on the field, he'd talk more about it to Junior on the ride home and at the house. Charlie was getting a deep explanation of why athletes moved how they did and why defenders did certain things or offenses did certain things. I believe that as a very young man, he began to look at a football field or a basketball court through a coach's eyes, so the game was much slower for him than everyone else his age. You combine that with his natural athletic abilities and you've got a young man set completely apart from his peers. He was remarkable. His football abilities were beyond anything I had ever seen as a radio guy and fan of the sport."

• • •

There's a scene in the movie *Good Will Hunting* where Matt Damon's character, Will, is trying to explain his genius to his girlfriend, who is baffled as to how organic chemistry and complex math and science problems come so easy to him. To try to shed light on his intellectual gifts, he brings up Beethoven.

> "Beethoven," Will says. "He looked at a piano and it just made sense to him. He could just play."
>
> "So what are you saying, you play the piano?" the girl asks.
>
> "No, not a lick," Will says. "I look at a piano and I see a bunch of keys, three pedals and a box of wood. But Beethoven, Mozart... they saw it and they could just play. Well, I couldn't paint you a picture and I probably couldn't hit the ball out of Fenway and I can't play the piano."
>
> "But you can do my org-chem paper in under an hour," she says.
>
> "Yeah, I mean when it came to stuff like that I could always just play," he says.

Talking to Charlie Ward about his athletic ability is strikingly similar to the above conversation. Except in his prime, he probably *could* have hit the ball out of Fenway, and when it came to sports, he could always just play.

• • •

Our conversation is taking place in the foyer of his parents' house. Charlie has just driven an hour from a football camp he was coaching in Valdosta, Georgia. He's wearing standard coaching gear, a zipped-up windbreaker and workout shorts. He's forty-six but looks almost exactly like he did in his NBA playing days. Like his father, he has a natural glide when he walks.

"I've always had the gift of eye-hand coordination, and a lot of things came easy to me when it came to athletics," he says. "I was able to pick things up quicker than anyone else, and I even recognized it when I was very young. Things that other people had to practice I didn't have to practice. When it came to sports, so many things were innate for me. I was able to think through a process on a field very quickly—quicker than others—and it made me almost see things before they happened. That's just how it was."

When asked specifically about skills he possessed that other kids had to work at, he brings up throwing a football.

"I always had a sense for how to throw the ball with speed and accuracy," he says. "I didn't need any technique or coaching. I didn't go to any camps. I was very raw, but that came from spending so much time playing outside and honing my skills in the street."

The asphalt on Plum Street, South Street and Magnolia Street was the de facto gridiron for the neighborhood kids when they weren't at the middle school field or playing basketball. The most popular game, seeing as they were playing on the hard street, was two-hand touch football.

The field was the width of the street, with out-of-bounds marked by the curbs on each side. The end zones were marked by mailboxes, parked cars, driveways, telephone poles or whatever else was easily visible. Games were paused to allow cars to pass and the ball was live until it touched the ground, even if it hit a telephone wire or pole or anything else while in the air. Parked cars on the side of the road were considered out of bounds.

When people would later cap off stories of incredible feats Charlie pulled off on the football field with the phrase, "and he wasn't even touched," this is where it all began.

The Wards' house was set up in such a way that Charlie Sr. often found himself grading papers inside while keeping an eye on the street football action outside. He noted that Charlie was always picked first and he was the most talented player in every single game. He also observed that it didn't affect him one way or the other. He never gloated, never rubbed it in anyone's face, and he was silent regardless of how many touchdowns he threw for or ran in. This quiet dominance would become a hallmark of his stoic leadership on the field as he got older, a surprising development considering how young he was and how good he was compared to his peers.

A nine-year-old who hadn't learned humility yet could be forgiven for feeling full of himself after weaving through his buddies for a ridiculous street touchdown. He could even be forgiven for spiking the ball or shouting or doing the Ickey Shuffle—but that wasn't Charlie's way. Like his athletic ability, humility came natural to him as well, which was probably for the better considering how many older kids he made look foolish on those streets.

"When he was five years old, most seven- and eight-year-olds couldn't catch him," Charlie Sr. said. "When he was seven and eight there wasn't a ten-year-old around who could chase him down. When he was ten? The only kids who challenged him were already in high school."

When there weren't kids around to push him, he'd use the street itself to raise the level of difficulty of his pick-up games. He'd throw over station wagons, behind bushes and, as was his specialty, thread the needle on his passes through electrical wires.

There is a series of telephone wires in front of the Wards' house that hangs about twenty feet in the air and runs diagonally across the street. Depending on which direction a team was heading on offense, the wires could be a problem because the kids weren't able to get the proper arc or height on a long pass without hitting them. Kids knew this and adjusted their defenses accordingly—except when Charlie was quarterback. He had a knack for slinging the football through the wires, on the run, like he was some kind of sports act on *America's Got Talent.*

"That was the pressure back then," he said. "You're either accurate or you break stuff."

He also credits the street with developing his pocket awareness and the ability to throw accurately while scrambling.

"When I'd go back to pass, I had to avoid kids trying to tag me in a small space on a narrow street, so I got a sense of what would eventually be pocket awareness," he said. "I learned to move my body and keep my balance while not getting touched. And naturally, when you're throwing a football in the street you have to be on target or you'll hit a car windshield or a mailbox or a house window or something like that. I wasn't afraid of interceptions; I was afraid of damaging someone's property. But I wanted to win so I never stopped throwing, and I was never scared to play hard."

Throughout his grade school and early middle school years, Charlie built a reputation as a quiet athletic genius. A savant, really. Everyone who watched him play recognized they were seeing something special, whether it was parents watching through windows or neighbors driving by or kids playing with him. It was accepted dogma that they were witnessing some form of child prodigy.

Most stories involving neighborhood legends culminate with the young upstart beating his rival in one-on-one or leading his pick-up team to a memorable win to take the top spot in the athletic pecking order. Or at least that's what happens in movies. In real life, sometimes, there really is just one singular talent that doesn't have a rival, and in Fruit City that was Charlie. When asked if there was anyone in the neighborhood he couldn't wait to take on or challenge as he got older, he paused for a minute and breathed deep, thinking.

Anyone?

"Honestly," he said. "When I think of kids in the neighborhood and who we played with, if you asked people who they thought the person to beat was, they'd say me. Just being honest."

Honest and correct. Every person I spoke to concurred. Even as a boy, Charlie was the man to beat. And he hadn't even played organized sports yet.

Chapter 5

The Phenom

Mark Lastinger was loading lumber at a Lowe's Hardware store in 1986 when he got the call. The voice on the line was Randy Young's, a classmate of his at both Thomasville Central High School and Valdosta College. The question asked was, would he be interested in becoming the radio color man for Thomasville's Central High football games?

Lastinger couldn't say yes fast enough.

Unbeknownst to him, he would be accepting the job on the cusp of what was about to be the golden years for high school football in southern Georgia. In addition to his radio job, he would eventually join the *Thomasville Times-Enterprise* and spend almost thirty years there as an editor.

After accepting the position, Lastinger took it upon himself to do a deep dive on not only the high school football situation in Thomasville, but also the Pop Warner teams and middle school teams. He wanted to have his finger on the pulse of pigskin in Thomasville, and to do that he began interviewing coaches and teachers and dads in the area about what the next crop of Central superstars looked like.

In those interviews, one name came up over and over again, and each time it did it was spoken with a sense of wonder: Charlie Ward Jr.

He was told stories of one-minute scrambles, fifty-yard throws, eighty-yard touchdown runs, incredible comebacks and absurd feat after absurd feat achieved by a kid who was about to enter high school.

"Every single person I spoke with to get up to speed on my new job mentioned Junior," Lastinger said. "It was unanimous that he lit up every single youth league and middle school league he played in. I knew about his dad from going to Central, but that was the first I'd heard of Junior's legend. It preceded him before he even got to high school."

Win-loss records and stats for middle school sports in mid-1980s Thomas County don't exist, but if word of mouth is to be believed, Charlie threw for a million yards, with a few thousand touchdowns and another several thousand rushing yards. He could also throw the ball a mile, run circles around people, and, as one teammate said, "blow by you so fast it looked like his legs were moving slowly—like rims on a tire."

When it came to basketball, his hands were as fast as rattlesnakes and he could dribble the ball like it was attached to a string. He could make any pass or steal any pass. He was unguardable and he could guard anyone. He knew what you were going to do before you did it. He was playing chess while everyone else was playing checkers. He could not be rattled. He never showed any emotion. He was the most competitive kid you'd ever seen but he was also the most quiet. He was the best teammate and the best individual player. He wanted none of the spotlight but he got it all. His play was as brash and bold as he was shy.

The superlatives and the hyperbole and the seeming contradictions in personality and performance flow endlessly.

And it's all true.

• • •

In fifth grade Charlie was finally allowed to play organized sports. After having spent years honing his skills on playgrounds, streets, fields and driveways, where the lack of a referee or official rules gave his opponents almost free reign to do what they could to stop him (not that it helped), the structure, in its own way, was freeing. In basketball, he found that with a ref calling fouls kids couldn't tee off on him or shove him or grab his shirt as he tried to dribble by them. Bigger kids could no longer shove him with impunity or hip-check him to the ground or elbow him. They couldn't get away with body fouls on shots or "the hand is part of the ball" slaps on his wrist while trying to shoot. The refs, simply by enforcing the rules of the game, tipped the athletic scales more in Charlie's favor than ever before.

Without the rule-bending physicality, which never fazed him in the first place, his opponents had very few tools left in their arsenal to stop him. And thus, he thrived on the court.

In football, as Johnny Depp says in the famous scene from *Donnie Brasco, forget about it.* Whatever level he had been playing at before Pop Warner, he was now nearly unstoppable with a helmet and pads and an offensive line providing him time to scramble—no more of the unenforceable, barely-followed "three Mississippi" that was supposed to be counted out loud before anyone on the opposing team tried to rush him. It was one thing when kids his own age had to try to lay two hands on him to call him down. In that task they often flailed and failed and looked foolish. It was quite another to actually have to, you know, *tackle* him.

Old videos make it appear as if Charlie is covered in grease. One moment he's about to be wrapped up; the next he's spinning or sliding free. One moment a defender has him dead in his sights, the next he's tackling air. Occasionally, in older grainy footage with unsteady camera work, it looks like he actually teleports away from a defender, disappearing in their grasp and reappearing as a streak down the sideline.

And then there's something Charlie rarely had in his street football days: space—glorious, open, free space to roam left-to-right between the sidelines. Gone were the curbs and cars and pebbles and potholes that reined him in. And gone was the advantage opponents created by loading up one side of the street to force him to play on half the asphalt space.

For the first time, Charlie could have receivers run out-routes and flares and all sorts of patterns that went horizontal rather than mostly vertical. Now he could spread the field, find the open man, and, as if using a new toy for the first time, unwrap his powerful arm and unleash frozen ropes to kids ten or fifteen yards away. With all those routes came another thing Charlie never had: time.

He had time to evaluate the defense and see how it ebbed and flowed after his receivers and running backs; time to let plays develop down field while he scrambled; time to set his feet if he needed to or take off.

For the first 12 years of his life, Charlie had only put on replica NFL football helmets as Christmas gifts and had never stepped foot on a field with actual shoulder pads. Now, already a phenom, he was playing on a real field with real teammates and a real coach—finally discovering the real game of football.

"We used to put on the toy helmets and replica pads and try to hit each other in the yard," Charlie said. "Me and Shawn Jones and his brother would do all kinds of things to get a chance to play and hit. But that was just messing around. When I finally got to play Pop Warner, it was such a great experience. We had practices where we'd be able to get better and then games to look forward to every Saturday."

If there is one "welcome to real football" moment for Charlie in middle school, it was complete with the joy, pain and punishment that the gridiron provides. It took place with no time on the clock and Charlie's team behind on the scoreboard. He grabbed a snap, didn't see anyone to pass to, juked the first guy who came after him and then took off down the field.

"I wasn't a big believer in getting hit," he said. "So I'd avoid getting touched at all costs. That play I was running around, and just as I finally broke free I sprained my ankle. I kept on sprinting for the end zone, and as I got caught I crossed the goal line for the game-winning touchdown—but my head and face were slammed into the chalk they line the field with. My head was buried in it and I had a mouth full of chalk and dirt and that was the first time I really went down and ate mud and got hurt. But it all felt good."

Such is football.

Behind Charlie's arm, rushing and punt returns, his team won the first of many championships he'd take home across several sports in his middle school career

• • •

Once the floodgates of organized sports opened, Charlie signed up to play anything that involved a ball. Tennis. Baseball. Golf. If it was available to play, he played it. He was even an excellent swimmer, like his old man.

A good rule of thumb when exploring Charlie's middle school exploits is that each of his coaches believed the sport in which they coached him was his best sport. This obviously goes for football and basketball and can be debated on tangible results like an NBA career, an Elite Eight appearance in college basketball, and a National Championship in college football. But it doesn't end there.

There are almost as many stories about Charlie in Little League as there are in Pop Warner or middle school hoops. At that time, he was a shortstop with uncanny footwork and a pitcher with, as we've mentioned, a strong arm. He could also hit for power and fly around the bases.

Earl Williams, who was the principal of Central Middle School and a former mayor of Thomasville, watched Charlie play Little League games and swore by his skills on the diamond. He was interviewed by Bill Vilona for a Gannett News Service story on the eve of Charlie winning the Heisman, and he was effusive in his praise.

"Charlie stands above everybody. There is something about Charlie that is magical...I still believe baseball is Charlie's best sport. He's such a tremendous athlete."

Charlie's Little League team would win the championship, and he'd make an all-star traveling team to play against other leagues. At that time, he didn't think of baseball as his third or fourth favorite sport. If it involved a bat or ball he loved it, speaking about sports more like children than hobbies and finding it hard to pick one he loved more than the other.

"Baseball, basketball and football were really one-a, one-b and one-c to me," Charlie said. "But back then I couldn't tell you which was which."

He'd give up baseball after eighth grade for track, but that didn't last long.

Several years later, after having not picked up a baseball or bat at any point in high school, Charlie headed over to the diamond to help out the varsity baseball team in a pinch to start the season. He was a senior by that point and the coach had been trying to beckon him back to the dugout for years to no avail. Charlie rolled the bat around with his wrists, took a few practice swings and dug into the batter's box against the opponent's starting pitcher. At this point, you know where this is headed.

First pitch.

First swing.

Home run.

Charlie then decided to play baseball his senior year of high school.

"The home run story is true," he said. "First time I got up there I hit one out. First pitch I saw. It was fun. If I got on base, I was stealing. Every time. I enjoyed it."

Back in middle school during the summers, a bus would stop by the house early in the morning to take the Ward children to the YMCA for camp. They'd play sports all day every day, and it's at the Y where Charlie learned how to swim. Almost immediately, he stood out. Talk to someone who watched him race around the pool in those days, or friends on his swim team, and they'll tell you that swimming might have been his true athletic gift.

"If Charlie decided that all he wanted to do was swim, he'd have been able to master it," Henderson said. "With his natural ability he could beat everyone in the pool."

This story, too, repeats itself across witnesses and across sports.

Charlie tries a sport. Charlie is good at a sport. Charlie is soon the best at that sport.

Charlie Ward Sr. was the golf coach at Thomasville and once brought his son to the course and showed him how to hold a club. Charlie took a few hacks. Sliced a few. Hooked a few. Then decided to play a round.

"Charlie went out and beat everybody on the team," Williams said.

There are several legendary tennis stories about Charlie as well, usually involving him beating someone much older, much more skilled, or both. His eye-hand coordination allowed him to strike the ball with unnerving accuracy, while his athleticism gave him the advantage of being able to cover the whole court. Few could match his natural gift for anticipating what his opponent was going to do. He even went deep into an Arthur Ashe AIDS Tennis Challenge fundraiser in 1994. His doubles partner in that event was none other than John McEnroe.

When it came to sports, Charlie Ward Jr. could just play.

Chapter 6

A Brief Pause Before Greatness

The cartoon bulldog at the center of the billboard at Veterans Memorial Stadium, home of Thomasville High School's football team, has huge, yellow-shot eyes; sharp, protruding teeth; a long, lolling tongue; and spikes on its collar. It looks like a rabid dog straight out of an old Tom and Jerry cartoon. The image is framed by an orange doghouse that appropriately says, "THS DOG HOUSE" in thick, red lettering. Footballs surround the doghouse touting the years of Thomasville's state championships. Not mentioned on the billboard is a contest South Georgia residents call the "Game of the Century," a reference to the 1987 Region 1-AAA Championship football game between Thomasville—led by Shawn Jones—and their arch-rival Central High School, quarterbacked by Charlie Ward Jr.

Lines to get into this game stretched to the practice field across the street. To top it off, three future Division I college football national champions, for three different programs, were present at the coin toss: Ward (Florida State), Jones (Georgia Tech) and Eric Curry, who was an All-American and played on Alabama's 1992 National Championship team.

Charlie Ward Jr. was destined to play in a game of this magnitude in Thomasville. He was born for it. Heck, his dad was born for it. All he had to do was avoid the proverbial injury bug. Unfortunately, he was bitten hard early in high school and it put his whole career in jeopardy.

Freshman year.

Knee surgery.

The injury presented itself during the last basketball game of ninth grade. He was playing for his dad, starting on the varsity team after an uneventful freshman football season. To this day, Charlie isn't sure exactly when he hurt himself. It was possibly during practice… or possibly lifting weights on a leg press machine… Who knows?

What is certain is that during his final game that season, his knee swelled up to the size of a balloon and surgery was needed. For those who watched him play on the fields at the YMCA or on the streets of Fruit City or the rec leagues throughout Thomasville, this was always the fear in the back of their minds—that some freak injury or accident would deprive Charlie of reaching his full potential, depriving him of high school all-star games and state titles and collegiate glory at a major program and, maybe one day, the NFL.

Up to this point, he had excelled so easily and so effortlessly at athletics that only a cruel twist of fate could rob him of his destiny. Family members and friends prayed that this wasn't that twist.

"After Junior hurt his knee his freshman year, I remember very clearly the discussion about the high school teams he was going to be a part of moving forward having a big question mark hovering over them," Randy Young said. "This was the mid-1980s. Knee surgery wasn't an assembly line like it is now. We all knew how talented Junior was, but back then, we just didn't know how well he'd recover. Everyone was concerned."

Everyone, that is, except Charlie.

His parents both say he handled the surgery and recovery without a moment of panic or fear. He was calm and confident, believing in his heart that things would be fine.

"That's just always been Junior," his dad said, smiling in his family room. "Nothing rattles him. Not even surgery."

Don't believe him?

I present to you Exhibit A, a tremendous photo in the Ward family photo albums from early 1986.

The picture is of Charlie Ward Jr. wearing a sleeveless #33 Tony Dorsett Dallas Cowboys shirt and gray shorts in the family room. He's standing next to a three-foot high by six-foot wide school project. The project consists of three panels of giant white poster board, with a red-patterned border as boundaries for each section. The headline of the project, in red stencil lettering, reads: Knee Injuries.

There is a section on the "Procedure" and on the "Classification of Data," as well as a spot to define the problem and present a hypothesis—standard high school science project stuff.

The right panel is labeled "Results Data," and then the most important part is underneath, titled "Conclusion." At that point, when it came to Charlie's athletic future, the conclusion to be drawn from his surgery—namely whether or not it was successful—was uncertain. The symbolism of the image however, was clear.

Not only is Charlie, a future Heisman Trophy winner, wearing the jersey of Tony Dorsett, a man who also won the Heisman, but he's standing next to a presentation on knee injuries, when it so happens that a knee injury ended Dorsett's NFL career and that same injury could derail Charlie's entire, supremely bright athletic future.

Did I mention that Charlie has a huge smile on his face in the photo?

Like his dad said, he wasn't afraid of the surgery or the recovery or the rehab. The only thing that seemed to bring him down was that he had to rest, meaning for the first time since he was two years old he couldn't play sports.

It was a long four months for Charlie to wait for his knee to heal, and it was a rough four months as well for Charlie Ward Sr., who knew first-hand what a leg injury could do to a promising young football career. He watched Charlie walk around on crutches, watched the bandages get taken off, watched him work his way off the crutches, all the while praying that the surgery would end up being just a tiny bump in the road and wouldn't affect his son's future in any way.

• • •

Charlie rehabbed throughout that summer, throughout football season and throughout his sophomore year. As the months ticked toward the start of what would be his junior year at Central, those who cared for him and cared about the football team breathed easy as it became apparent he would make a full recovery. However, the timeline of his return didn't perfectly align with the start of the football season. He was still able to compete for the varsity quarterback job for the Yellow Jackets, but he wasn't going to be medically cleared to play in an actual game when the season kicked off.

In fact, the only activity he was cleared to perform on a football field when the first game of 1986 arrived was punting. So, he prepared for week one as a punter, taking any chance he could get to be back with his team.

"I had a strong kicking leg, and at least I was on the team helping out," Ward said. "That was my mindset. Happy to be back on the field any way I could be."

His punting also gave the community a chance to punt on the controversial issue of having an African-American starting quarterback, something that was still a rarity in the south and throughout football in general.

The NFL at the time had only two starting African-American quarterbacks in Warren Moon and Randall Cunningham. Most of the major college conferences likewise either had zero, or at most two, starting African-American quarterbacks as well. Charlie Sr.'s beloved Florida State had never had a black starting quarterback (something we'll dive much deeper into later) at that point in time.

While many football fans acknowledged that, when healthy, Charlie was the superior player to the white upper classman quarterback, there was still some "old south" sentiment in the region that believed he didn't have a place under center.

As fate would have it, there was never a full-blown controversy or rift in the town. Charlie's injury gave everyone an out; no public benching of a white quarterback in favor of a black quarterback meant no public outcry from those hanging on to a once-segregated and ugly past. As far as Charlie was concerned, his injury allowed the team to avoid any of the major issues in terms of tension.

"I knew some people may have tried to make something of it, but to me it was a non-issue. We had a senior who was the starting quarterback, and since I wasn't cleared to play, he was the starter. That was it," he said.

And then suddenly, it wasn't.

Chapter 7

Starting Quarterback

Happily, the 1986 Central High School Yellow Jacket football team was not mentioned in a preseason column in the *Tallahassee Democrat* with an all-time great sports headline by Don Watz: *If Experience Were Hair, These Teams Would Be Bald.*

While the 1985 Yellow Jackets went 7-3, they were a young group, having lost most of their starters on offense and several on defense from the '84 squad.

The 1986 team, on the other hand, was coming off that 7-3 season with 14 starters returning, chock full of seniors and leaders. The *Atlanta Journal-Constitution* had them ranked #1 in Georgia's I-AAA Division. They had a strong tailback, an offensive line with several massive young men and an all-region linebacker.

"We're looking for a pretty good football team this year," Head Coach Charles Greene said on the verge of his fourth season leading Central.

Greene, who served as a longtime assistant at perennial Georgia high school football powerhouse Valdosta, was no stranger to winning games in general—titles in particular. He was on staff for several state championships at Valdosta under legendary coach Wright Bazemore, and took over when Bazemore retired after winning his final championship in 1971. Greene went 17-3 in two seasons at Valdosta but was then fired, as only the regional champion earned a playoff berth in those days, and eight- or nine-win seasons weren't good enough. If that seems harsh, keep in mind that Valdosta is an iconic high school football program, and to this day has won about two-dozen state titles, with several alumni having reached the NFL.

After the firing, Greene wound up at Stephens County, where he had only one losing season from 1975 to 1983 before taking the job at Central in 1984.

Greene was a Christian and a winner who ran his teams on the philosophy that the locker room was a family and tough love ruled the day. There was no swearing allowed, and no disrespecting coaches or teammates. He also surrounded himself with as many true-blue football lifers as he could at all his coaching stops. At Central, that included Charlie Sr., Eugene Conner and Ken Manwaring, the strength and conditioning coach.

The culture was supportive yet demanding. There were days in the weight room with so-called "burnout sessions," when players would get on a bench and press the bar as fast as they could and as many times as they could until their lungs were on fire and their arms were numb. The goal was to break the boys down during weights and conditioning and then build them back up on the field through practice and repetitions.

Charlie Sr. and Coach Conner were in charge of the offense, and they were also responsible for keeping the boys in line. Sometimes it involved yelling, other times a pat on the back, and occasionally even a hug.

For Junior, having his dad on staff proved to be a huge benefit.

"I always knew my dad was the social studies teacher and coach at Central and that we'd be at the same school when I got to ninth grade," Charlie said. "There was nothing negative about it. I know that he didn't want to show any favoritism, so he coached me harder than he coached anyone else, but it didn't bother me. I never felt any extra pressure to perform or to be at a higher level than my teammates. I just went out and did my job. I also knew that there were plenty of kids whose dads weren't even around, so I was fortunate to not only have mine as a coach but I was able to talk to him about strategy and ask questions after practice."

Charlie Sr. was the running backs coach and Coach Greene worked specifically with the quarterbacks. In addition to having Junior on his 1986 roster, Greene also had senior Chris Taylor to develop and prepare for the season. He preached that the role of the quarterback was to make everything go. He drilled into Charlie and Chris that a QB not only had to lead the team down the field, but he had to lead them mentally as well: If he was out of control or erratic, the team would be too. Greene harped on having poise and patience, both of which Charlie had shown natural gifts for. Greene's offenses typically ran the Pro-I formation, in which the offense was built on the running game, not the quarterback. This is why, regardless of injury, Chris Taylor was Greene's planned QB1 at the start of the year.

In fairness to Greene, Charlie hadn't taken a meaningful snap under center in almost a year-and-a-half, and without a crystal ball he had no way of knowing that he was sitting on one of the greatest high school football talents in the history of the sport.

At the time, with the information Greene had, his depth chart was, at the very least, defensible. His team appeared to be loaded top to bottom.

"Going into 1986 they had a stud running back in Steve Fleming who was going to be running behind an offensive line that averaged dang-near three hundred pounds per man," Mark Lastinger said. "[Greene] probably didn't think he'd need Charlie when the season started, but he soon found out that big necessarily didn't mean better."

When asking members of that Central High team to describe Fleming, they all use the same NFL player as a comparison: Herschel Walker.

"He was loaded with muscle," Ward said. "Just a strong, muscle-bound guy who was fast."

Fleming was the definition of a power back, with quick feet, a low center of gravity and the force of a freight train. He could either run through guys or juke them. The offense Coach Greene ran was built for a back like Fleming.

Central also had speedy Steve Garland, a 5'6" wide receiver who had played with Charlie since middle school. Honed over years of throwing to each other in Pop Warner games, on the playground and in practice, their timing on patterns was impeccable. Quite often, they knew what the other was thinking, forming a QB-receiver mind-meld that left other teams wondering how they found each other in such tight spots.

Up front, the offensive line was filled with mammoth high school players and was led by Scott Cooley, who would go on to play at South Carolina.

And then there was the 6'2", 210-pound freshman phenomenon Tommy Rainge, who deserves a brief interlude and introduction.

• • •

By the time Tommy Rainge arrived at Central High School, he had already lived a long life for a fourteen-year-old. He grew up in Rochester, New York and suffered the loss of his mother from heart problems when he was only nine years old. At age twelve, he moved to Valdosta, Georgia with his father, where he fell in with the wrong group of kids, and following a minor brush with the law was sent to a youth development center. After spending almost a month there, he was moved to a group home in Thomasville. While in Thomasville, he participated in the first week of practice for the football team and caught his first passes from Charlie. It was apparent to everyone that they had immediate chemistry on the field.

Following that week of practice, Rainge had a meeting with what was essentially his guidance board—a probation officer, his dad, Central Head Coach Charles Greene, and Valdosta Head Coach Nick Hyder—to discuss his future.

"I just thought about it," Rainge said in a retrospective piece in his hometown paper. "Should I go back to Valdosta just to play with the Valdosta Wildcats, or should I stay here in Thomasville where I have guidance and also play for a great team in Central High School? I don't think anybody influenced me in that decision. I didn't want to go through the experience I went through, hanging out with the wrong group of guys. I knew the circumstances I would be in. If I went back, I wasn't going to have someone to guide me in the right direction, so I decided to stay in Thomasville."

Coach Greene believed in Rainge and felt good about having him stay. Rainge also gained a strong support group that included Ken Conner, the son of Central's assistant coach Eugene Conner, Coach Greene, and Charlie Ward Jr.

In Charlie, Rainge saw a teammate and friend who made smart decisions, stayed cool under pressure, was a leader, and didn't get into trouble.

"Charlie was a phenom. He was so smooth. He didn't sweat," Rainge said. "We gelled well. I can't explain it."

In Rainge, Charlie saw the big, speedy target he'd always dreamed of playing with when he watched the NFL with his dad on Sundays—namely one of Roger Staubach's favorite receivers and Charlie Sr.'s old Florida A&M teammate, "Bullet" Bob Hayes.

"Tommy was before his time as a wide receiver," Ward said. "He was six-two, about two hundred and ten pounds. He was big but had great speed. He was powerful too. I threw a lot of deep balls to him and he'd jump up and get them."

Often times, Charlie would throw the ball ten to twenty yards in front of Rainge and let both him and the ball outpace the opponent's defense. After several diving, leaping and soaring catches, Rainge earned the nickname "Superman" from his teammates and high school football fans around southern Georgia. The tandem quickly became must-watch football.

"It was magical," Rainge said. "Charlie threw me all of my touchdowns. We were always in sync. He'd have his eye on me, and I could cut off my route and he'd know where I was headed. He was just so far above everyone else talent-wise. It was fun to see the looks on the faces of the other team's coaches and players during a game. Man, you could just see it. After a quarter or two of scrambling and throws, they'd watch Charlie with this look, like, *who is this guy?!*"

• • •

Incidentally, all of the offensive fireworks and head-shaking runs and mind-boggling throws and video game scrambles would be a bit delayed, because for the first two games of the 1986 season Charlie Ward Jr., future Heisman winner, national champion and College Football Hall of Famer, was on the bench.

Despite entering the season as the #1 ranked team in their division, Central opened the year with one disastrous loss after another.

The offense couldn't score.

The morale was low.

They couldn't win.

"Frankly, the offense sputtered under Taylor," Lastinger, who announced the games, said. "They started out 0-2 due to anemic offensive production."

Anemic would actually have been an improvement. After two games, their monstrous offensive line had combined with their freight train of a running back to score zero touchdowns. They lost the first game of the year 7-3 to Dougherty and fell 15-3 to Tift County the next week. Heading into their third game against the Colquitt County Packers, the Yellow Jackets hadn't scored a touchdown or even topped seven points on the season. Then, during the game with Colquitt, Taylor got hurt and had to be taken off the field.

Suddenly, Charlie, who as mentioned earlier was only medically cleared to punt at this point, was now the only viable option at quarterback. He was also, basically, an enigma wrapped in a riddle in pads.

His knee was sore but it was structurally sound. He was cleared to punt, but not to play without restrictions. He was the best quarterback on the team, but not technically on the depth chart. He looked completely healthy and recovered, but he hadn't gone all out in a practice yet.

Then there was the most important aspect of all: his dad was at the stadium and his mom was not. Charlie Sr. was a coach on the team, and his mom wasn't in the stands yet because Junior was only supposed to be kicking the ball on fourth and long.

As Taylor was removed from the field, Coach Greene and Charlie Sr. went over their options. Charlie Sr. had overseen Junior's recovery throughout the entire process and believed that his knee was 100%. He felt that the "punting only" mandate was just a precaution. However, it was a precaution that Charlie's mother, his wife, was 100% in favor of. After some deliberating, a split-second decision was made.

"Sure, it's been long enough. Let's put him in," Charlie Sr. told Coach Greene, looking around to see if Mrs. Ward was in the stands.

She wasn't.

Yet.

As Willard Ward made her way into the stadium feeling carefree, with none of the usual motherly nerves about her son getting hurt or taking a big hit or suffering a tough loss, she heard something over the PA system that changed all of that.

Now entering the game, Charlie Ward Junior!!!

What in the world? Willard thought.

She hustled into the stadium and tried to steal a look at Charlie Sr., who did his best to avoid eye contact. She proceeded to watch the game, searching the field to see how her son would hold up.

"When they finally made the call to put in Charlie, we all kind of held our breath," Randy Young said, remembering the feeling in the stadium. "He hadn't really played in almost two years. During his first series we all went, 'Okay, he's fine.' Because he just dominated. He was a man amongst boys. He is one of the only high school players that I've seen in all my years who single-handedly, by themselves, could completely take over a football game."

As would become the norm, Charlie led the Yellow Jackets to a win.

The real battle, however, took place at the Ward home that night.

"You can only imagine what happened at my house that night between my mom and my dad," Charlie said. "My mom was upset, saying that I wasn't cleared to play and that I was only supposed to be punting. And then my dad was saying that if I could punt and be on the field anyway then there was really no reason I couldn't play quarterback. It was just back and forth... But I ended up playing the rest of that season."

• • •

Central's home stadium, aka the Jackets' Nest, is located at the corner of North Pinetree Boulevard and East Jackson Street, across from a Days Inn, a Nissan dealership, a Honda dealership and a McDonald's.

Today, the giant billboard hovering over the northwest corner of one end zone stands as a testament to the foundation of excellence Charlie helped build, as well as to his accomplishments after his high school playing days were over. Two giant yellow jackets flank the words STATE CHAMPIONS in huge, yellow letters. Below that reads the years of the titles. Under that, more giant yellow letters read REGION CHAMPS and twelve years are listed. Beneath those years, a wide, blue rectangle sign says, CHARLIE WARD, JR., 1993 HEISMAN TROPHY WINNER.

Looking at the billboard today gives the impression of a football powerhouse steeped in state and regional titles. Back when Charlie took over in that home game against Colquitt, however, they could have painted the billboard with a single brush and can of paint. The only thing on it would have said REGION CHAMPS, 1972 & 1974. No other titles. No Heisman winners—nothing but Central High's mascot and two regional wins from the early 1970s.

With Charlie under center, the billboard was going to start filling up quickly.

Almost overnight following the 17-6 win against the Packers, the mood around the football team and the town changed. It was as if a fog had been lifted. As if suddenly the team was a juggernaut.

"When Junior stepped on the field, everyone instantly believed they were going to win," Lastinger said. "He was the coolest customer I had ever seen. Looking back, the only way to explain how he played was to say he was like Michael Vick as a runner with Joe Montana's arm. He was unstoppable. Defenders would have him dead to rights and he'd disappear. At the last second he'd slip away or step back or roll like a bull fighter and he'd be gone."

Highlight tapes are filled with scenarios where defenses seemingly had the perfect play called to force Charlie out of the pocket, only for him to escape and toss a perfect thirty-yard pass, on the run to his receivers.

"His anticipation was off the charts," Lastinger said. "In addition to his athleticism, he truly had the knowledge of not only what everyone on his team was doing at any given time, but also of what the defense was doing."

His number one target, Tommy Rainge, echoes the sentiment, explaining that there were times when he'd break off a route, and almost before he knew where he was headed, the ball was in the air leading him exactly where he wanted to go.

"People still come up to me around town asking about certain plays or talking about certain things me and Charlie did," Rainge said. "He always had one eye on the field and one eye on me. It was just phenomenal. I'd cut off a pattern, make a move and man, the ball just showed up where I needed it. It was such a privilege to play with him. He was so smooth and calm and confident."

Even at the age of seventeen, it appeared to everyone involved in his sports career that Charlie was impervious to pressure. Rainge talks about how it would be ninety degrees out and they'd be backed up in their own end zone against an opponent and Charlie wouldn't even be sweating. Childhood friend Aloysius Henderson recalls watching Charlie on the sideline during games when Central would fall behind, and he'd quietly be telling his teammates that they were going to win. No yelling and shouting, just matter-of-factly telling his teammates to relax because they were capable of coming back for a victory. Charlie Sr., when asked to really think about it, can't recall a single time when Charlie was rattled or thrown off his game on the football field.

"Stress. Pressure. That stuff has just never fazed him," his dad said. "He never talked about anything to us. He knew he was a target as the quarterback and leader, and he knew he was going to take shots, but it didn't change how he played. If you tried to hit him, most likely he'd do a little Jim Brown move and you'd miss and he'd be scrambling for a throw or he'd take off on a run. If you did manage to hit him or even hurt him, he'd never let you know. Once he got the reputation for being a star, other teams would hit him late, after the whistle, try to take him out or beat him up and he'd have no reaction. He'd just get up, go back to the huddle and do his thing."

After taking over the starting quarterback job with a comeback win, he began a confidence-building undefeated streak to start his career, each game taking the once-dormant offense to new heights. After Colquitt, Central beat Cairo 30-0. Then they smoked Albany 41-7.

By the time the Thomasville versus Central rivalry game appeared on the schedule, Charlie had established himself as the unquestioned leader of his team. He had also picked up a trademark "look" that was soon recognizable to both teammates and opponents.

The "look" started with his signature towel, tucked into the edge of his football pants and always hanging slightly off to the right. It was most often white, but sometimes it was navy. Occasionally, on game films, the towel fluttering between defenders is the only way to keep track of Charlie as he carves through would-be tacklers from schools like Bainbridge and Appling County and Coffee County.

There's even a legendary story about the towel that goes like this:

It's third down (or fourth) and Charlie was under center in the pro set. He took the snap and dropped back, faking a handoff to the fullback. After the fake, he put the ball on his hip as if he was going to pitch it to the running back. As the defender closed in, he pitched the towel (which the defender went after), tucked the ball and sliced up the field for a touchdown.

"One of the most incredible things I've ever seen," Henderson said.

He also had a white armband that he wore over his right forearm. Because it was bright, it would help distract defenders with ball fakes, pump fakes and flea flickers. Combine that with the golden pants the Yellow Jackets wore—and for a young man who said little—Charlie's uniform had a modicum of Deion Sanders swag to it. This was no accident, as right about the time Charlie was taking over the reins at Central High, Sanders was lighting up Doak Campbell Stadium in Tallahassee for the Florida State Seminoles with his cornerback play, punt returns and interceptions.

"We watched every Florida State game, and you couldn't miss what Deion was doing out there," Charlie said. "His style and confidence influenced a lot of guys in our area. Me included."

Ward's flare and his three-game winning streak brought the Yellow Jackets' record to 3-2 heading into their October 17 match-up against their crosstown rivals, the Bulldogs, who were 4-1 and ranked fourth in the state. It would also be the first official meeting between Charlie Ward Jr. and Shawn Jones, aka the Thomasville Twins, in a meaningful high school football game. The town could barely contain itself. These were perhaps the two best quarterbacks South Georgia had ever produced, and they were leading excellent teams onto the field in a game with playoff implications (Central had climbed back into the top ten in the county rankings). And to make matters more interesting, they were best friends off the field.

"They're practically brothers," Willard Ward said.

Charlie and Shawn were born in the same hospital on the campus of FAMU and delivered by the same doctor (Dr. Brickler) only four months apart. Their moms were sorority sisters and their dads were fraternity brothers. They played the same position and had the same experiences growing up as gifted athletes in a small town. Despite their friendship, which would outlast any of their clashes on the field, the people of Thomasville were champing at the bit to watch them square off.

"If you wanted to rob the city of Thomasville, you'd never find a better time than Saturday between 4 p.m. and 6:30 p.m. The city will stop. Everybody will be watching their televisions. There isn't too much bigger in [Thomasville] than Charlie and Shawn playing against each other," Karl Abrams, a longtime coach at Thomasville's YMCA said at the time.

Abrams coached both of the Thomasville Twins in basketball and said the town would completely focus on them when they faced off in football.

"When they went to high school and played against each other, there would be 12,000 people in the stands and 24,000 eyeballs glued to two players. They would keep people on the edge of their seats," he said.

In total they would face each other four times in high school.

Round one went to Charlie.

Up to that game, Thomasville's defense had been fairly stout, holding several opponents to one touchdown each and a few others to just two and a smattering of field goals. Central's defense was even more formidable, having allowed only four touchdowns in five games. None of that mattered on this particular day.

The Thomasville Twins led their teams to a combined 63 points that day, with Charlie scoring on a variety of passes and runs the likes of which the Bulldogs (or anyone in South Georgia) had never seen.

The final score was 35-28, and the win gave Charlie and the Yellow Jackets their fourth straight victory. That Sunday, from Walmart to grocery stores to gas stations, Charlie was the talk of Thomasville.

How good is he?

Can Central win State?

What if he doesn't lose again?

Can he go pro?

On October 18, 1986, Charlie Ward Jr. was just a kid who was a little over one month into having the starting quarterback job on his high school team. State, national and professional accolades were all off in the distance. Nobody knew the level of greatness they were witnessing or how far it would eventually go. But everyone in Thomasville *sensed* that they were on the brink of being a part of something, and someone, special—or to use a word that often comes out of people's mouths when talking about Charlie: magical.

"There is something about Charlie that is magical," Central Middle School Principal Williams said.

"He was just…magic," Rainge said several times while talking.

"Football was his gift," Randy Young said. "He was magical out there."

And really, could you blame anyone who was watching for thinking that way?

After beating Thomasville in the shootout, Charlie led Central to two road victories in a row: the first a tightly fought 13-9 win against Coffee, and the second a 31-7 blowout against Bainbridge, which moved them up to be the third-ranked team in the region. They then squeaked by tenth-ranked Appling County at home, 31-29, before finishing the regular season with a win against Ware County, 26-18.

Charlie had now led Central to eight straight wins and a playoff berth. The team had gone from averaging three points a game on offense to nearly thirty. The "Junior" effect was in full effect. Yet, it had almost no effect on Charlie.

"It's always been my nature to be calm," he said. "I had my hands in a lot of plays, but any good player needs other good players to be successful. I had a few guys like Rainge and Garland to throw to. I had a great running back. We had a big line. Our defense was very good. We all had been playing together for a long time so we had chemistry too. I felt like it was *our* winning streak, not mine. I was the quarterback and when a big play was needed, [I stepped up because] that's what leaders are supposed to do. That was my job so I did it."

To keep him humble and focused at practices during the winning streak, Charlie Sr. would go out of his way to be hard on Junior. He was on him for putting the ball in the wrong hand while running. He was on him for not recognizing a defense early enough…or for staying in the pocket too long. He was all over young Charlie, picking at him and calling him out whenever he could in front of the team. It was all part of his plan.

"When your son is on your team, you can never go easier on him than any other player," he said. "But since he was my son, I knew what he could handle and I could use him as an example. I know how Charlie is and I know he lets things go in one ear and out the other. I know he can take a whole lot and shrug it off, so I'd throw a whole lot at him. I wanted the other kids to think two things: one, that if I expected this much out of my son, I expected the same out of them; and two, if they saw him taking the criticism like a man and learning from it, which I knew he would, they'd follow suit."

The only problem with the plan was that Junior's maturity and lack of emotion almost caused it to backfire several times, leaving Charlie Sr. in a position where he was almost forced to go easy on him for the sake of the other kids.

"When kids would mess up during practice, we'd make them run suicide drills and jumping drills," Charlie Sr. said. "Nobody wanted to run suicides in the South Georgia heat. But when Charlie would mess up, I'd have him run first in front of everyone, and it didn't bother him at all. He'd run forever. I'd have him do jumping drills and other stuff, and he took whatever we threw at him and moved on without getting upset. The other kids doing the drills with him wouldn't be able to hang with him, so we'd have to stop it before he showed any signs of being punished. The only person who would get upset was Mrs. Ward because she wanted me to ease up on Junior."

Meanwhile, at the Ward house back in Fruit City, the toast of the town still had to put his dishes in the sink after eating toast for breakfast. He still had to do chores and homework and clean up his room. Humility ruled the day in the Ward household, no matter how many wins he'd rack up or how many yards he'd run for. There was zero special treatment.

"He was just Junior to us," his sister Leta Ward said. "We knew he was good at football and that maybe at that point he could get a scholarship to play in college. We had a sense that he was headed in that direction."

• • •

The Associated Press had Central ranked third in the region to start the postseason and the *Atlanta Journal-Constitution* had them ranked fourth. The first game was a rematch against Appling County that in no way resembled the 31-29 back-and-forth offensive game the first time around. This game was a 13-6 slugfest that the Yellow Jackets were lucky to come out of with a victory.

On the other side of the playoff bracket, Thomasville beat Bainbridge to set up Charlie Ward Jr. versus Shawn Jones, Round 2.

This time, the game would be played on Central's home field in slightly different conditions. It was late November, just around Thanksgiving—the field was in bad shape and the weather wasn't very good. The Thomasville Twins would lead their teams to only a combined 20 points, more than forty fewer than their first match-up. Charlie and Central would again be victorious.

The win would put Charlie's undefeated streak at ten games and put Central in the driver's seat for a state title.

"Charlie saved the day so many times," Lastinger said. "The belief permeated the team that if he was on the field, they would win. And to that point they were correct."

On December 5 the Yellow Jackets traveled to Augusta to play Westside in the hostile road environment of Richmond Academy Stadium for the state quarterfinals. The bus ride was almost five hours, taking the team across the entire state of Georgia right to the edge of South Carolina. The concern leading up was that it would be a long, disappointing ride home if the Jackets lost.

They didn't.

Charlie put on a display of offensive wizardry, leading his squad to a 41-14 win and setting up a semifinal showdown at home against Worth County, who had only one loss on the season and their own seven-game winning streak on the line.

"Ohhh, the Worth County game," Charlie Sr. groans. "So many things should not have happened in that game. Fumbles. Bad play calls. Bad reads in the end zone. That was our game to win."

"That game was disappointing," Lastinger says. "Central fumbled a couple kickoffs early and really set up Worth County. We were a better team and were in a hole the entire game."

Finally, after starting the season on the bench and watching his team muster two field goals in two games, then taking over the starting QB job in week three and leading the team to more than four touchdowns per game and a double-digit win streak, the magic, as it were, ran out.

Central lost to Worth County in the Jackets' Nest, 21-14.

"We were disappointed, for sure," Charlie Jr. said. "We should have won. But I knew we had most of us coming back, and that the next year we'd probably enter the season as favorites to win the state championship. That's what I told the guys after the game."

"Yeah," Charlie Sr. said. "He got those natural leadership qualities from his mom. He wasn't too high with the highs or too low with the lows. We were all upset that we lost—hated it—but the season was the most fun any of us had had in a long time. Junior knew we were set up well for the next year. He processed the loss and moved on. Plus, with football ending, basketball season was about to begin."

Chapter 8

A Brief Basketball Interlude

The pushing and shoving had gone on for a while. Fouls had long-since stopped being called. There was no courtesy or checking or complimenting each other on a nice shot or a great spin move. This was vintage driveway hoops. One-on-one. Few rules. Just two people, a ball, a hoop and pride on the line.

Charlie had faced his nemesis too many times to count at this point and had yet to win. Month after month, year after year, he would take a beating. Shots would be blocked. Dribbles would be stolen. He'd get backed down and embarrassed and dominated in the post.

Each time he played, he'd try a new move he learned from watching his favorite basketball players on TV. Maybe it would be a crossover from Philly's Andrew Toney or a quick jumper from Detroit's Vinnie "The Microwave" Johnson or a soaring layup from Magic Johnson.

None of it worked.

This day was no different.

Despite dribbling himself to exhaustion and trying step-backs, fade-aways, driveway threes and pull-up jumpers, Charlie would once again lose.

To his older sister, Leta.

"He was such a sore loser back then," Leta said. "I'm five years older and he always wanted to play me, and it so happened that I had a little skill on the court. He'd go out with his friends and beat all of them and then come home and ask to play me, thinking he'd win but I'd end up beating him. He would literally cry sometimes when he was really little."

It wasn't until Charlie was in seventh grade that he finally was able to play David to his sister's Goliath role on the court.

"Once he started playing organized ball in fifth grade his game took off," she said. "I held him off for a while longer because I was taller and could shoot, but once he really learned how to play, and he finally beat me, that was it. Then, really, almost nobody in Thomasville could beat him in basketball by that point. He loved to play."

"As good as he was in football, he played basketball with more passion," Randy Young said. "You could kind of see it, at least from my perspective of watching him. It looked like he enjoyed it more."

The point guard position in basketball, same as the quarterback position in football, put Charlie in control of the action and allowed him to play to the strengths he possessed beyond his superior athleticism. With the ball in his hands, his uncanny ability to absorb what was happening on the court faster than everyone else made it appear as if he was playing at a different speed—like he had a supercomputer in his brain while the rest of the players on the court had a calculator. This was almost more pronounced in basketball than football. Whether you call it court vision or anticipation or basketball IQ, Charlie had it.

Had he never played football or had he been born in a basketball-crazy town somewhere in Kentucky where his on-court play wasn't in the shadow of his on-field heroics, maybe he would have had a bigger high school hoops profile nationally. Maybe he'd have been a part of the 1988 McDonald's High School All-American team that included Christian Laettner, Alonzo Mourning, Shawn Kemp, LaPhonso Ellis, Malik Sealy, Chris Mills and Anthony Peeler. Maybe.

"As much as he loved basketball, football was where he was most impressive," Young said. "He was an exceptional high school basketball player, but in football he was just remarkable."

Charlie, for his part, refused to pick a favorite between the two sports and just enjoyed the transition from one to the other. After sustaining the injuries and recovering from the surgeries he endured earlier in high school, he wanted to drink sports from a fire hose now that he was healthy—the more, the better. Off-seasons weren't for time off, they were for dominating with a different ball.

Following Central's football loss to Worth County, Junior and Senior, player and coach, transitioned to basketball and didn't think about football until hoops season was over.

The basketball team, however, didn't begin Charlie's junior year ranked number one like the football team had been. They weren't ranked at all.

"We just didn't have the type of team to get it done on a nightly basis," Charlie said. "It didn't mean we didn't practice hard or have good kids, we just weren't blessed with much talent. We played hard and we played together, though."

Translation:

The basketball team wasn't very good, but he had fun.

While Charlie racked up an untold number of steals and assists (many to his wide receiver/power forward, Tommy Rainge) during basketball season, the rest of Thomasville was still buzzing about what took place in the fall. Even as he ran track in the spring, it felt as though there was an omnipresent giant clock counting down to the start of the 1987 high school football season, with one question looming over everything,

How far could #10, Charlie Ward Jr., take the Yellow Jackets?

Chapter 9

Exceeding the Hype

There's a road in Thomasville that connects the North Thomasville Bypass with Pinetree Boulevard. It runs right through the heart of Thomas County Central High School's campus. Teenagers have stolen the sign for the road numerous times, and it has been replaced numerous times. The latest version of the sign on display isn't even entirely accurate, as it says CHARLIE WARD BOULEVARD, when the official name registered with the town—and with Google maps—is Charlie Ward Junior Boulevard.

The sign is set back to the left next to Victory Baptist Church, so as you approach it off Pinetree, the Google Maps voice says, *"take a left on Charlie Ward Jr. Boulevard"* before you actually see that you're about to drive on Charlie Ward Jr. Boulevard, which is all the more meta if you're in Thomasville to research a book on Charlie Ward Jr.

Relaying this story to Charlie Ward Sr. in his family room brings a big smile to his face. He bounces off the couch, slides a box away from the wall and reveals a pristine blue sign with yellow lettering that says CHARLIE WARD JR. BOULEVARD.

"This is the commemorative one, and it's the only one that's left," he laughs. "Kids kept stealing the sign off the street and they finally stopped printing the whole name like this one. Now this one right here is Junior's, but the one at the school doesn't have the 'junior,' so I guess that street's named after me."

In the front of the school, directly before the main entrance, is another sign that says, HOME OF CHARLIE WARD JR. — WINNER OF 1993 HEISMAN TROPHY.

"Oh, that one's definitely his," Charlie Sr. says, laughing. "He earned that one."

For those keeping score, that's one street sign, one sign at his high school, one sign at that school's football field and another entering the town that lets visitors know Thomasville is Charlie Ward Jr. country.

While this type of legacy may have seemed plausible to football fans in south Georgia following Charlie's junior year at quarterback for Central, it certainly wasn't considered likely. Charlie was really good, even great up to that point, but the football faithful had seen great football players before. What they hadn't seen was excellence, bordering on gridiron perfection.

They were about to—and they'd have some famous company.

• • •

The Quality Inn sitting across from the Thomasville Shopping Center on US-Road 19 used to be a Holiday Inn back in the 1980s. This is crucial information when it comes to telling the story of Charlie Ward Jr. because there is now a different Holiday Inn in Thomasville down the road and the two cannot be confused. The new Holiday Inn is sandwiched between an International House of Pancakes and a Waffle House, and was not the secret getaway for the Florida State Seminoles teams on Friday nights before big Saturday home games decades ago. That distinction goes to the current location of the Quality Inn, aka, the old Holiday Inn. Why does any of this matter? Because the old Holiday Inn is less than a half-mile from the Jackets' Nest, where Charlie Ward Jr. performed weekly on Friday nights in the fall of 1987 in front of sold-out crowds that were loud enough to get the attention of the FSU head coach Bobby Bowden, who would occasionally wander over, unofficially, to catch the action.

"We knew Coach Bowden took his team to the Holiday Inn to get them out of Tallahassee and to keep them isolated and focused the night before a game," Yellow Jackets radio announcer Randy Young said. "There were many Friday nights where we'd see him on the outskirts of the stadium, leaning against the fence. He wasn't recruiting or anything. He was a football fan like us and he got to witness some awesome games."

Legendary University of Georgia Head Coach Vince Dooley also made a few official appearances to watch Charlie play live. At this point in time, Dooley was less than a decade removed from a national championship and several one-loss seasons. His presence was felt the moment he came within one hundred yards of the stadium. After all, he coached Herschel Walker, a virtual football super hero to the young men in Georgia at the time.

"I've always felt that Bowden had a big advantage in recruiting southern Georgia, and Central High in particular, because of his Friday nights in Thomasville," Young said. "So many nights we'd be in the booth and we'd kind of glance down and see him hanging out near an end zone taking in the action. He saw a lot of players that you'd think would end up at Georgia or Georgia Tech, but he eventually recruited to Florida State."

The 1987 version of Coach Bowden differs quite a bit from the modern coaching icon that retired in 2009 with two national championships and nine one-loss seasons. In the fall of 1987, Bowden's Seminoles were coming off a 7-4-1 season in 1986 and a 9-3 season in 1985. He was entering his twelfth year in Tallahassee, and aside from back-to-back strong seasons in 1979 and 1980 that both ended in Orange Bowl losses, Bowden's teams consistently finished outside of the top 10 in the AP Polls final results.

Back then, Bowden had built his reputation on being an excellent recruiter, an innovator, a program-builder and a man who could win bowl games (the only two he lost were the Orange Bowls in '79 and '80). His teams were good, but he had not yet won a national championship or cemented his legacy as one of the top coaches in the nation. He seemed to hover one tier below Penn State's Joe Paterno, who won the national championship in '86; Jimmy Johnson of Miami; Barry Switzer of Oklahoma; Tom Osborne at Nebraska; and Bo Schembechler at Michigan, all of whom competed for titles year in and year out.

No doubt, one of the things that drew Bowden to the Jackets' Nest all those Friday nights was the hope of finding a talent that could help him get to the promised land. In that hope, Bowden was not alone. As the 1987 Georgia high school football season got underway, Central's Head Coach Charlie Greene wondered if he had enough talent to do the same.

The *Atlanta Journal-Constitution* had Central ranked third heading into the year, and so did the Associated Press. Don Watz's preseason review for the *Tallahassee Democrat* also placed Central among the top teams in the Class AAA region, citing few holes in the squad.

"The Yellow Jackets are loaded with experienced regulars who helped post an 11-3 record last season... Nine starters return on offense, six on defense," he wrote. "The complete Yellow Jacket backfield will return, with senior quarterback Charlie Ward at the helm. Junior fullback Steve Fleming and senior running back Keith Christopher will carry most of the load. Coach Charlie Greene, in his third year there, will say only that he feels his team will be competitive."

"It will be a five-team race," Greene was quoted as saying in the piece.

He was being generous.

Everyone in Georgia knew that the road to the state championship went through Thomasville and the Thomasville Twins. It was unclear which of the two teams would come out on top, or even which one had an edge, but the community was aware that they had entered a Golden Era of football. The city of roughly 17,000 people was now the hub of the high school football universe in the Peach State, with Charlie Ward Jr. and his buddy Shawn Jones on a collision course to decide the title.

The season began for Central on September 5 with an impressive 21-0 shutout of Dougherty. They followed that up with a tight win against Tift County, the fifth ranked team in the state, and then a win against Colquitt County. By week four they were the number one team in the state, rolling over Cairo 34-14 and then beating Albany 20-13, giving them a five-game winning streak to add to their résumé.

While the Yellow Jackets were taking care of business on their schedule, the Thomasville Bulldogs had been doing the same, crushing one team after another, including the 1986 champions, Worth County. They also beat Westover, Coffee and Cairo, catapulting themselves to the number two ranking in the state, with their own five-game winning streak heading into their October 16 rivalry game at the Jackets' Nest. Finally, south Georgia high school football fans had the game they'd been dreaming about for years.

Thomasville vs. Central.

#2 vs. #1.
Shawn Jones vs. Charlie Ward Jr.
Round three.

• • •

If you were to rank the most important moments involving electricity and the city of Thomasville, the first would have to be when it arrived in the city in 1889. A group of private investors installed a small generator at the old Thomasville Variety Works on Stevens Street that had the capacity of only fifty lights. Following that, one could argue that the second-most valuable moment in Thomasville's history with electricity came when it powered the Friday night lights for the Thomasville Twins' football game on October 16, 1987.

Though this was more than a mere game; it was the biggest event to that point in 1987 in Thomas County. There were parades and pep rallies and marching bands. There was live music and dancers and singers. Vendors were selling balloons and t-shirts and hats. Fans arrived hours before kick-off to enjoy the festivities and grab a seat in what turned out to be a standing-room-only crowd of roughly 10,000 people. If you exclude the elderly and infants and others not able to attend the game, about 75% of the entire town was in the stadium. Another 10% or so hung out around the stadium and listened to the game on the radio so they could hear the roar of the crowd live.

"The anticipation for that game was something I had never seen before," Charlie said. "It was the only thing people talked about all week. Friday night seemed to be on everyone's mind no matter where we went. School. Church. Everywhere."

The hype was all consuming, and by kickoff the stadium was a powder keg ready to be lit. An opening kick return for a touchdown or a big scoring drive might have driven the stadium into a frenzy. Instead, the game began with a long, steady, seventeen-play drive by the visiting Bulldogs, who fed their stud running back Ronnie Gardner over and over again to try to take the home crowd out of it. In the end, the drive covered 64 yards, took up most of the first quarter and ended with a 24-yard field goal by Mark Futch.

As often happens in games of this magnitude, there are unpredictable contributors and story lines. In this case, that contributor was Futch, who had just taken over the kicking duties. The field goal in this game was his first successful try of the season, on the road, in the biggest game his town had ever seen.

Central, finally, got the ball on their home field—and quickly did nothing with it. They were forced to punt on their first series. When Thomasville got the ball back, they went on another long drive (ten plays) and Gardner scored on a one-yard run. The snap on the extra point was fumbled, so the Bulldogs took a 9-0 lead.

The next possession for Central led to another punt—and so did the possession after that. The Yellow Jackets, who were coming off a combined 54 points in their previous two games, entered halftime against their rivals with an abysmal stat line:

13 total offensive yards.

3 punts.

0 pass completions.

0 points.

The game was unfolding in the exact opposite way that Coach Greene wanted it to. In an interview he gave before the game, he laid out what his concerns were and what he thought Central had to do to win. His team was doing none of them.

"I tell you, the real key for us is to stop that wishbone. And we have to get good field position. We can't be hoping to drive from our twenty every time," he said.

So much for best-laid plans. After thirty minutes of football, Central couldn't stop the wishbone, they had crummy field position over and over, and forget driving from the twenty—they weren't driving at all.

"We got taken out of our game," Charlie Sr. said. "Coach Hodges [Thomasville's head coach] had a good game plan and we couldn't execute ours. We knew we needed some fire to open the third quarter."

As always, Charlie was a sphinx. To look at him, you wouldn't have known if his team was up twenty or down thirty. Internally, he knew what his team was capable of and he was confident they would be able to move the ball in the second half. After all, he figured, it couldn't be worse. And they were only down nine points. They could make that up quickly.

"He had such a strong mindset," said Rainge, who had zero catches in the first half. "He was confident all the time. Not cocky. Not that at all. Confident. He was poised, and he knew exactly what he was supposed to do on the field and what you were supposed to do, and he usually knew what the other team was going to do before they did it. This so happened to be one of those games when nothing was going right."

Charlie and the Yellow Jackets came out passing in the second half and finally moved the ball some, but when the clock ran to 0:00 in the third quarter they still could not get in the end zone. The game remained 9-0, with both teams locked in a defensive struggle. Neither side had scored in two full quarters and the sold-out crowd was getting anxious. The Thomasville fans could see Charlie getting comfortable and were worried that he would finally break through and explode in the fourth. The Central fans were feeling positive for the same reason, but they were concerned that their own defense was worn out and that Shawn Jones might make a few plays early in the quarter to put the game out of reach. Both sides had valid concerns, and Jones would make his mark first, hitting a receiver for a 36-yard touchdown and putting his team up 15-0. The Bulldogs' Head Coach Mike Hodges tried to make it a three- or four-score game and went for two, but the attempt failed, still leaving the Yellow Jackets with a monster hole to dig themselves out of.

With less than twelve minutes on the clock and his high-powered offense still being shutout, Ward lined up on his own twenty yard line and surveyed the field. He knew he needed to make something happen soon. Nothing to that point had worked. Not shotguns or swing passes or deep balls or dives or rollouts. Instead, he decided to pick up the pace.

"When you're a leader on a team, your teammates look to you in the biggest and bleakest moments to make something happen," he said. "I felt that it was my responsibility to get us going any way I could."

Four plays, eighty yards and fifty-six seconds later, Central made it to the end zone for the first time that night on a pass from Ward to Andre Hunter. Central fans went flat out crazy. In a game where positive yards were hard to come by and points even harder, Coach Greene decided to gamble and go for two to cut the lead to one touchdown and one two-point conversion. The attempt didn't work, but the scoreboard gave Central and its supporters new life. Thomasville fans, on the other hand, went into full-on nail-biting, don't-jinx-this mode.

Jeannie Roberts covered the game for the *Tallahassee Democrat* and captured the mood in the stadium in the fourth quarter.

"Even after the Bulldogs led the entire game, no Thomasville fan in Thomas County stadium rested easy...Ward, a serious running threat from anywhere on the field, could strike at any time," she wrote.

Following the Yellow Jackets' score, the two teams traded several possessions, with the Bulldogs doing their best to milk the clock and sit on their lead. As the clock wound down, Thomasville found themselves facing a fourth down that could potentially end the game. Central's defense would have none of it, hung tough, and gave Charlie and his offense one last chance.

Moments later, Charlie and his squad were facing their own fourth and one with the game seemingly on the line. After dropping back, Charlie scrambled to find an open receiver. Nobody was free. As he desperately searched the field for a target, Eric Curry, the future Alabama standout, caught up to him for a sack, making the biggest play of the game.

After beating Thomasville his first two times as a starter, this one simply wasn't meant to be for Ward and the Yellow Jackets. The final score was 15-6.

"This was a team victory," Coach Hodges said afterward. "I tell you, these boys have worked four years to get this win."

Charlie, always economical and positive with his words, didn't dwell on the loss for long.

"That was a tough one," he said. "We had a few turnovers and plays that didn't work out for us. I knew if we could win the rest of our games we'd probably play them again in the playoffs, so that's the mentality I took after the game was over. They were a really good team. We lost. We had a lot of games left though."

• • •

The loss to Thomasville only dropped Central to third in the region, so a playoff berth was still likely as long as they took care of business the last four games of the regular season. And the Yellow Jackets did just that. Despite the calm, taciturn exterior that Charlie exuded, his competitive juices were raging inside. His natural disposition was not one in which that rage manifested itself outwardly with yelling or shouting or the old "wear your heart on your sleeve" mentality of a quarterback like Brett Favre. No, in Charlie's case, the way he would express how furious he was about losing to his crosstown rival was to unleash his skills on his upcoming opponents.

"Charlie never said much," Charlie Sr. said. "That phrase 'he let his play do his talking' was never truer than with him. He just closed his mouth, put his head down, and went to taking apart these teams the rest of the year."

First up was number ten-ranked Coffee, whose defense had the misfortune of directly following Thomasville. Charlie didn't see the Trojans' defenders so much as he was seeing red from the loss to the Bulldogs. The Trojan linemen and defensive backs were simply obstacles to be thrown over or run through. Central would win that game easily, 41-14.

Then they'd beat Bainbridge 34-28, annihilate Appling County 42-14 and wear out Ware County, 33-6. For the record, in the month following the loss to Thomasville, Charlie led the Yellow Jackets on an offensive blitz that would total 150 points in four games heading into the postseason.

The first round of the playoffs pitted Central against Coffee for a second time, and for a second time they were no match for the Yellow Jackets, who won 29-15, running up their total against one of the top teams in the region to 70 points in two games.

And so, six weeks after the toughest loss of Charlie's young career, he'd have his chance at redemption against his friend Shawn Jones and Thomasville one final time in the regional round of the playoffs on November 27, 1987.

This time, however, the Bulldogs were number one in the state and Central was third. The game would be on the road at Thomasville's stadium, and for the seniors on the losing side, their high school careers would be over. Then there was this, not to be overlooked: Charlie, though he'd never show it or say it, was playing for revenge. He was not about to lose to Thomasville a second time.

• • •

Eleven thousand, five hundred people would show up for Ward vs. Jones, round four. Thus far the series was 2-1 in favor of Ward, but a loss here, in the playoffs, and following the loss in the regular season, would cement the Bulldogs' supremacy over the 1987 Yellow Jackets. It would also allow them to finally cash in on what was perceived to be an edge in talent.

"[1987] was probably as talented a football team as we had at Thomasville while I was there," Coach Hodges said, looking back on the game.

According to Randy Young, had the playoff brackets broken differently, and given the way the two teams were playing at the time, the game should have been for the state championship.

"There were stud college athletes all over that field," he said. "So many of those guys played at the next level and the headliners were going to big time programs and would win national championships."

In this moment though, it was all on the line: hometown pride, bragging rights and legacy.

"Standing room only was a misstatement," former Thomasville offensive lineman Renny Thompson said. "It was from Jackson Street all the way to the practice field. It was pretty incredible."

"I don't think it could've gotten any better," former Thomasville assistant coach Andy Jones (father of Shawn Jones and Mike Jones, both star players for Thomasville) said. "With what we put on the field and what Central put on the field, I mean, we had college coaches from all over."

This game would turn out to have an entirely different feel and tempo than the previous match-up. It would not be a defensive slog where both teams put up a string of zeroes on the scoreboard.

Central received the ball first, and on the second down of the first series of the game, Charlie dropped back and unloaded a 75-yard touchdown pass to Tommy Rainge for a quick 7-0 lead.

"We were just in sync," Rainge said. "He had that look like he'd get me the ball if I got open, and I did. As soon as I had my defender beat I knew Charlie could get me the ball. He was special. I don't think too many other guys in high school can make that throw."

The elation wouldn't last long.

Within minutes, Thomasville scored on their own 75-yard touchdown pass from Shawn Jones to Jerome Williams.

The game would remain 7-7 at the end of the first quarter. To start the second, Charlie got into an otherworldly rhythm and led the team on an eleven-play, 80-yard drive that would end in a rushing touchdown for Steve Garland. Central would then get the ball back with time running out before the half, and Charlie executed the two-minute drill like he was a ten-year NFL veteran. He quickly marched his team down the field and hit Garland on a four-yard pass for a touchdown.

"We didn't go for the field goal because the clock was running, so we just called the play that was working," Coach Greene said.

At halftime Central led 21-7 and Thomasville's Mike Hodges was more than impressed with what Ward was accomplishing against his team.

"I've never seen a quarterback with Ward's awareness and field presence. That's what sets him apart," he said. "I mean, he's a great athlete with good quickness and a strong arm, but it's his ability to create something from nothing that makes him tough."

Despite the Yellow Jackets' strong finish to the first half and momentum clearly on their side, the defense came out a little flat in the third quarter and gave up two touchdowns while the offense briefly stalled, putting the game at a 21-21 stalemate with only fifteen minutes left to play.

A subplot during the third quarter involved Charlie's favorite deep threat, Tommy Rainge. Rainge dislocated his shoulder returning a kickoff in the second quarter, and the medical staff wasn't sure if he could return to the game.

"They carted me off the field and they told me I couldn't go back into the game," Rainge said. "But I told them my team needs me and if I can move it [his shoulder], I'm going in. I got a little mobility on my shoulder, put on my pads and got back out there."

With roughly ten minutes left in the game, Charlie would find Rainge in the end zone on a twenty-five yard pass to break the tie and put Central up 28-21.

At that point, Coach Greene thought his team might have a slight advantage.

"I saw Thomasville getting a little tired in the second half," he said. "We played more four-quarter games…and I think that helped us."

The offenses would trade possessions for the meat of the fourth quarter. With just under four minutes left and Thomasville marching down the field, Shawn Jones and the Bulldogs faced a critical fourth and six. Sensing their season on the line, the Yellow Jackets' defense stepped up and Scott Taylor sacked Jones.

Charlie then ran the clock down until finally giving the ball back to the Bulldogs with just over a minute left, but there would be no last-second heroics from his fellow Thomasville Twin. With around fifty seconds left, Jones was hit while throwing and his pass was intercepted and returned for a 65-yard touchdown to put the final score at 35-21, Central.

The Yellow Jackets had just won arguably the biggest high school football game in south Georgia history and their fans, the sidelines and the coaches were in a frenzy.

"It was truly a great high school football game. They don't come much better than this one," Coach Greene said.

The final tally for Charlie would be 204 yards passing with two touchdowns and several drive-saving scrambles. The teams would combine for 400 yards in the air and more than 425 on the ground. The win would also put Charlie at 3-1 against Thomasville and Jones.

"I've never seen a quarterback who sees the field like Charlie does,"

Greene said. "It's just uncanny. It's like he's aware of everything going on on the field at the same time. You have to see it to believe it."

The coach on the opposing sideline, Mike Hodges, had now seen "it" four times and was a believer. After the contest a reporter asked him what the turning point in the game was, and he answered with a reply that is now famous around Thomasville: "The turning point? When Charlie got off the bus."

• • •

After the game there were no *Friday Night Lights* or *Varsity Blues*-level parties and debauchery for Charlie. Yes, he was elated and celebrated with his team, but his close friends weren't partiers and he wasn't the type to go out and drink alcohol or get into trouble. He didn't drink then and doesn't drink now, in fact. Despite being the most popular young man in Thomasville—especially on that night—taking advantage of it with a raucous evening on the town simply didn't interest him.

What did interest him was being there for his friend, who just lost not only the biggest game of his high school football career on the biggest stage, but also lost the last game of high school football he'd ever play.

That friend was Shawn Jones.

"After that final game Charlie came home, called Shawn and the two of them went out together," Willard Ward said. "For as long as I can remember, it's been that way."

Jones' father echoed that point as well.

"They were both very quiet. I used to have people ask me if Shawn ever talked," he said, laughing. "They didn't like the attention. After the games, they'd go to Burger King and have a Coke."

Karl Abrams who worked at the Thomasville YMCA, thought that was par for the course for their friendship.

"When they were growing up, you never saw them hanging around," he said. "They're quiet, private people. I'm sure they spent time together and confided in each other."

Some people had a hard time understanding how a person could put their blood, sweat and tears into beating somebody on the field and then put it aside immediately afterward.

"Only immature people can't handle these situations," Charlie said when asked about it. "Everyone who is a competitor wants to win no matter who you're playing. You can't lose a friendship over a game."

This point of view was vintage Charlie—thoughtful and opinionated with wisdom that felt slightly beyond his years. His graciousness in winning and his quiet persona were part of the reason it was easy for Bulldogs fans to now shift their energy toward rooting for Central to bring a state championship to Thomasville. In order to do that, they'd have to win three more games.

In the state quarterfinals Central played Butler and won 27-19, setting up a December 11 rematch against Worth County, the team that beat them in the playoffs the previous year.

"Worth County, Worth County, Worth County," Charlie Sr. said, shaking his head on his couch many years later. "We had to face them again and again. Things didn't go well."

"That game just didn't go our way," Charlie said. "We knew what we had to do on the road and we didn't get it done. That one hurt."

Central's state title hopes and Charlie's high school career would end on Worth County's home field with a 28-21 loss.

The dream season was over.

In the end, the Charlie Ward Jr. era at Central would be recognized as the beginning of the "Golden Years" for Thomasville, when both the Yellow Jackets and the Bulldogs would compete for state championships the next several years.

"I truly believe that the level of play laid the groundwork for the teams from both high schools from 1987 on," Randy Young said. "It was just the beginning of a special time."

For Charlie, it was the beginning of another stage in his life, one that would involve awards, accolades and national attention, three things he wasn't inherently comfortable with.

At the end of the year, the *Atlanta Journal-Constitution* would select Charlie as their Region AAA Offensive Player of the Year. During the season he passed for 1,891 yards and 15 touchdowns, completing 109 of 190 attempts. He also rushed for 1,007 yards and nine touchdowns, giving him a grand total of 2,898 yards and 24 touchdowns on the season. And not to be overlooked in another area, he was one of the top punters in the state, averaging more than 40 yards per punt.

Chapter 10

The Recruit

Throughout the 1987 high school season Charlie was considered the prize recruit for many of the top colleges in the country, including Notre Dame and most of the major ACC and SEC schools in the south. For Charlie Sr., whose own options for playing college football had been limited by segregation, watching his son have the red carpet laid out for him by some of the biggest coaches and universities in football was a small form of redemption.

"All the major schools in the area sent letters and called and asked for game tape," Charlie Sr. recalled. "They sent scouts to Junior's games his whole senior year. Georgia, Florida, Florida State, Georgia Tech—all of them. We had dozens of introduction letters and offer letters and letters asking Charlie to visit from all over the country. They came in the mail every day."

"We wanted Junior to go somewhere he'd feel comfortable and where he could play quarterback," Willard said. "We didn't want a coach saying one thing and then trying to turn him into a receiver once he agreed to attend."

While that thought might sound ludicrous to the modern reader, with African-American quarterbacks like Cam Newton and Jameis Winston becoming the faces of the NFL and winning titles as quarterbacks in college, there was a time not too long ago when athletic black quarterbacks were recruited and immediately turned into receivers or running backs once they arrived on campus.

Despite all the progress made from Charlie Sr.'s days as a college athlete, the quarterback position was still largely considered a job for white kids.

This happened to be something that Florida State Coach Bobby Bowden strongly wanted to rectify.

"I had two black quarterbacks at West Virginia, and there was probably some criticism back in those days from some fans," Bowden said in his book, *Tales from the Seminoles Sideline*. "But Florida State had not had a black quarterback before Charlie."

"I remember the discussions very clearly," Randy Young said. "It all revolved around what coaches were promising him. In that period of time, black quarterbacks in the south were just starting to become mainstream. But you still had places like Georgia who didn't have their first black starting quarterback until Charlie was in high school. A lot of people were convinced that if Charlie went to Florida State he was going to eventually be forced to play wide receiver."

In addition to receiving guarantees that he would remain a quarterback, Charlie added another wrinkle in the recruitment process: he wanted to play both football and basketball. Following his titanic senior year of football, he quietly played hoops on a team that wasn't bound for any post-season glory or even a .500 record. He did, however, completely own the competition, averaging twenty points, twelve assists and eight rebounds per game his senior year.

"He was on another level than his peers in basketball, we just weren't any good," Charlie Sr., the head coach of the team said. "Junior and Tommy Rainge were the two talented guys we had. But Junior put together some performances...boy...he could play."

There was the time that the Yellow Jackets played Monroe High School on the road and Charlie ended a ten-year losing streak.

"Monroe's coach had been there a long time and I'd never beaten him," Charlie Sr. said. "He was twenty or thirty years older than me, and we could never really compete against them. Junior's senior year, I don't know if he knew about the streak or just decided on his own he was going to end it, but he went away from his normal passing and distribution game and decided to score. I don't think he missed two shots. He had thirty-eight or thirty-nine points and probably a dozen steals and we finally won. When we were walking out of the gym the coach came up to me and said, 'You finally got me.' All I could do was smile. It was all Junior."

Then there was the game against Bainbridge, who used to have a very small, very intimidating gym where they simply did not lose. It was hot and sweaty and almost claustrophobic. Teams showed up there and were immediately psyched out.

"You just did not beat them in that gym," Charlie Sr. said. "Nobody did—until Junior went in that last year and did it. I saw the coach a few times after that and he'd always mention how Junior was probably the first person to beat them there in too many years to count."

The Bainbridge game is memorable in the Ward household for another reason as well. After it was over, the University of Georgia took Charlie Jr. for a visit to the school that night.

With the storied history of the Bulldogs, a legendary head coach in Vince Dooley, star player alumni at the next level like Herschel Walker, and the pull of his home state, Georgia was neck-and-neck with Florida State in Charlie's mind as to where he'd like to attend college.

"Georgia was a real possibility," Charlie said. "So was Georgia Tech for a while. I knew people at both schools and grew up watching both schools."

"When Junior got his list down to a few schools, we sat with the head coaches and asked them the same two questions," Willard Ward said. "Will Charlie stay at quarterback and can he play basketball as well?"

Georgia, as much as they wanted Charlie, said no.

"They came back to us and said that they didn't think it was possible for Junior to compete in both sports," Willard said. "So that was it for Georgia and Georgia Tech."

Now the question boiled down to whether or not Charlie and his parents believed that Florida State would truly let him be the team's quarterback, which was a legitimate obstacle, because early in the recruiting process Bowden himself felt that maybe Charlie's best chance to be a Seminole might be as something other than a quarterback—though it should be noted that his reasons had nothing to do with race. It just so happened that in January of 1988 Florida State was absolutely stacked at QB. Peter Tom Willis and Chip Ferguson were set to fight for the starting job that spring, but more important for Charlie's sake, Bowden had two red-shirt freshmen, Casey Weldon and Brad Johnson, who would eventually become starters, already on the depth chart.

At most, the assistants on Bowden's staff thought they might need one quarterback in the '88 recruiting class, and if they were going to take one it was unanimous that it should be Terry Jordan from Tampa, a classic drop-back quarterback who would fit right into FSU's system. Up to that point, they hadn't run a shotgun, running-style offense that suited Charlie, and there were plenty of questions as to whether it would be worth trying, which led to Bowden's initial assessment of Charlie.

"What I saw was a great *running* quarterback," Bowden said. "I said we would take him if he'd consent to play another position."

Enter Wayne McDuffie, a former Florida State lineman and Bobby Bowden's offensive coordinator from 1983-1990.

McDuffie was a 6'2", 220-pound physical specimen with Hollywood action-hero looks and the disposition of a Navy SEAL Master Chief. His nickname in college was Tarzan because of his dominance in the weight room. On the field and as a coach, he fought hard for what he believed, and his belief in Charlie Ward Jr. led to a now-legendary recruiting story.

The scene took place during a meeting about recruits with Bowden and his assistants. Charlie's name came up, and one assistant after another passed on the idea of giving him a scholarship while Bowden himself showed only fleeting interest. With each setback, McDuffie got angrier and angrier. He could not comprehend that his colleagues did not see what he saw in Charlie.

"I was standing there when Charlie got off the bus [before Central's final game against Thomasville]," he said about the meeting. "He got off that bus with more confidence and faith. He had a look on his face like Michael Jordan. A look that said, 'I'm totally in charge.'"

He couldn't get that look out of his head as his fellow assistants nitpicked what he believed to be a once-in-a-generation talent. He could barely contain himself in his seat.

He fumed.

He snorted.

And then finally, he exploded.

"He beat his fist on the table," wrote Gerald Easley in the *Tallahassee Democrat*. "He stood on his chair and shouted. He may have even used some profanity."

"[He] bounced his fists off a table, then stood on a chair and roared," wrote Ian O'Connor for the *New York Daily News*.

In short, he reached back to his Tarzan-inspired college days and went totally and completely ape. And it worked.

"It was the persistence of Wayne McDuffie that convinced us to sign Charlie," said FSU assistant coach Brad Scott, who was the FSU recruiting coordinator then. "He kept saying, 'This guy is a winner.'"

FSU assistant John Eason was lured in by McDuffie early on to help convince Bowden, as Eason was familiar with the Ward family because he had been a teammate of Charlie Ward Sr.'s at Florida A&M. Eason was on board with how good a quarterback Charlie was, but he truly became a believer after watching him play basketball in the winter of 1988.

"When I got courtside and saw the calmness in his face—despite the intensity of his actions—I knew he was special." Eason said.

At the time, Coach Bowden wasn't necessarily arguing that Charlie wasn't special; he simply wasn't convinced that Charlie would be a special *quarterback*. That notion put him at odds with his assistants and put his assistants in a bit of a pickle.

"When Mr. McDuffie and Mr. Eason were talking to us, I made them promise that if Junior committed to Florida State he would remain a quarterback," Willard Ward said. "We had been told that Florida State would never start a black quarterback so we wanted assurances. I told Mr. Eason that I wasn't handing my son over to Florida State, I was handing him over to Mr. Eason to look after."

"I had to make sure Charlie was treated right," Eason said. "I didn't want to answer to his mama."

Now Eason and McDuffie had their marching orders: Convince Coach Bowden to give Charlie Ward Jr. a scholarship and promise his parents he'll remain a quarterback.

At no point did Willard Ward request Eason or McDuffie pounce on a chair and roar like a lion to make their arguments, but in the end that's what it took to convince Coach Bowden to agree to visit the Wards.

"It was one of those years when we didn't need a quarterback, but you still don't want to let a great one get away," Bowden said. "Wayne and John were convinced he was a great one."

And so, after casually watching Charlie for years on his Friday night visits to Thomasville, and after hearing McDuffie rant and rave about how great he would be as a quarterback, Bowden finally found himself on the Wards' couch in their family room…getting absolutely grilled by Willard Ward.

"I asked Mr. Bowden all of the same questions I asked Mr. Eason and Mr. McDuffie," she said. "He was the head coach. I wanted him to tell me Charlie was going to be his quarterback."

"She was tough, boy," Charlie Sr. said. "But Coach Bowden answered everything right."

Once he removed himself from the hot seat, Coach Bowden had one question for Charlie.

"Are you patient?" he asked.

"Yes, sir," Charlie said.

"Good," Coach Bowden answered.

He then went on to explain his current depth chart, how deep with talent it was, and how all Florida State quarterbacks had at least a two-year learning period before they could truly compete for the job.

Charlie was not scared off and said that yes, he could be patient. That only left one other issue.

Would Coach Bowden let him play basketball as well?

"Brad Johnson played basketball at Florida State for a few years so it wasn't anything new to them," Charlie said. "I hoped it wouldn't be an issue for me."

It wasn't.

After laying out a few conditions (get good grades, attend class, etc.) Coach Bowden offered the pride of Thomasville, Georgia, Charlie Ward Jr., a full scholarship to Florida State University with a guarantee that his position would remain quarterback.

Chapter 11

Tallahassee Community College

The National Collegiate Athletic Association's (NCAA) Proposition 48 took effect in August of 1986. It was officially called Bylaw 5-1-(j) and required incoming college freshman athletes to score at least 700 on both the math and verbal sections of the Scholastic Aptitude Test (SAT), or the equivalent 15 on the American College Test (ACT). In addition, student-athletes must have a cumulative 2.0 grade point average in eleven core curriculum classes.

Athletes who couldn't meet Prop 48's standards were allowed to accept a grant-in-aid and enroll in school. However, if they accepted a grant they would lose a year of athletic eligibility. If they enrolled and paid their own way for one year, they would have four years of eligibility remaining. Most important, however, is that those affected by Prop 48 were not allowed any contact with the school's athletic program during their freshman year. The only activities they could participate in were those available to any student, like intramural sports and going to football games as a fan.

It was a game changer.

"Back then [before Prop 48], many high school athletes knew as much about the ACT and the SAT as they did about Bulgarian cuisine," wrote Barry Temkin and Linda Young for the *Chicago Tribune* in a four-year retrospective on the controversial proposition. "Now they know them for what they are: tough tests for college admission and the most feared opponent some of them will ever face. Feared because they can do what no coach ever would: bench them for a year without the chance to play or even practice with their college teams."

The effect on some potential college athletes the first few years was devastating. Long-discussed scholarship offers were rescinded or never made. Kids found out at the last minute that they weren't eligible for a scholarship. Schools shied away from recruiting kids who didn't have the grades. No less than Bobby Bowden himself weighed in on its one-year anniversary in 1987 by acknowledging how eye opening the Prop was.

"I think the kids are finally starting to realize that this thing is for real," he said in an interview at the time. "I really think the first year that the rule was in effect, an awful lot of players never thought it would affect them. Now, all the players know that if they don't pass Proposition 48, they're not going to be able to play that first year in college."

One player it did affect was Charlie Ward Junior.

Charlie had good grades in high school but his ACT score was a little low, and had he attended college right away, he would have been swept up in the new Prop 48 fiasco.

"I didn't want to lose a year of eligibility," Charlie said. "So I decided to sit out a year and take some classes at Tallahassee Community College and prepare for the SAT in the spring."

Charlie's mom also had an ulterior motive in encouraging her son to wait to attend college as a fully qualified academic freshman: his legacy.

"I knew what the ramifications would be for Junior beyond eligibility if he enrolled at Florida State under Prop 48," she explained. "He would have had that proposition associated with him for the rest of his life. Every good thing he did at Florida State and after would be tagged with that Prop 48. Charlie was smart. We made sure he had good grades. He just didn't take certain tests well. I thought he could use a year to mature academically as well before going to college. I was sure the spotlight would be on him one day."

Willard Ward knew her son and knew what he was capable of when he applied himself. She'd been through something like this before with him. When Charlie was in third grade his teachers were concerned he was falling too far behind his peers in class. Mrs. Ward took it upon herself to help catch Charlie up. Though she'd sit with him while he did his homework and she'd give him extra assignments, nothing seemed to break through. He still lagged behind where he should be.

"It was frustrating because we'd go over a chapter in history or English or science and then he wouldn't remember anything," she said. "He wouldn't commit anything to memory."

Then, like all things Charlie, sports would somehow intervene. One Sunday night in the fall, the Wards were eating dinner and Charlie was talking about the football games he had watched on TV that day with his father. He was animated and excited and remembered every score, every pass and seemingly every play of the game they watched, including names, numbers and things the announcer said.

"Here I was thinking something was wrong with Junior's brain and then it hit me, *There's nothing wrong with him; he just doesn't want to learn,*" Willard Ward said. "The things he recalled and the memory he had of the game proved that to me. I couldn't believe a child as young as he was could remember so much. That meant that when he *wanted* to know something he could know it. I got on him extra hard after that once I knew what he was capable of."

She even got his elementary school principal in on the act, asking him to bring in copies of *Sports Illustrated* to motivate Charlie to read. The ploy was successful. In no time, Charlie had caught up to his classmates.

As the decision about what to do regarding Prop 48 approached, Willard believed her son had again reached a point where he could use some time to catch up. She didn't want him to get to Florida State and struggle and then be labeled with having an academic weakness. A year in community college would give Charlie a chance to focus solely on his studies, learn how to prepare for class and tests at the college level, and gain a leg-up once he did begin playing big time football.

An added bonus was that he could live with his sister Leta, who was in school at Florida A&M, right next to Florida State.

"I think Junior would have been frustrated if he was home preparing for his test and doing nothing else around Thomasville," Leta said. "I was able to help keep him upbeat. But he understood the long-term goal. My parents were educators and they wanted to make sure that the Prop 48 thing wasn't something that would stick with him his whole life. They were very forward thinking. They knew before anyone that it was important for Junior to enroll at FSU as a full-time student right from the start. Testing just wasn't Junior's thing and it was smart to give him time to work on it."

• • •

Tallahassee Community College's campus is 2.2 miles due west of Florida State's Doak Campbell Stadium, with West Pensacola Street running from TCC directly to the 50-yard line of the practice facility on Stadium Drive, next to FSU's home field.

In 1988, that practice facility was home to the top ranked preseason team in the country according to the Associated Press. It was a team that would eventually include more than a dozen NFL players and nearly as many future All-Americans, including Deion Sanders, Pat Tomberlin, Chip Ferguson and Dexter Carter.

That team would be memorable for two things: Getting crushed 31-0 in the opening game of the season against arch-rival Miami, dropping them from #1 to #10 in the rankings; and then not losing a game the rest of the year and climbing all the way back to the #3 spot in the country with a tough Sugar Bowl win against #7 Auburn. In between, they would be on the winning side of their own share of blowouts, including a 59-0 win against #15 South Carolina and a 52-7 win over the hated University of Florida Gators.

Meanwhile, their future Heisman winner and national champion, Charlie Ward, was busy decimating practice squads in TCC intramural football and basketball games with his friend, training partner and confidant, James Marable.

"The coaches at Florida State gave me a few workouts to do and I'd occasionally hang out with some of the guys on the team, but for the most part I was on my own until I was really enrolled," Ward said of his time at TCC. "I really needed something to do and someone to train with."

Into that void stepped Marable and old-fashioned intramural sports, which would provide a much-needed outlet for a world-class competitive drive that, for the moment, was forced to stay idle.

"I met Charlie in high school. I was a senior when he was a freshman," Marable said. "When I'd go home to Thomasville, of course I'd watch him play and I was amazed by what he did, but we didn't strike up a friendship until his gap year. I was a friend of his sister's at Florida A&M. When I found out he was in town I reached out to him. I was heavily into fitness at the time and I thought he'd want to work out together."

Though Marable was not a college athlete, he was a beast in the gym and he challenged Charlie every chance he got. They pushed each other in the weight room, running sprints and on the basketball court.

"I knew my only opportunity to beat him in the gym would be upper body training," Marable said. "There was no way I could take him in any lower body work. When we'd do leg workouts I couldn't lift more than him. He was very powerful."

The workouts. The motivation. The competition. It was all exactly what Charlie needed in what otherwise could have been a depressing and quiet year. Imagine going from the excitement of his high school football team's playoff run, to getting a scholarship offer to the number one football program in the country, to…nothing. For the first time in a long time, he wasn't officially part of a team or school or anything. It could have been a disaster to his psyche, but Marable and his friends gave him an escape—and a purpose.

"I was in Kappa Alpha Psi and I'd invite Charlie to come hang with me and my frat brothers," Marable said. "He'd hang around us, and when we'd practice for intramural football he would play quarterback and get us ready for our games."

On the intramural football fields of TCC, few people knew who Charlie was from his high school days and that suited him just fine.

"I'd just introduce him as my homeboy Charlie who was going to Florida State next year," Marable says. "They didn't know what he did in high school or what he'd eventually do with FSU, but all it took was for him to start playing with us to know he was special."

Leta Ward says that occasionally some of the big names on the Seminole roster would come to take Charlie out and keep him engaged with the team. During those brief breaks from TCC he'd get a taste of his future. He'd spend some time with Dexter Carter and talk with Deion and get a feel for what Florida State's culture was like during the season. Still, he wasn't allowed near the practice field or to officially spend time with the team.

And so, while Chip Ferguson and Peter Tom Willis and Casey Weldon and Brad Johnson mastered the Florida State playbook, honed their footwork and perfected their throwing motion on what is now Bobby Bowden Field, Charlie Ward Jr. was firing lasers and carving up frat football practices with some FAMU Kappas.

"It was what it was," Charlie said. "I made the best of it and had fun with those guys. I'm the kind of guy that can have fun wherever I am. Those games kept me active and involved since I didn't have much contact with the team yet."

"Most of the guys in my frat had been good athletes in high school and many were several years older than Charlie, who was only 18 at the time," Marable said. "None of that mattered. He was so far ahead of all of us out there. He'd tell us things to look for and help us practice, but he was the most gifted and poised athlete any of us had ever seen. When he finally got to FSU and started having success, I walked around with my chest poked out. I was so proud of him. Watching his ascension felt like I was watching my real brother. That's honestly how I felt."

When intramural football season ended Charlie turned to the Dade Street Rec Basketball League to try to feed his competitive fire. Here, too, he dazzled teammates and made strong impressions, one of which would directly affect his future at Florida State. This time though, rather than wow some frat guys, he'd catch the attention of a third-team All-American athlete and an NCAA head coach.

• • •

John "Patrick" Kennedy's college basketball career lasted two seasons at King's College in Pennsylvania before he swapped his white high tops for a whistle and became coach of the junior varsity team his last two years in school. After graduation, he spent a few years as an assistant coach at Lehigh and then joined legendary coach Jim Valvano at Iona College in New Rochelle, New York. After back-to-back NCAA tournament appearances and a combined record of 51-10 in his last two seasons, Valvano left to take over North Carolina State, where three years later he'd win one of the most famous national championships of all time in 1983.

When Valvano left Iona in 1980, twenty-eight-year-old Kennedy was promoted to head coach. After a slow start he reeled off four straight seasons of twenty-two wins or more and notched two NCAA tournament appearances and two conference tournament championships. In 1986 he left New Rochelle for Tallahassee to become Florida State's head coach. By the time Charlie Ward arrived at TCC, Kennedy had two 19-win seasons under his belt, and his 1988-89 team went 22-8 and he made his second NCAA tournament as Seminoles' head coach.

His star player on that squad was 6'6" senior guard George McCloud out of Daytona Beach, Florida. McCloud was a smooth-shooting righty who loved launching long-range jumpers with his straight-up, quick release style. As the team's leading scorer, he often had the green light when he got hot, leading to five 30-point games his senior year and a scoring average of 22.8 points per game. After graduating he played twelve years in the NBA, leading the league in three-point attempts in 1996.

The year after he graduated from FSU, McCloud stayed in shape in the summers by playing in the city league at Dade Street Community Center. One day he found himself matched up against a teenager named Charlie who was supposed to be getting ready to play football for the Seminoles. McCloud knew that Kennedy was looking for guards to take his place, and after going toe-to-toe with Charlie for a few games he believed Kennedy's search was over. The new guard he was looking for was right in his own backyard.

"Charlie Ward is your point guard," he said when he called Kennedy.

Kennedy had been aware of Charlie in high school but had backed off his recruiting when it was apparent that Charlie was making his decision about college based on where he'd play football.

"My recruiting staff had heard of Charlie as a basketball player, and my assistants had gone to see him play in high school in Thomasville," Kennedy said. "They loved him as a point guard, but at the time I wasn't sure if the football program was sold on him. I knew Bowden wanted a drop-back passing QB so I didn't know if he'd end up at Florida State. I told the football coaches that we'd love to have him as a basketball player, but I knew football was Charlie's number one option, so while he made up his mind about college we went about our recruiting without him."

Up to that point, Kennedy had never actually seen Ward play in a game, but he had experience in juggling a player between the football team and the basketball team with another FSU quarterback, Brad Johnson.

"I thought of Charlie the same way I thought of Brad," Kennedy said. "I thought this player is here on a football scholarship and if he's available we'll see how he can help. Of course if he can help us, we'll surely use him. We heard that Charlie was the best guard out of Georgia after his senior year in high school."

Now Ward's reputation was preceding him on both the football and basketball teams at Florida State. All he had left was to increase his SAT score in the spring—which he did—and officially enroll as a student in the fall—which he also did. In August of 1989, Charlie Ward Jr. was finally, officially a college student at FSU.

Chapter 12

The Punter

This wasn't supposed to happen. Bobby Bowden liked to end his preseason camps on a high note and give his first-team offense and defense a chance to get into a rhythm before the first game. He did this by letting them scrimmage straight up against the best remaining Seminoles who were occupying the lower parts of the depth chart. It was meant to be a confidence booster, a predetermined, good old-fashioned butt kicking to fire everyone up. Like clockwork, the offensive starters rolled over the defensive backs-ups and then the defensive starters locked down the offensive back-ups. Ten minutes into the game at the end of the 1989 preseason, however, Bowden was on the sidelines, flabbergasted, wondering what in the world was going on. Rather than his first team being in a traditional cakewalk, they found themselves in a tooth-and-nail showdown.

"We took our best guys against the rest," Bowden said. "All the good players are over here and all the other guys are over yonder, and this team of good players is supposed to run up and down the field. And the game is going to end up 50 to nothin'. But Charlie Ward nearly beats the first team. Game probably ended up 33-28. We could not stop him—he was just making stuff up."

At this point, Charlie had been a member of the Seminoles for a few months. He was officially listed as fourth on the quarterback depth chart behind starter Peter Tom Willis and back-ups Casey Weldon and Brad Johnson. The only snaps he took under center that preseason were as the quarterback of the scout team offense as they faced FSU's first team defense, which was loaded with future NFL talent and college stars.

LeRoy Butler.

Terrell Buckley.

Kirk Carruthers.

Odell Haggins.

Big names, to be sure, but Charlie didn't blink. That day, despite the fact that he hadn't worn pads and a helmet in over a year, he treated the All-Americans and eventual pros the same way he treated Bainbridge and Coffee while he was at Central High School.

After that scrimmage, Bowden became a believer.

"That's when you really realized we got something here, boy. It was just amazing. It made you feel like maybe we're not very good, but then you realize we got this one individual you couldn't stop—running and throwing the football. He could throw better than I realized," he said.

Coach Mark Richt came on board the Seminoles staff as a quarterback and offensive coach in 1990, and already Ward's scrimmage performance was a thing of FSU lore.

"I joined the team from East Carolina a year after that scrimmage, and when I got to training camp people were still talking about that game. It was the first time I heard about the legend of Charlie Ward," said Richt, who would go on to win 145 games at Georgia before leaving to coach his alma mater Miami. "They said he single-handedly almost beat the first unit because of his performance that day."

But he could also punt the ball a mile, which is ultimately how he made his way onto the starting roster for the 1989 football season. This did cause confusion amongst some of the team's freshmen players, who routinely watched Charlie, their punter, pick apart their nationally ranked defense in practice. One freshman in particular, future Super Bowl champion William Floyd, couldn't help but wonder how a single athlete could have all that talent.

Floyd was a 6'1" 240-pound wrecking ball of a man who went to Lakewood High School in St. Petersberg, Florida. He graduated as the number-one ranked running back in Florida and the number-two ranked fullback in the country. When he arrived in Tallahassee he had expected to be enamored with their defensive stars and offensive stars like Dexter Carter, but time and again in practice that summer, he'd find himself watching the punter.

"I'd see it every day and I couldn't believe it," Floyd said. "We had a great freshman punter who could be the next Reggie Roby, and he'd kick these deep, long spirals...and then the same guy would be our scout team quarterback and make our first-team defense look bad. He was blessed by the man upstairs for sure, but I became a believer in Charlie Ward the person before I became I believer in Charlie Ward the player."

Floyd says that even as Charlie was making a name for himself as perhaps the best scout team quarterback in the country, his poise, his demeanor and how he treated his teammates was making a bigger impression. It would not be a stretch to imagine a nineteen-year-old getting full of himself after routinely making All-Americans look average in practice, but that simply wasn't the case. He remained humble even as it became clear he was the future of Florida State.

"Man, there were days where he'd be running the scout team and he would just destroy our first-team defense," Floyd said. "We'd be watching and he was making us look silly sometimes. I knew then that he was eventually going to be the leader of the team."

That future was still a few years off. As far as the 1989 season was concerned, the team would have to settle for his contributions as a punter. And that was cool with Charlie.

"Any way I could help the team, I'd do it," Charlie said. "I had faith that my time would come and until then I'd do what I could to contribute and make my teammates better."

• • •

Charlie's first game as a Seminole took place on September 2, 1989 at the Gator Bowl in Jacksonville, Florida. Their opponent was the Southern Mississippi Golden Eagles, to whom they paid over half a million dollars for accepting the opportunity to be an opening-day punching bag on a neutral site. The teams had faced each other the previous two seasons, and Florida State had won by a total of 110-23. By all accounts, it was supposed to be nothing more than a warm-up for the Seminoles' game the following week at Clemson.

"To us, Southern Miss was like playing a junior college," LeRoy Butler said in Jeff Pearlman's book *Gunslinger.* "A fly on our shoe—that was Southern Miss."

"We knew they had this quarterback who was very good," Peter Tom Willis said. "But I don't think any of us knew how to pronounce his name."

Florida State jumped out to a 10-0 lead on a Dexter Carter touchdown and a subsequent field goal, and the game quickly seemed to be headed in the direction of the previous two. Charlie Ward was on the sideline, wondering if he would even have to punt in a game where the offense might score on every possession.

"It was very hot and humid that game," Charlie said. "I think the stadium was about one hundred and ten at kickoff. We moved the ball easily in the first quarter. They were wearing black uniforms and helmets and it looked like they might just tire out."

Then that quarterback whose name Willis couldn't pronounce went to work, leading his team to a field goal after a 64-yard completion. He followed that up with another quick drive after a turnover that led to a touchdown, and suddenly FSU and Southern Miss were tied in the beginning of the second quarter.

Oh, the Golden Eagles quarterback leading the charge was Brett Favre.

"Nobody really knew who he was then," Charlie said. "We'd know him after."

While Florida State players were cramping and crumbling and taking IVs due to dehydration, Favre's trademark swagger and guts kept his team in the game. When the Seminoles punched, he counterpunched harder. Between the heat and the pressure and pain they were inflicting on each other, every possession became a battle of wills.

In the end, the game came down to Favre hitting tight end Anthony Harris for a go-ahead touchdown that would leave Florida State with next to no time on the clock, which turned out to be just enough time for Bowden to call one of the most bizarre plays of his coaching career—and it involved Charlie Ward. Here it is in his own words, from his book, *Tales from the Seminole Sidelines*:

> I got the idea for this play from watching Dean Smith's four corners offense in basketball. The idea was to freeze the ball. What I was trying to do was keep my quarterbacks happy because I couldn't play them all. We put in Brad Johnson, Charlie Ward and Casey Weldon at the same time. And P.T. [Willis] was our starter that year. And sometimes I believe he was in there with it, too. Every day after practice I would meet with the three quarterbacks and practice this little thing we called the "four corners." Bill Peterson, when I was an assistant under him, would always do tricks at the end of practice. I picked it up from him and did it at West Virginia and some here [FSU].
>
> With this play, we did it for fun against our defense and thought that it just might win a ballgame sometime. I would put two of the quarterbacks out wide, about eighteen yards back so nobody could get to them real quick. One would throw the ball to the other quarterback, and that person would hold on to it. And when the other team would get close, he would throw it to this guy until somebody opened up downfield.
>
> That last time we had the ball against Southern Mississippi, we put the three quarterbacks in there—Brad Johnson, Casey Weldon and Charlie Ward. But they just laid everybody back there and let you do all of that. We didn't get any pressure. Where a play (usually lasts) five or seven seconds at most, it seemed like it ran for twenty seconds. What happened is when we tried this against Southern Mississippi, the clock ran out. Can you believe that? The dang clock ran out.

When the clock hit 0:00 after Weldon's pass to Ward fell incomplete, it would solidify the biggest win in Southern Mississippi history and alternately one of the biggest upsets in Bobby Bowden's storied Seminole career. In addition to the triple quarterback play, Charlie was called upon to punt four times and totaled 156 yards, giving him roughly 40 yards per attempt.

• • •

The loss to Southern Mississippi dropped the Seminoles from sixth in the rankings to sixteenth, with #10 Clemson scheduled to visit Tallahassee the following weekend. That week, Charlie ran the scout team to mirror Clemson quarterbacks Chris Morocco and DeChane Cameron, a fellow stud-Georgia quarterback from LaGrange. Morocco was the starter, but Cameron, much like Charlie, was a running threat in addition to having a great arm. Had Clemson head coach Danny Ford been given a free pass to Florida State's practices that week, he may have chosen to start Cameron, as Charlie was simply magical running Clemson's offense.

"Part of it was that I started to know our defense from playing them every week in practice," Charlie said. "Eventually I figured them out, and if I exposed some things it would help the defensive coaches fix them for the next game."

In between learning the Florida State playbook and running their opponents' plays, Charlie remained quiet and committed to his classwork and his bible. As electrifying as he was in practice, his personality off the field stood in stark contrast to his performances, which is why there were rarely any instances of resentment or frustration from the teammates who were occasionally embarrassed on the field by their nineteen-year-old punter. Because he didn't taunt, trash talk, or complain about playing time, they respected that Charlie played as hard as he could at all times and then went about his business.

"He was definitely quiet and kept to himself, but he'd talk to you," Floyd said. "He just knew he was a leader even when he was only punting. We were neighbors for three years at school and he was just beyond reproach. He was such a special person even without football."

It's important to remember that in the late 1980s and early '90s, Florida State wasn't just ranked regularly as a national powerhouse in football, they were also consistently one of the top party schools in the country, with multiple #1 rankings by the prestigious *Princeton Review*. Add that to the team's success on the gridiron, and many players took full advantage of the popularity of being a football player and the nightlife available to them.

Not Charlie.

That stuff just wasn't his style.

Instead of the Run DMC or LL Cool J poster that seemed to be mandatory for college freshmen in the late 1980s, Charlie had a purple and black velour image of Jesus on the cross. Instead of *Playboys* and other men's magazine lying around as reading material, he had the bible. His faith was (and is) where he found comfort. It was the source of his strength, and while his friends on the team were out on the weekends partying he preferred to stay home and watch TV, preferably whatever sports were on, and then fall asleep on the couch. But he never judged. Never preached. Never said anything to his teammates one way or another about how they conducted their lives. He treated everyone well and the end result was that for many players, he kind of became their spiritual anchor.

"The more time I spent time with him, the more he became a center of peace for me," Warrick Dunn said. Dunn would eventually become a star at Florida State and in the NFL, but he was also Charlie Ward's roommate when Charlie was a senior and he was a freshman. "He never asked for attention or accolades or even talked about it. He never worried about what others did. He led with a quiet strength that everyone respected."

But it would be several years before that strength would be needed to take the Seminoles program to new heights, so that first year all Charlie could do was punt and prepare for each upcoming contest.

The Clemson game on September 9, 1989 was the first time that Charlie, after a lifetime of watching Florida State on television with his father, finally got to suit up and run out of the tunnel in Tallahassee.

"That was special for us," his dad said. "To see him on that field in that uniform."

The game, unfortunately, would not be so special.

Clemson took a 28-10 lead into halftime, and despite a few touchdowns in the second half Florida State would lose 34-23 and tumble out of the top 25. Charlie punted four times for 168 yards, raising his per-punt-average to well over 40 yards.

"I certainly didn't expect us to start 0-2," Charlie said. "Or lose that game."

Bowden was much more blunt.

"Clemson's better than I thought they were," he said after the game. "That was just a good whipping."

• • •

The Seminoles would not lose another game the rest of the year, relying on a defense that improved every week and an offense that could barely be stopped. They'd score 195 points over their next five games against Louisiana State, Tulane, Syracuse, Virginia Tech and Auburn, before heading into a game against the number one team in the country, the undefeated University of Miami.

Florida State had lost four times in a row to the Hurricanes, and in 1987 and 1988 they were the only two losses for the Seminoles on the season—and they were gut wrenching.

"Last year, the attitude we had was overconfidence," Bowden said before the game. "We don't have to worry about that this year."

The game would be head coach Dennis Erickson's first in the rivalry, as he took over for Jimmy Johnson in the off-season. Erickson left Washington State for the chance to run one of the most successful college football teams of the 1980s, though he was a little surprised at how high the heat had been turned up on the series with the Seminoles.

"Since I have been in Florida, football seems more important to people," he said in an interview the week of the game. "The rivalry is more intense. I can feel that this week."

The reason for the intensity was that year-in and year-out when the two teams faced each other, they'd be loaded with future NFL talent who often played against each other in high school and wanted bragging rights over the state of Florida. Many of the players had been either friends or rivals in high school and this was their chance to show that the school they chose was the right one. The Seminoles alone had 20 players in this game that would go on to the NFL.

On offense, Erickson would be starting freshman quarterback Gino Torretta in only his third game, along with Leonard Conley and Wesley Carroll, while the defense was anchored by Russell Maryland.

"It should be a classic," Erickson said.

It wasn't.

Torretta managed to throw four interceptions in the first half, including a pick on the first play of the game and another later in the end zone. Star Florida State linebacker Kirk Carruthers grabbed two of the interceptions himself, forced a fumble and recovered another fumble. Florida State also had a fumble, an interception and a botched fake field goal. One of the highlights of the game was Charlie's 57-yard punt to back up the Hurricanes deep in their own territory. The punt was one of five for him, totaling 220 yards on the day, far outpacing Willis' 129 passing yards. When the comedy of errors was all said and done, the Seminoles ended their losing streak against the Hurricanes with a 24-10 victory. When the AP poll came out early the next week, they found themselves all the way up to number six in the country.

Looking back on this game almost thirty years later, perhaps the most remarkable fact is that the freshman who punted five times and the freshman who threw four interceptions would both go on to win Heisman trophies.

The Seminoles would follow up this win with another and another and another and another, closing out the year with 10 straight. After Miami they beat South Carolina, Memphis State, Florida and then Nebraska in the Fiesta Bowl. After starting the season ranked sixth in country and then losing twice, their ten wins in a row placed them third in the final rankings.

John Wimberly, the injured punter who Charlie replaced in the preseason, returned to the lineup for the Memphis State game and split the kicks with Charlie. He did the same against Florida, and then in the Fiesta Bowl Wimberly handled all three punts, making that game the first all year in which Charlie never saw the field. Peter Tom Willis finished his career as a Seminole by throwing for 422 yards and five touchdowns in that game. With the quarterback spot now vacant and Charlie's scout team dominance fresh in his coaches' minds, the off-season would be a quandary about what to do with him.

"His second season, Charlie was set to compete with Brad Johnson and Casey Weldon, who were two years older and one year ahead of him. The question we had was, 'do we have him compete or redshirt him and give him two years separation from those guys?" Coach Richt said.

Chapter 13

To Redshirt, Or Not To Redshirt

While Peter Tom Willis was being drafted as the sixty-third overall pick in the 1990 NFL draft by the Chicago Bears, Bobby Bowden and his coaches in Tallahassee were spending their spring figuring out who was going to replace him.

"We'll give everybody equal work at the start and hope somebody moves out front," Bowden said in an interview that spring. "You want somebody to be set apart…you don't want to end up with three or four equal players. You want the choice to be easy."

Of course Bowden wanted it to be easy, but the likelihood of that happening was next to none. Brad Johnson and Casey Weldon were both excellent athletes who had waited patiently for their turn and who were capable of picking up where Willis had left off. Charlie had the highest upside of the three but he'd spent more time running opponents' offenses than FSU's. Also, Wayne McDuffie, Charlie's number one fan and the reason he was in Tallahassee, had left for a job with the Atlanta Falcons in the off-season. Brad Scott, also a fan of Charlie's, was promoted to offensive coordinator, so his input would be in the mix.

"I am not foolish," Scott said upon taking the job. "I know this offense has been successful and I am not going to make major changes in what we've been doing."

With Willis gone, a certain amount of change would be necessary to adapt to whomever would be under center. Bowden felt it would be tough to fully replace a guy who set fifteen team-passing records and five Florida State career records at the time, including a passing efficiency of 148.5.

"I doubt anyone can come in and do what he [Willis] did," Bowden said. "The more you think about it, the more remarkable it was." Prior to spring practice, Bowden gave this quick assessment of where he felt each quarterback was in terms of taking over as the starter. "Casey and Brad are equal right now. Casey is a little more mobile and Brad is more focused. Charlie probably has the best arm of them all."

The classic coach non-answer answer left Seminoles fans, Charlie and the other quarterbacks without a clue as to what Bowden was thinking as spring practices got under way. One small, but not insignificant, piece of the puzzle was the addition of Kenny Felder, a 6'3", 215-pound quarterback/baseball player from Niceville, Florida.

Felder was not in the mix for the starting job, but if Charlie was going to have any chance at redshirting, the ability of Felder to be an emergency third option behind Weldon and Johnson was critical. As a player in a redshirt year (extra year of eligibility), he can practice with the team, attend class and be an otherwise normal student, but he can't participate in any games. The benefits of redshirting, especially for someone in Charlie's position, is to not only give an athlete the chance to mature as a person and a player but to also extend eligibility beyond the normal graduation years. For Charlie that meant ceding the starting job in 1990 to either Weldon or Johnson, then giving him 1991 to compete with Johnson or back him up with the path clear for him to start in both 1992 and 1993.

An important consideration for Charlie regarding redshirting was his ability and availability to play basketball at Florida State, something he made clear was important to him during recruiting. Without a hard answer as to what Bowden was going to do heading into the '90 season, Charlie couldn't get a clear idea of how or when he'd be able to play hoops.

The spring football practices came and went without Bowden tipping his hand as to whom he was favoring as a back-up, though it was becoming clear that Johnson would be the starter. The quarterback competition was forcing the guys to perform under pressure, and Bowden needed to know who could step up and who couldn't. When school ended and the players scattered for the summer, Charlie was convinced that the back-up job was going to Weldon, and his desire to play basketball grew.

"I barely even threw a football that summer," he said. "I played so much basketball. I missed it. I knew my time would come as quarterback and I wanted to see what I could do on the basketball court. At that point I hadn't been on a basketball team in two years. I was hoping that I could redshirt for that 1990 football season and join the basketball team."

One of the reasons this idea held so much appeal was because Brad Johnson had played both football and basketball at Florida State, and he credited his two-sport status for his success at eventually winning the starting job over Weldon.

"The two years I played basketball helped me out," Johnson said. "Traveling, getting ready for big games, playing in big ballgames. Competing really helped me."

Johnson, like Charlie, treated football as his primary sport but loved basketball just as much. Before he became the starting quarterback, he was known to head to the gym after football practice to get his shots up until he found his stroke. Standing at 6'5" and weighing close to 240 pounds, Johnson was much bigger than Charlie and played small forward on the basketball team. Since he wasn't the point guard and the offense didn't run through him, he could sometimes pop in and out of FSU basketball games and still have an impact.

One year, Florida State was practicing for the Sugar Bowl in New Orleans and the basketball team had a game in Orlando. Johnson bolted the football team immediately after practice, joined the basketball team for their game, dropped 13 points, hightailed it out of there when the game was over and was back practicing football the next day.

"It was fun for me," Johnson said.

Fun or not, Johnson had also paid his dues in Bowden's infamous "wait your turn" development of quarterbacks. In addition to playing hoops, he'd spent three years in the system, watching film, watching other starters like Peter Tom Willis prepare, and participating in quarterback meetings. When it was announced in early summer that he had won the starting job, there was no doubt amongst the team that he had earned it.

"Brad was the steadiest and most productive of all of our quarterbacks," Bowden said in assessing the spring practices that year. "Brad seems to be more consistent at this time. Casey is more dramatic. He'll make a great play he shouldn't have made then he'll make a boo-boo he shouldn't have made."

Charlie knew that his day, too, would come. Until then, the idea of following in Johnson's footsteps on the basketball team sounded good. He just needed Coach Bowden's blessing.

• • •

There were three days at the end of August in 1990 when the temperature was over 95 degrees and the humidity was at 100%. Scientifically speaking, the air was superheated water vapor. To walk through it was to instantly be drenched. To practice football in it, in pads and helmets, was to experience sauna-level sweat. Despite many of the players on Florida State's roster having grown up in Florida and Georgia and thus being adjusted to the climate, the string of days at the region's extremes had pushed even the toughest athletes to pine for air conditioning.

In this crucible of sweat and steam a quarterback battle ensued.

With only a few weeks left until the start of the 1990 season, Charlie's play had put him neck-and-neck with Casey Weldon for the back-up spot. In truth, Charlie the football player was Charlie the basketball player's worst enemy. While Weldon struggled, throwing eight interceptions during the summer's four main scrimmages, Ward excelled. He became known by the defense as an escape artist, turning sure sacks into first-down runs or completions. He spun, side-stepped, stutter-stepped and shimmied around so many defenders that his teammates thought he had mystical powers, like he was a football wizard or something.

"He had eyes in the back of his head," William Floyd said. "He is one of those guys that feels the game. It's almost like he's so tuned in to the game that he knows when people are around him without looking. He could feel people on his backside when there was *no way* he should know it. He'd do a twirl move at the last second when the guy thought he had a huge hit on him. Then he was gone."

The coaches were fast becoming enamored with what he could do. Bowden in particular began backpedaling a bit on the whole redshirt talk, going so far as to declare Charlie almost "too good" to not have on the team.

On September 2, following the last Friday night scrimmage of 1990 when Charlie led a reserve unit to two touchdowns, Bowden declared, "Charlie Ward is a very dangerous quarterback, and I'm not even thinking about redshirting him now. It [the back-up quarterback battle] will be close."

On September 10, after a season-opening 45-24 blowout against East Carolina, Bowden was still talking about Charlie's value to the team, while only giving cursory attention to redshirting. "He is so dangerous," Bowden said. "He is pushing the other quarterbacks right now. We are trying to hold Charlie out."

By this time, the coaching staff's wavering on the redshirt decision was starting to frustrate Charlie. He wanted a definitive answer and he wanted that answer to be that he could redshirt and go play basketball. From his perspective, he had stated his intention to play basketball during the recruiting process, and even though he was providing healthy competition for Weldon and the other quarterbacks on the roster, he did not want to waste a year of eligibility in that role. Even though his play in practice did not show it, he was not happy.

"That was about as upset as I can remember Junior ever getting," his mom said. "We spoke on the phone all the time while the redshirt question hung out there, and each time he got more aggravated. He'd say, 'Mama, didn't Coach Bowden sit in our family room and say I could play two sports?' And I'd say, 'Yes, he did tell you that.' And he'd say, 'He said if I got good grades and kept up with my studies and with football, I could play both, right?' And I'd say, 'Yes, he said that.' Then he'd get agitated and say, 'Now Coach is telling me that he has to think about it because I'm doing pretty good at football and he isn't sure if I can play basketball, and I want to play. I did everything he asked.'"

Willard Ward would hang up from her phone calls with Charlie and wonder what as a mother she could do. She had sat in her own living room and listened to Coach Bowden and his staff say they'd let Junior play basketball if he met certain conditions, and he did that. She also knew that Junior had not been shy about his desire to play two sports. The more she contemplated it, the more she felt that the FSU coaches were going back on their word, and for the first time she took Coach Bowden up on his offer.

What was the offer?

He told Mrs. Ward, like he told most of the parents he met during recruiting, that if they ever have any problems or questions or concerns about their child, to please feel free to call him at any time.

"And I did just that," Willard said. "I called and left a message and Coach Bowden called me back when he got the note that said CHARLIE WARD'S MAMA WANTS TO TALK TO YOU."

The phone call was fairly straightforward.

"How can I help you?" Coach Bowden asked.

"Well, Charlie is a little concerned, upset really, because he said he asked you about playing basketball and you said you had to think about it, when he thought he'd done what you'd asked and made it clear that he wanted to play both sports," she said.

"I know I told him he could play both sports," Bowden said. "But I said I wanted to think about it and I wanted him to think about it to see if this is really what he wants to do."

"It's what he's wanted to do from the beginning," she said. "He believes he's earned it."

"The truth is he's not going to play a whole lot behind Brad. Casey is capable of backing him up, and I told Charlie it would be a couple of years before he'd play," Bowden said. "Let me think it over and talk to him soon. You're right, Mrs. Ward, he has done what we've asked of him."

Coach Bowden thanked her for calling and they hung up with no definitive answer. No answer came the next week. Or the week after.

Florida beat Georgia Southern and Charlie was still on the roster.

Then they beat Tulane and Virginia, and every Monday when Charlie showed up to practice he was still officially part of the team and available to play.

It was maddening.

"I never stopped practicing as hard as I could," Charlie said. "But basketball season was coming up and I wanted my answer so I could be prepared and let Coach Kennedy know. I didn't know what the hold up was."

On October 6, Florida State lost to arch-rival Miami on the road. It was a tough loss considering both teams were in the top ten and were once again playing with national championship implications on the line. Charlie figured the last thing on the coach's mind was his redshirt issue.

Then on the following Thursday, Charlie Ward Jr. was finally set free to play basketball with Coach Bowden's permission, beginning with his availability to participate in Midnight Madness that upcoming October 15.

Charlie was elated.

"I have been waiting for this a long time," he said immediately after hearing the news. "I know I'm not in basketball shape right now, but I played with lots of guys at the Dade Street Community Center this summer, and I'm ready."

Coach Bowden was happy for his young star, but cautioned that he could be called into service.

"He knows with injuries to the quarterbacks we might have to call him back," he said. "Or if we have to get our defense prepared, we might call him over for one day to imitate the opposing quarterbacks. But I'm hoping that won't happen."

The Florida State football team would follow up the loss to Miami by falling to Auburn, then close out the season with six straight wins, including one against Florida and a victory over Joe Paterno's seventh-ranked Penn State team in the Blockbuster Bowl.

By that time, Charlie was a few months into his career as a college basketball player.

Chapter 14

Back to Basketball

His chest heaved and his lungs frantically vacuumed in the warm air from the gym. His gold Florida State basketball shirt was doused with sweat. Whenever he could, he'd put his hands on his knees and clutch the bottom of his shorts for a break. It was the third basketball practice of Charlie's college career and he was gassed. From the first whistle, the team had gone from drill to drill to drill at a ferocious pace; the tempo made his calves burn and his heart pound. It had been two years since he'd been properly conditioned to play basketball and with each minute that passed, it showed.

"On my second or third day, I really got blown up," Charlie said. "In football you might run four hundred yards after practice, but in basketball you're constantly running up and down the court. Football shape is nothing like basketball shape."

In the beginning, Coach Kennedy and his staff felt like Charlie was trying to combine the two sports on the court.

"He hadn't played organized basketball in a few years and it really looked like he was playing football out there for a while," Coach Kennedy said. "Or at least street ball. I didn't know what my expectation should be."

Heading into Charlie's first practice, Coach Kennedy said he was hopeful that Charlie would be able to contribute in some way during the season. By the end of the first week, he was thinking that there was a good chance Charlie would be a regular in his rotation. By mid-November he was all-in, believing Charlie was the missing piece to his team's puzzle.

"Charlie could be the difference in our whole season," he said as the first game approached. "He's definitely our sixth man. He can play point guard, second guard or small forward if we want to go with a quick team. I'm not sure that of the guys getting the bulk of the minutes that he won't be the one shining."

Not bad for a kid who about one month earlier was spending most of his time with Florida State's quarterback coach Mark Richt.

Aside from getting his conditioning up, Charlie was learning how to fit in with a new group of teammates and a core of guards that included 6'3", 200-pound Chuck Graham, 6'6" passing wizard Aubrey Boyd and 6'1" community college transfer Derrick Myers. Day by day his basketball muscle memory returned, his instincts came back and his basketball coaches, like his football coaches before them, began to "gush with praise" over their new guard. One stark difference was that while much of the gridiron talk focused on Charlie's quick feet and ability to get out of trouble, the coaching staff on the basketball team was mesmerized by his hand speed.

"We were out there early that first year, and Charlie was running up and down with our second unit and it felt like he was stealing the ball every few possessions," Coach Kennedy said. "One of his steals happened so fast I wasn't sure how he even did it. I pulled my coaches together and said, 'Those are the quickest hands I've ever seen in my life.'"

In high school, Charlie was looked upon to score and be the ultimate playmaker. On Kennedy's team that first year, he was asked to be a spark off the bench and the defensive stopper in the final minutes of tight games due to his ball-stopping skills. This required him to focus on different aspects of his game than he had in the past.

"I've matured a lot since high school," Ward said at the time. "I was good in my league and everyone came looking for me to put the ball in the basket. Now I'm just one of the guys. I'm looking to get the ball to the open man or create something. As we continue to play, and I get used to playing in front of crowds, I will improve. It takes time."

Coach Kennedy also wanted to make sure he was ready for crunch time.

"The biggest thing we want him to improve on is free throws," Kennedy said. "We are going to need him back there late in the game. He really bolsters our backcourt."

A week before the first game of the season, the Seminoles played an exhibition game against the Brazilian National team and things started to fall into place the way Kennedy had envisioned.

Before a crowd of 3,492 at the Tallahassee-Leon County Civic Center, the Seminoles grabbed an lead early against the Brazilians and didn't let up. They led 42-36 at halftime, held off a Brazilian surge, and won 86-81. Most important, the guards complemented each other perfectly. Chuck Graham scored eighteen points in seventeen minutes of play and Charlie completely stifled the Brazilians' offense, especially in the second half as the lead was cut to four.

"The guard situation is a lot clearer," Kennedy said. "Charlie Ward really showed he can play defense. He's coming along fast. Both Charlie and Derrick [Myers] can get all over the opposition, and they make things happen."

That dual-guard defensive pressure was something that Kennedy hoped their conference opponents would not be prepared to handle once the season began. At that time, Florida State basketball was in its last year of participating in the Metropolitan Collegiate Athletic Conference, aka the Metro, whose major programs were the University of Cincinnati, the University of Louisville, Tulane University, the University of Memphis, the University of South Carolina and Virginia Tech.

Though Louisville and Memphis, and occasionally Cincinnati, were basketball powerhouses, by the end of the 1980s Florida State had made its intentions clear that the Seminoles were looking to bolt the conference for shinier courts, bigger rivals and a more visible tournament. For a brief period of time, the Metro toyed with forming a "Super Conference" with the Big East and the Atlantic 10, but those plans never came to fruition. After that, Florida State decided it was time to leave, and as fate would have it 1991 would be its last year participating in the Metro. The conference would only survive in tact until 1995, when it merged with the Great Midwest Conference to form what is now called Conference USA.

Little of this was known before tip-off of the 1990 basketball season for the Seminoles, but it's important to note because they've been a member of the ACC for more than twenty-five years, and Charlie helped make their transition into a conference with basketball titans like North Carolina and Duke a successful one in the early '90s.

• • •

The 1990 season opened on November 27 with a 24-point blowout win against Texas Southern. Four players scored in double figures, including Charlie, who had ten points, six rebounds and two assists in only fourteen minutes of play. The Seminoles would then lose their next game by twenty-four to the University of Florida. A lone bright spot was Charlie grabbing four steals in less than twenty minutes of playing time.

For the first month and a half of the season, the Seminoles struggled to have any consistency. They'd win one, lose two, win two, lose one and on and on. It was up and down, and it drove Coach Kennedy crazy. Coming from the Northeast, he was used to adding a little "seasoning" to his language to get the guys fired up, especially when he was aggravated. As the erratic play continued, the verbal "seasoning" started to get spicier and harsher in the pre-game pep talks, and occasionally in the post-game breakdowns. After a string of choice words prior to a game, the team would often put their hands together to say a prayer. As Coach Kennedy looked into the faces of his men during these moments, he sensed that Charlie was feeling uncomfortable. He thought it might be about the losing. It wasn't.

"He said to me, 'You know, Coach Bowden gets us fired up and he doesn't use language like that,'" Coach Kennedy said. "It was a really great moment for me because I decided to cut back on the saltiness of my language, and the coaching staff cleaned up their language too."

This was an early instance of the gravitas and respect that Charlie seemed to emanate naturally. Some players described it as an aura; others, as a presence. Whatever they called it, there was something about him that made people, even hardened coaches like Kennedy, want to alter their behavior for the better. How else can you explain a tough, middle-aged East Coast coach to be willing to watch his mouth around a nineteen-year-old college freshman?

A lack of profanity, however, didn't immediately produce wins…or the much-coveted consistent play. Doug Edwards and 6'7" forward Michael Polite traded off leading the team in scoring, with Chuck Graham pitching in a few times as well. The team was 5-5 after losing to Southern Mississippi in the tenth game of the year. Charlie played only nine minutes after tallying ten minutes, fourteen, seven and five in the previous run of games.

Kennedy's squad was running too much on emotion with not enough discipline, and his gut told him he needed to make a major change. He had to find a way to both stabilize and ignite the team for the final stretch of the season. For that he turned to Charlie, the man he took to calling the team's "spark plug" in almost every post-game interview he did. Rather than continuing to limit Charlie's playing time, he unleashed him against Cincinnati on January 10 with a season-high 31 minutes on the floor. The Seminoles won. Then they beat Louisville, Stetson and South Carolina, with games featuring more and more of Kennedy's "spark plug." Against Stetson, Charlie had fourteen points, seven rebounds and nine assists. A week later when they played Arkansas, the #2 ranked team in the nation according to the Associated Press, Charlie turned in his second-best game of the season with thirteen points, four assists and seven steals in thirty minutes of play. His best game was the regular season finale against South Carolina, when he nearly had a triple-double the hard way—eight points, nine assists and nine steals (a Florida State record).

With Charlie logging heavy minutes, the team finished 12-5 heading into the Metro Conference Tournament as the #2 seed. Their first game against seventh-seeded South Carolina was relatively uneventful. The teams were tied at halftime, and then the Seminoles pulled away to win by ten. The second game, against sixth-seeded Virginia Tech, was never even a contest. FSU was up by twenty at the half and went on to win by twenty. Florida State was now in the conference championship game for a fifth time, having lost the previous four tries to win the tournament.

Coach Kennedy's swearing in his pre-game talks was also down about 80%.

• • •

Louisville had won eleven previous Metro Conference Tournaments, but they had to fight their way into the 1991 finals from the eighth seed after one of their worst regular seasons in recent memory. Legendary Cardinals Coach Denny Crum, with his two national championships and 400 wins, didn't sugarcoat how the year had gone in an interview with the *Los Angeles Times* before the tournament.

"Coach [John] Wooden told me that you only prosper through adversity," he said. "Well, guess what? I'm going to be rich when this season is over."

Not withstanding the bottom seed and the down year for the perennial conference champs, when Florida State took the floor of the Roanoke Civic Center for the finals, the familiar site of Crum with his signature blazer and a program rolled up in his hand let the Seminoles know they were in for a dogfight.

The Civic Center had been a rotating host of the Metro Tournament for years, along with Freedom Hall in Louisville and the Mississippi Coast Coliseum. It had a nondescript interior, with a beige court and a navy paint. At center court was the small, minimalist logo of the Metro Conference in a tight circle, with a larger circle containing the stencil-like letters of the Roanoke Civic Center. Hanging over the partition at center court was a half-hearted twenty-foot banner that said "1991 Metro Tournament" in big block letters, much like a furniture store offering a blowout sale on couches. At full capacity the venue held roughly 8,500 people, giving it the feel of a giant rec center rather than a major arena.

Compare this setting to that of the ACC Tournament. FSU's future conference held its tournament at the three-year-old Charlotte Coliseum, which seated 24,000 people and boasted more than 300 consecutive sellouts for the Larry Johnson and Alonzo Mourning-led Charlotte Hornets. This made the Roanoke Civic Center seem like a quaint place to play basketball, and one the Seminoles felt they had grown out of. One way to put an exclamation point on their time there, and in the Metro, would to be to win the title and never look back.

"If we could win the Metro Tournament, it would be a storybook finish," Coach Kennedy said. "I couldn't think of a better way to go out."

For the first twenty-three minutes of the finals, the pages of Kennedy's storybook finish seemed to have been thrown into a furnace and burned.

The Seminoles had no early answer for Everick Sullivan and tournament MVP LaBradford Smith and found themselves down eleven points at halftime. A few minutes into the second half, with none of their adjustments working, the Seminoles were down by twenty and Crum's boys were feeling it. The arena was filled largely with fans dressed in the classic Cardinals red and black, and suddenly the Metro Final felt like a blowout home victory for Louisville. With FSU reeling, the Cardinals' band blasted "Rock and Roll Part II" and their fans stood and screamed and tried to get the Seminoles to give up. A few players hung their heads. Others got down. A few more looked distracted. One, in particular, showed almost no emotion. He simply chose to lead.

"Charlie had a real calming effect on the guys," Coach Kennedy said. "He believed we'd win and went to work. I don't think I even took him out in the second half."

One possession at a time, Florida State began to creep back into the game, and with every defensive stop and offensive score, the bench gained more confidence. Sam Lunt was an associate director of sports medicine and had been with the FSU basketball team for twenty-nine years at that point. He remembered the energy and excitement on the bench during the comeback decades later.

"That was some good basketball," he said.

"It took a while but we did turn around the momentum by the end of that second half," Ward said. "When we cut it to four or five we all believed we could win. We believed in each other."

Florida State was down five points with just under three minutes to play when Chuck Graham nailed a three to cut the deficit to two points.

"That was a real big shot by Chuck," Ward said. "We had a lot of confidence in him and he came through. Then after a few turnovers, Chuck hit two free throws to tie it."

The game was now 69-69 with one minute and thirty seconds left. The Seminoles had clawed their way out of a twenty-point hole in just over fifteen minutes of game time. For those in the crowd and on the coaching staff, it was an astonishing reversal.

"That comeback was one of the greatest comebacks I was ever involved with," Kennedy said. "But we needed to finish."

Louisville had the ball after Graham's free throws and quickly gave it to their star player and go-to guy, LaBradford Smith. He looked for his spot on the floor, found it about fifteen feet from the basket, pulled up and... missed. Charlie grabbed the rebound and took the ball across the court with one minute remaining.

"They had pretty big guards like Smith you had to play against, so we looked for a match-up where we could get the ball to Doug Edwards down low," Ward said. "But it wasn't open."

The shot clock slowly wound down as the Seminoles moved the ball around.

Twenty seconds left.

Fifteen seconds left.

Ten seconds left.

Once again, Charlie found the ball in his hands. He looked up at the shot clock and decided he had to make a move.

Eight seconds left.

He worked his way to the top of the key.

Five seconds left.

Just as three seconds ticked on the shot clock, Charlie lifted off the ground and got his jumper off.

"I can still remember Charlie taking that jump shot from the top of the key," Coach Kennedy said. "In typical Charlie fashion, there was no question the ball was going into the basket."

The shot was a nothing-but-net, no-doubt-about-it swish

The Seminoles were somehow up 72-69.

There was time for one more Louisville possession, but Doug Edwards stole the ball to lock up the unlikely, unbelievable comeback.

In the post-game frenzy, a reporter asked Charlie about the final play and he answered in his succinct, humble manner.

"I stepped up and made a shot," he said.

When all was said and done, Charlie played thirty-eight minutes in the game, which was the most on the team and a far cry from a few months prior when he could barely make it through a practice. For the game he had eighteen points, eight rebounds, six assists and two steals.

"There's no doubt that when Charlie played well, we played better as a team," Coach Kennedy said. "That game his composure, leadership and stamina may have been the two biggest factors."

• • •

Winning the Metro Conference Tournament not only netted the Seminoles a trophy but also an automatic bid into that year's NCAA tournament, where they were a #7 seed in the Southeast Regional. Their first round game was against the University of Southern California and their star guards, Harold Miner, soon to become 'Baby Jordan' in the NBA, and hyper-quick Robert Pack, another future pro. At the time, Florida State hadn't won an NCAA tournament game in more than ten years. That losing streak, just like the Metro Conference Finals losing streak, ended. Once again, Charlie led the team in minutes and assists, and Doug Edwards led with twenty-four points in the team's three-point win over USC. This set up a second-round match-up against #3 seed Indiana, led by Calbert Cheaney and iconic coach Bobby Knight.

The first half against the Hoosiers could not have gone better. Even though they shot 50% from the floor, the Seminoles played fast and loose, owned the boards and took a six-point point lead into halftime.

"They were very aggressive and confident in the first half," Knight said.

Kennedy was pleased.

"We did a great job controlling the boards in the first half," he said. "We needed the type of first half that we had. Our guys knew what a strong second-half team Indiana was."

Indiana opened the second half on fire, knocking down four three-pointers to take a 45-40 lead that they would continue to stretch.

Longtime Florida State beat writer for the *Tallahassee Democrat,* Steve Ellis, covered the game and wrote, "Red-hot shooting from the perimeter and red-hot shouting from the fans was exactly what Indiana needed to counter FSU's height advantage, and an 11-point deficit."

Charlie fouled out as the Seminoles scrambled on defense and tried to stay in the game, but the Hoosiers proved too good.

"We'd hoped they wouldn't heat up, and not only did they heat up, but they got the crowd right back in it," Kennedy said.

That combined with a ton of missed shots would spell the end of the road for Florida State, who would go on to lose by twenty-two points and fall one game shy of the coveted Sweet Sixteen. Doug Edwards had eighteen points and fourteen boards, while Charlie had eight points, four rebounds, four assists and five steals.

It was a triumphant return to the hardwood for Charlie Ward Jr.

After a two-year hiatus from organized basketball, and without even knowing if he'd be cleared to play until about a month before the season started, Charlie led FSU in assists and steals and was second to Edwards in postseason minutes. He hit the championship-winning shot in their conference tournament to secure an NCAA tournament berth, then helped lead the team to its first March Madness win in more than ten years. He was named to the All-Freshman Metro Conference team and established himself as a steadying force, a leader and a "spark plug" for a team that sorely needed all three. And he helped Coach Kennedy drop his ratio of swears to clean language during pep talks by a factor of ten. Not bad for a redshirt freshman on a football scholarship.

Chapter 15

Welcome to the ACC

Charlie Ward Jr. isn't in the official team photo for the 1991-92 Florida State Seminoles basketball team. The picture is one of those awkwardly staged team shots where chairs are arranged in a semi-circle around the Seminoles' logo at half-court of their practice facility. All of the coaches are wearing blazers with white or gray button-down shirts and what can only be described as classic dad ties in odd patterns and stripes and colors. The big men are standing in the back with Coach Kennedy in the middle, over a head shorter than Byron Wells and Andre Reid who flank him on either side. The trainer and team managers are sitting on folding chairs in the front row with the backcourt players, including Chuck Graham and a few new guys who will soon become FSU legends.

"I don't know where I was that day," Charlie said. "Must have had something going on with football. But I knew Sam and Bobby were practicing with the team and I heard that they could help us get to the next level."

The "Sam" and "Bobby" he was referring to were future fellow NBA players Sam Cassell and Bobby Sura. Cassell is the last player seated on the right. He's wearing white Nikes with white socks pulled halfway up his calves and a big smile on his face. Those who know him would say the moment the photo was snapped was most likely the only time all day he wasn't talking. Cassell was loud and proud and brash, and talked a mile a minute to Charlie's word-per-hour. Where Charlie kept to himself, it often seemed that Cassell had ongoing conversations with practically everyone on campus,—even himself.

"Nothing wrong with talking to yourself," Cassell once said. "As long as you don't start answering yourself, you're alright."

As Charlie would slip quietly in and out of both locker rooms and classrooms, Cassell couldn't help but announce his presence. Kenny Smith, who would play with Cassell on the NBA's Houston Rockets, put it this way: "It doesn't matter if it's 2 am or 2 pm, you'll hear Sam coming before you see him," he said. "When he gets on the bus I fake sleeping. Or I put on the headphones of my Walkman and start nodding to the music—even when I don't have a tape in. And I know he was louder at Florida State."

He was.

"Sam came from one of the worst ghettos in Baltimore and listened to rap music," Coach Kennedy said. "Charlie came from a small town in Georgia and listened to gospel music. But they were kindred spirits when it came to basketball."

Just as Charlie balled up socks while growing up and turned everything from hampers to trash cans into hoops, Cassell did the same thing. As Cassell moved through his middle school and teen years, he constantly sought out bigger and better competition as Charlie had, although he didn't have a hoop in his driveway like the Wards. Instead, he'd have to walk twelve blocks to Baltimore's famous hoops mecca, the Madison Square Recreation Center and The Dome, an outdoor court with a roof on it where the city's best players often gathered. It was Baltimore's version of New York City's famed Rucker Park.

Cassell's high school, Paul Laurence Dunbar High, was also nearby, and that too had a strong reputation in basketball. When Cassell was a freshman, the team had compiled a 59-0 record over two seasons with a roster that included Tyrone "Muggsy" Bogues, Reggie Lewis and David Wingate.

When Cassell graduated from high school he, like Charlie, could have enrolled at Florida State under Prop 48 but chose not to. Instead, he attended San Jacinto Junior College in Pasadena, Texas before eventually choosing to become a Seminole over offers from Arkansas and Oklahoma.

Bobby Sura, at 6'5", was a slightly bigger guard than the 6'3" Cassell, but he came from a much smaller high school with far less of a basketball tradition. Sura was from Wilkes-Barre, Pennsylvania and was voted the 1991 Small School Player of the Year. He averaged thirty-four points a game and set a school record with sixty-eight points in a single contest.

"He played in a horrible high school league, but he was perfect for us," Kennedy said. "I always loved Bobby and he was a great fit. With Bobby, Sam, Doug Edwards and Chuck, we had an emotional team. Charlie was our stabilizer."

So, rather than ease their way into the ACC pool with minimal ripples in the shallow end, the loud-talking Cassell and smooth-shooting Sura and slashing Chuck Graham and slick-passing Charlie couldn't help but cannonball into their new league.

"Nobody knew that FSU played hoops back then," Cassell said.

He was exaggerating to make a point, but he did have one. When comparing FSU football to FSU basketball, Coach Bowden and his team resided at the center of the college sports solar system, while the hoops team typically orbited somewhere between the Oort Cloud and Saturn. That was what Cassell wanted to change.

"All the ACC teams thought we'd be a pushover," he said. "We knew we just needed an opportunity to showcase what we could do. And that first year in the ACC we ran through almost the whole conference."

The "almost" is in there because the 1991-92 Duke University Blue Devils had an all-time great college team, featuring Christian Laettner, Bobby Hurley, Grant Hill, Thomas Hill and Cherokee Parks. The University of North Carolina also had a strong team, with stars Hubert Davis, George Lynch and Eric Montross. Both teams would battle Charlie and company for supremacy of their new league, but as the Seminoles' inaugural ACC season got under way, Coach Kennedy could sense something special happening in practice. He loved the team's early chemistry, loved the confidence, loved the energy and couldn't wait to add Charlie.

"We just clicked," Cassell said. "All there is to it. It was great."

Charlie got Bowden's blessing and began practicing with the team in late November, though he wasn't available for the first game of the year against Jacksonville as he continued to get into basketball shape. FSU won that game, with thirty-three points from Chuck Graham, twenty-two from Cassell and twenty-two from Edwards. Charlie then played only four minutes in the second game against Syracuse, which they lost by almost twenty points. By the third game he was up to playing eighteen minutes, and when

Florida State's first ACC match-up against North Carolina arrived at the Dean Dome in Chapel Hill, he was ready to go all out.

• • •

Seeing the Carolina blue, in person, on the actual floor of the Dean Dome, is basketball's version of visiting the Sistine Chapel. Officially called the Dean E. Smith Student Activities Center, the building with the famous white dome at its peak was named after the iconic Tar Heels coach. Unlike most multi-use college campus arenas, the Dean Dome was designed specifically for basketball by architect Glenn Corley, and the results are hard to refute. Since the doors opened, the Tar Heels have won 80% of their games at home, including a five-year stretch when they were undefeated on their own floor.

This hallowed ground would be the site of Florida State's first road game in the ACC—December 15, 1991, against the #5 ranked North Carolina Tar Heels. Cassell being Cassell, evaluated the situation this way: "This is not like the Duke crowd," he said. "I'd put it like a cheese and wine crowd. Laid back. You've just got to come in here and play hard."

Since it was the first game between the two as conference rivals, Carolina made a kind gesture before tip-off by giving the Seminoles the game ball. "What a great psychological thing, giving them the game ball," Dean Smith said. "We surely showed our hospitality."

Florida State was gracious, and then promptly thanked the Heels by jumping out to a quick 14-3 lead behind two Cassell three-pointers.

Prior to the game, Coach Kennedy had told his squad over and over that if they could get ahead and be up five points at halftime, they'd have a good chance at winning. Suddenly, they were up big and were riding a wave of positive emotion. Kennedy knew Carolina was too good to roll over, especially at home, and he was curious to see how his team would perform when the Heels made their inevitable run. The first push brought UNC to within five points, 18-13. The second push put UNC up 33-29 with about five minutes remaining in the first half. All the momentum and energy the Seminoles had been feeding off since the game started had been squandered. They'd just given up a huge lead on the road in a hostile environment. Kennedy had several competing thoughts going through his head: Would they go into halftime down big or would they rally? And if they rallied, whom would they rally around? Who would lead the response to show that they weren't intimidated?

The answer was Charlie Ward, whose two three-pointers, steady demeanor and overall leadership led a 13-0 Seminoles run, giving them a halftime lead of 46-39.

"We were up a lot early so I knew we were capable of playing with them—and even playing better than them," Ward said. "We took their shots and it was time for us to fight back. Everyone stepped up."

At halftime, Kennedy continued to preach his plan. "We're exactly where we want to be," he told them.

The second half picked up where the first left off, with FSU continuing to score and stretching the lead to eighteen points on a lay-up by Charlie with about ten minutes left. They then made the mistake of slowing down the tempo and milking the clock, which let Carolina get back in the game and cut the lead to four on an Eric Montross bucket. Fortunately for the Seminoles, UNC went ice cold after that while they made a steady stream of free throws to put the game away and give the Seminoles their first ACC win—and their first win against North Carolina in twenty years.

Cassell scored twenty-two. Graham had nineteen and Rodney Dobard had eleven points and twelve rebounds. Charlie had eighteen points, five rebounds, four assists and two steals.

"Florida State has had some great wins to get to the NCAA Tournament, to the Final Four," Kennedy said after the game. "But I would have to say this probably ranks among the greatest moments and greatest victories in school history."

It was a blockbuster opening act in the ACC that announced both FSU's arrival as a team to be reckoned with and Charlie Ward's potential as an elite college basketball player and bona fide two-sport star.

"Our football folks believe he's going to be a great, great quarterback," Kennedy said. "I've said this before: If he's the quarterback that can lead Florida State to a national championship-type season in football, and does what he does out here [on the basketball court], I don't believe there's a better athlete in the country."

There was no doubt that the Seminoles looked like a more cohesive, fluid team on both offense and defense with Charlie on the floor, and no less than Dean Smith took notice.

"Ward is just an incredible player," he said. "Of course, Cassell did some nice things too. But Ward is just amazing. I don't know if Bowden will get him back."

The irony of Coach Smith's last quote is that at almost the exact time he was joking about Coach Kennedy locking down Ward as a basketball player, and while the Seminoles players were celebrating their landmark victory, Charlie was on a plane back to Tallahassee so he could practice with the football team as they prepared for the upcoming Cotton Bowl against Texas A&M.

"He's got to work on being a quarterback," Kennedy said. "But I thought he looked pretty good as a basketball player."

• • •

After the victory against the Tar Heels, the Seminoles reeled off three out of four wins against non-conference opponents, and then went 10-5 the rest of the way against the ACC. They swept North Carolina State, Georgia Tech, Wake Forest, Clemson and North Carolina in the regular season, and split a pair of two-game series with Maryland and Virginia. The only team they didn't beat in two tries was Duke.

Florida State would finish the regular season 22-10 overall, ranked second in the conference and #19 in the AP poll. The only Seminoles player who would lead their new conference in a major statistical category was Charlie and his 75 steals. He topped a group of future NBA players and stars that included Christian Laettner with 74 steals on the year, Jon Barry of Georgia Tech with 71, followed by George Lynch, Tom Gugliotta, Thomas Hill, Walt Williams, Cassell, Edwards and Travis Best. Charlie also finished tenth in total assists, right behind Duke's Grant Hill. Cassell would be in the top ten in almost every major scoring category.

The Seminoles would beat North Carolina State in the first round of the ACC tournament and then finally lose to UNC in the semi-finals, 80-76. Charlie put up fifteen points, five rebounds and five assists. Though they failed to beat UNC a third time and reach the finals of their new conference's tournament, the Seminoles' top 25 AP ranking and strength of schedule gave them a #3 seed in the West Regional of the NCAA Tournament, with their first game against 13th-seeded Montana in Boise, Idaho. While they would have little trouble handling the Grizzlies, Charlie dislocated his shoulder with just over four minutes left in the first half. He'd end up playing only fourteen minutes and watched the second half of the game in a sling. Cassell was able to take over point guard duties while also scoring twenty-three points in the 78-68 win.

Charlie's injury kept him out of the Seminoles' second-round game against Georgetown and their star center Alonzo Mourning. Once again, Cassell took over Ward's point guard duties and did a great job.

"I hated being out, but I knew Sam would step up for us," Ward said. "Coach told us that if we could contain Alonzo we'd control the game, and we were able to do that. It was one of those unfortunate situations where I wasn't able to help my team in a big game, but I was also proud of how they played."

Coach Kennedy's plan was to essentially smother, frustrate and thwart Mourning at every turn, and it worked. They threw body after body at him, fronting him with big guards like Bobby Sura when necessary. The strategy paid off as Mourning had only one point at halftime.

"Going in, we believed everything revolved around Alonzo Mourning," FSU assistant coach Tom Carlson said. "The idea was to always have two people on him."

Florida State battled back from an eleven-point deficit in the second half, and when Mourning fouled out with a few minutes left, the scales seemed to tip in FSU's favor.

"We lose him [Mourning] and it creates a psychological disadvantage for us," Georgetown's coach John Thompson said. The end result was a 78-68 victory and what Coach Kennedy called the biggest win he'd had at Florida State.

"We said the next step after last season was to get to the Sweet Sixteen, and we did that," Kennedy said.

• • •

Florida State would have five days to prepare—in Charlie's case, heal—for the match-up against the #2 seed from the West region, Indiana University. The Seminoles players viewed the game as a way to avenge their 82-60 loss to the Hoosiers in the 1991 tournament.

"That was a tough loss after so many big moments that year," Charlie said. "We were hoping to pay them back and get a win."

They were also looking to cement their spot at the top of the ACC, as they were one of four conference teams to advance to the round of sixteen along with Georgia Tech, Duke and North Carolina.

"If we could get to the Elite Eight or past that in our first year in the ACC, that would really be something," Charlie said. "That's what we were all playing for."

The game took place in Albuquerque, New Mexico at The Pit, a subterranean-themed arena famous for having its court thirty-seven floors underground. As Charlie took the floor for warm-ups in front of roughly 16,000 people that night, he did what he could to test out his injured shoulder. He rotated it, swung it, stretched it, pushed it and pulled on it, trying to find a sweet spot or movement that would relieve the pain and soreness. Nothing worked, but the second his arm had come out of a sling he'd decided that he was playing.

"Just wanted to be with the guys and contribute any way I could," he said.

Cassell hit a three to kick off a run that put the Seminoles up 9-2 early, but that would end up being one of the few times during the game FSU had control. Indiana's man-to-man defense kept them off-tempo and Charlie wasn't close to his normal self, especially on defense. FSU kept the game within striking distance well past halftime but had no defensive answer for Indiana's Eric Anderson, who poured in twenty-four points as his team pulled away with the win. Cassell fouled out and Charlie played twenty-four minutes but was able to muster only three points. He didn't have a single steal, which were sorely missed, as quick scores and changes of possession keyed so many FSU rallies during the season. Without those momentum shifts, they were never able to impose their will on Indiana. "We were never really able to put together one of our runs," Cassell said. "You have to give them credit."

"Indiana's a really difficult team to beat from behind," Coach Kennedy said afterward. "They're very good shooters. They execute well. They look like a team possessed." Indiana would make it all the way to the Final Four before losing to Duke, who would eventually win the national championship over Michigan.

Despite the loss, it was hard for Coach Kennedy or anyone on the team to label the season anything other than a big success. They'd catapulted their way to the top of the ACC in their first year there, and made it to the Sweet Sixteen. They also had almost all of their biggest contributors coming back for the 1992-93 season, including Chuck Graham, Doug Edwards, Bobby Sura, Rodney Dobard, Sam Cassell and Charlie Ward.

Where at one point, as Cassell said, people barely even knew that FSU had a basketball team, now everyone knew, and nobody wanted to play them.

Chapter 16

Almost Famous

The period of time between the summer of 1991 and the summer of 1992 was the last stretch of Charlie's life when he enjoyed relative anonymity in public. Aside from a few die-hard Seminoles hoops fans that might recognize him after his breakout season on the basketball team, Charlie could stroll through Florida State's campus—and Tallahassee in general—without being stopped or recognized. He could move through classrooms, dining halls and dorms at will. There were no expectations, no autograph seekers, nobody wanting his picture. There were no demands. There was no pressure. No burden to win a national championship. No Final Four talk. No Heisman campaign to feed.

For those who had a front-row seat to Charlie Ward's ascension, it's hard to remember a time when someone didn't want something from him.

"To me, he was just Charlie, but his last year was crazy," Warrick Dunn, Ward's roommate his senior year, said. "People idolized him. As his roommate, it got annoying because every five minutes someone would knock on the door or would want a photo or an autograph. I eventually put a sign on the door when he was out that said, CHARLIE AIN'T HERE and I put it in broken English to make a statement. People were in awe of him, but he handled it all so well."

Cassell was Charlie's college teammate and roomed with him on basketball team road trips. "When he became a star, I'd see him on campus and it was unbelievable. He'd be walking with cameras in front of his face every day. Everyone wanted to interview him. He had no privacy at all," Cassell said. "It was good to see how he handled that. It never changed him."

Students, too, noticed how he handled the attention and were amazed at his ability to take it all in stride. Russ Vorhis got to see Charlie's fame from several different angles. He worked for the Florida State strength and conditioning coach, Dave Van Halanger, so he got a behind-the-scenes look at some of the demands on Charlie, but recognized that Charlie was also very much a normal college kid.

"Charlie was just special," he said. "He made our whole campus proud. He didn't want to be covered in media attention. He was refreshing and real. I saw him with the teams and on campus a lot. I don't think he was ever uncomfortable. We were both involved with the Fellowship of Christian Athletes and he was a regular guy. He was just himself."

This version of Charlie's self didn't manifest by accident. It was created through a combination of factors, including the positive influence of his parents, his faith and his own personal choices. By the time the rest of America knew his name, he'd already decided what was important to him and how he wanted to live his life.

"It was like Charlie had a goal in life and he was just going to do that," Cassell said. "We all have goals, but he stuck to his no matter what."

Cassell likes to tell stories of how Charlie made a point to try to get a good night's sleep every night, even on the road. Cassell would sneak out of his room,return at 12:30 in the morning, and wake Charlie up and they'd talk.

"It was great," Cassell said. "Charlie had his own sense of humor. He was serious but he's funny. He could be hard to talk to in the beginning, but I was always teasing him and getting him to open up until he became like family. He's such a great person. Everyone says it and it's true."

Cassell tells his stories using a killer impersonation of Charlie, right down to his cadence, and the short pauses between sentences.

"I'd come in the room and he'd say 'Hey, Sam, what are you doing?' and I'd say nothin', C-Ward, what are you up to?" Cassell said, laughing, fully aware he had woken Charlie up. "I liked to stay up late, but he wanted to get his eight hours of sleep and he was going to get it."

Staying in and prioritizing sleep was a decision he made after some trial and error. Early in college he'd succumbed to peer pressure and stayed out late, but he didn't like how he felt.

"I got caught up in the partying ways of college life," he said. "My morals dropped off a bit. That wasn't the life I wanted to be leading."

He was often tired the next day or underperformed on the field or in the classroom after a night out, so he simply decided to not stay out late. The same decision process was used when it came to drinking alcohol. It wasn't like Charlie never tried drinking. He did. He just didn't like it.

"One night when I was a kid, my parents were out and my grand mom was watching us and we got into my parents' alcohol," Charlie said. "Me and my older sister and my cousin snuck off to a part of the house where my grand mom wasn't hanging out and we found some white wine. My sister and cousin told me not to drink it but I did. I drank a good amount and I got dizzy and really sick. I decided then and there I didn't want to drink alcohol ever again."

To be fair, most people say they'll never drink again after an awful first-drinking experience, especially after getting drunk on possibly stale, forgotten-about mom-and-dad liquor cabinet white wine, but Charlie stuck with it. He has no problem with others drinking, but like staying out late, he didn't enjoy alcohol so he stopped consuming it.

And going down the list of things that could potentially derail a superstar college athlete, right behind partying and alcohol would be poor grades and poor choices with women. When it came to the latter, Charlie remained celibate in college while with his girlfriend (now wife) Tonja Harding, who was in law school at the time.

"I certainly wasn't an angel my whole life," Charlie said. "But at the time I felt that if I was going to marry a young lady and we had sex before marriage, what was there to look forward to?"

As for grades, Charlie knew first-hand how difficult A's and B's were to come by. He'd spent a big portion of his gap year learning how to study and applying what he learned in class, actively fighting the notion that football players weren't great students. His GPA, like his regular and on-time attendance in class, was something he took great pride in. During his senior year, the *Pensacola News Journal* bucked the trend of profiles on Charlie's athletic achievements, and instead wrote a feature on his academic success in the field of Leisure Services with a major in therapeutic recreation. The Florida State football academic adviser at the time, Mark Meleney, confirmed that heading into Charlie's last year he had earned a 3.0 grade-point-average for four straight semesters.

"He's very close to graduating with honors," Meleney said back then. "His self-discipline and ability to remain calm and focused in times of pressure—just as he does on the football field or basketball court—are what make him a good student."

"People see me all the time on TV and see how I am athletically," Charlie said in the piece. "But rarely do people see how you are academically. Whenever you are the quote-unquote 'star' of the team, people think you're a jock. They don't have an image of you being an academic."

Donna Fletcher, who was Charlie's academic adviser and also an associate professor of Human Service and Study, said she didn't know Charlie was an athlete until they'd been working together for over a year, including more than 40 hours a week helping patients during his final summer at the Capital Rehabilitation Hospital.

"He had such a wonderful relationship with the patients, the way he spent time with them and helped them. Charlie is just outstanding in every respect," she said. His work with disabled patients and his work in the classroom earned him induction into Rho Phi Lambda, a national honorary society for Leisure Service students.

"It's amazing what he's done," Meleney said, rounding out the *News Journal*'s piece. "Especially for a young man who wasn't nearly as prepared for college when he came here as he needed to be."

And yet, in three short years Charlie went from not being prepared for college to being completely prepared for super stardom because he knew who he was and was comfortable in his own skin. Compared to other flashy Florida State stars like Deion Sanders and Terrell Buckley, Charlie was "the other side of the coin" as Coach Bowden took to calling him.

Following Charlie's Heisman win, *Sports Illustrated*'s Rick Reilly wrote a feature on Charlie that described his co-existence in Tallahassee as both its biggest star and most famous homebody. In his December 1993 piece, he wrote:

> Smack in the middle of Cocktail U, in the heart of the school named

> No. 1 for fun in the U.S., lodged between Drink Til You Sink at Bullwinkle's and Nickel Beer Night at Calico Jack's, there is a very unusual place called Charlie Ward. It is a place where every day is 1951; a place where the only resident not only doesn't have sex, he also doesn't smoke, drink, swear, pierce, cheat, chew, drive by or get busy; a place where every reporter, ankle-taper and drive-thru box gets a "Sir" or a "Ma'am"; a place where the closest thing to trash talk is "Dad, you mind if I take out the garbage?"; a place where hopelessly outdated concepts like respect and decency are trying to get cool again.

Charlie's signature quote in the piece is this:

> "Being a real straight arrow is something that a lot of people are offended by, I guess," he said. "But that's the way I've been all my life. It's just fun to be one of a kind."

And that, right there, is why the anonymous Charlie Ward Jr. of 1991-92 was completely and totally prepared for the A-list, cover-of-every-sports-magazine, #1 college-athlete-in-the-country level of stardom of 1992 through1994. He was cool with being what some people might call "not cool." As Reilly wrote in his piece,

> Maybe it's just easier to put it in the record this way: In the year 1993, in the age of Beavis and Butt-head, shock radio, Marky Mark, and brassieres as outerwear, the best athlete in college sports is a former choirboy, vice president of the student body and honor-roll student who is no louder than a convent cat and about as trendy as a firm handshake.

All of which was fine by Charlie and his teammates, because at his core he was, as Cassell described, "just a good country boy from Thomasville, Georgia who loved sports." And no amount of media coverage or money or awards was going to change that—though all three would be coming his way very shortly.

• • •

There was one thing, however, that Charlie did want as he readied himself for the official role of Florida State's Starting Quarterback, and it was something that most college students covet: a car. To get it, he had to do something that most college students did as well: get a random, odd summer job to make money.

The story behind his first car and his job is one of those classic family tales that parents delight in telling to anyone who will listen. While the story is about work ethic and being financially independent and learning that effort equals outcome, it's also kind of embarrassing for their kids. This particular story is almost told as an afterthought as we sit on the couch at Charlie Sr. and Willard's house. The topic of conversation was Junior's preparedness for the spotlight that was about to shine on him heading into his junior year as the starter at FSU. Willard was tending to the dinner being made in the kitchen and floating in and out of the conversation. Charlie was leaning against the wall, forced to hear the story for probably the hundredth time.

"As an athlete he was ready to handle the role, no doubt about that," Charlie Sr. said, running his hand over his hair, leaning back on the couch. "He didn't come to us for much or have any stress about it. Didn't really need or want anything I can remember… Except… Well… He did come to us about a car."

"The car!" his mom said, laughing from the kitchen. "Junior *really* wanted a car."

"And we had a car for him!" Senior said, jumping up. "He just didn't want it. No. He. Did. Not."

Why wouldn't he want it?

Willard walked back into the room and sat down next to Charlie Sr., smiling.

"When my dad died he left us a little old red car," she said. "We gave it to my daughter who was at FAMU, and then offered it to Charlie but he wouldn't take it. He said, 'Mama, I'm not driving around in that thing. You've seen all those fine cars up on campus. I'm not driving that old red car.' So I told him, 'That's okay, Junior. If you're ashamed of your grandfather's old car you can take the bus whenever you need to come and go anywhere.'"

Turns out that even ever-humble Charlie Ward Jr. would simply not abide driving a dorky car around campus.

"He stood his ground and said he wouldn't drive that car," Willard said.

"Then you can go get a job, we told him," Senior chimed in. "And pay for a car yourself."

"So that's what I did," Charlie said.

But it wasn't easy. The NCAA has rules about what kinds of jobs scholarship athletes could take, so Charlie asked friends and coaches and teammates for help finding work. Casey Weldon told Charlie about a job specifically for student-athletes that he himself had done the previous summer and had made some decent money doing. Charlie was interested.

"One problem," his dad said. "It was a sales job."

Not that anyone doubted that if Charlie put his mind to it he could sell, but in order to sell you have to, well, talk. That was the part that confused those who know him. How was quiet, unassuming Charlie going to be a salesman? Maybe if he was selling football equipment or basketball shoes that would make sense. But...

"And then we asked him what he'd be selling," his mom said.

"Fire extinguishers!" Charlie Sr. said. "What does Junior know about fire extinguishers?"

"We bought the first one," his mom said.

"That we did," Charlie Sr. said, and then added, laughing. "Didn't know if it was gonna be the last one either."

"It wasn't," his mom said. "He was good at it."

"The boy wanted his car," his dad said.

After Weldon told Charlie about the fire extinguisher salesman job, Charlie signed up and was flown out to Nashville, Tennessee with other college athletes for a weekend seminar on fire extinguishers.

"It was a weekend deal," Charlie said. "They taught us all about the product, how to use it, how to pitch it and sell it and close a sale. It was really the first public speaking I ever had to do, and in that respect it was good for me. We had to practice our pitch over and over and rehearse. The whole nine yards."

After the weekend seminar, Charlie went back to Thomasville and set up appointments with family and friends to sell his fire extinguishers. The company also had a connection with the Florida State boosters, and they helped set up appointments too. In no time, he was booked solid with appointments.

"It was funny because he would have us sit down and he'd go through his whole presentation with us and he'd practice and we'd give notes," his mom said. "Soon the whole town was buying fire extinguishers from him."

"I was setting up parties where I could present, and also friends and Florida State alumni hosted parties, and I'd go in and give my whole speech and demonstrate the fire extinguishers," Charlie said. "It was a good product and helped me get a little more comfortable talking in front of people."

By the end of the summer, not only was Thomasville the safest town in America in the occasion of a fire, but Charlie was the top seller in his region and had finally earned enough money to buy a used car.

"It was a white Honda," his dad said. "I think an '87. One of the local dealers sold it to him."

"I earned that car," Charlie said. "I loved that car. It felt good to drive."

"He did it," his mom said. "The boy who didn't like to talk bought a car with money he made talking."

And he beat Weldon's sales record from the previous summer by a few units.

His son was Florida State University's only Heisman Trophy winner, and was responsible for their first National Championship. This is a photo of Florida A&M halfback Charlie Ward of Thomasville, Georgia. His son, Charlie Ward, Jr. went on to a successful career in the NBA.

Charlie Senior strikes a Heisman pose at FAMU. (*Photo credit: Leta Ward-Dawson*)

Charlie Senior and Junior. (*Photo credit: Leta Ward-Dawson*)

Charlie Ward official Florida State headshot.
(*Photo credit: Florida State University*)

Charlie punting from South Carolina's end zone.
(*Photo credit: Florida State University*)

Pre-Game warm-ups at FSU.
(*Photo credit: Florida State University*)

Charlie Confers with Coach Bowden.
(*Photo credit: Florida State University*)

Charlie Ward Heisman Trophy.
(*Photo credit: Ryals Lee*)

Posing with the Heisman Trophy at the Downtown Athletic Club.
(*Photo credit: Ryals Lee*)

Heisman Trophy on display in library.
(*Photo credit: Jon Finkel*)

Charlie celebrating with his parents and family.
(*Photo credit: Leta Ward-Dawson*)

New York Knicks headshot.
(*Photo credit: George Kalinsky for Madison Square Garden*)

Driving to the hoop with the Knicks.
(Photo credit: George Kalinsky for Madison Square Garden)

Setting up the Knicks offense.
(*Photo credit: George Kalinsky for Madison Square Garden*)

Receiving his College Football Hall of Fame Salute.
(*Photo credit: Florida State University*)

Charlie with his siblings.
(*Photo credit: Leta Ward-Dawson*)

Thomasville Central home field sign.
(*Photo credit: Jon Finkel*)

Chapter 17

QB1

A thin white towel dangled just off-center of the belt of his gold football pants. His garnet #17 jersey was tucked tight into his waist and wrapped closely around his shoulder pads. The white wristband on the left sat mid-forearm while the wristband on his right arm settled just above his hand. He held his yellow mouthpiece in his left hand as he barked out the play call in the huddle. It was third and sixteen on his first drive of the first start of his college football career. The Doak Campbell Stadium crowd was dressed entirely in white. As Charlie marched to the line of scrimmage, the famous FSU War Cry thundered across the stadium. Eighty thousand arms Tomahawk chopped the air and the band's horn section blasted in rhythm. Charlie settled himself under center, yelled the cadence and took the snap. His right shoulder dipped back as he raced through his seven-step drop. He settled ever so briefly in the pocket, glancing down field for receivers beyond the first down marker. *Gotta keep this drive alive.* A tenth of a second later, flanker Matt Frier broke free on a post route and Charlie uncorked the arm Florida State fans had been waiting three years to see. The ball rocketed through the air straight at his target…but it was about eight feet too high. It sailed directly over Frier and was intercepted by Duke University safety Tee Edwards, who returned it twenty-five yards to give the Blue Devils great field position.

Six minutes later, Charlie would find himself in another third-and-long situation with a chance for redemption. The play called for another deep drop back with several receivers crossing the middle of the field. This time he saw Kevin Knox gain a step on his man and he fired a laser for a sure first down…except he threw the ball about six feet in front of Knox and

Edwards snagged his second interception of the game. Shortly thereafter, Charlie threw another pick.

He went into the locker room at halftime having thrown three interceptions in his first thirty minutes of college football. He remained calm during the break. Florida State was getting the ball to start the third quarter and he was determined to march right down the field.

After a great kickoff return by Tiger McMillon, Charlie had decent field position to open the third quarter. On the first play of the drive, Sean Jackson ran eleven yards to get FSU to mid-field. The second play was stuffed at the line. On the third play, Charlie dropped back to pass, faked a toss left, changed direction and looked down field. As he sprinted to his right, he pump-faked, froze the defense, and dashed for fourteen yards and a first down. This was the added dimension the Seminole faithful had been waiting for. Two plays later he faked a handoff, dropped back and rifled a ball down the middle of the field to Knox...but it was deflected and once again picked off by Duke. Charlie now had his fourth interception in just over two quarters of football. By the time the game was over, he'd added a fumble to the mix for a grand total of five turnovers in his highly `anticipated debut.

That was the bad news.

The good news was that in between the moments that showed inconsistency and inexperience, Charlie displayed flashes of sheer brilliance as a runner. And when he was able to dial in his accuracy as a passer, he unleashed enough short bulls-eyes and long bombs to make the Florida State coaching staff giddy about the plays they would be able to call in the future. All told, Charlie threw for four touchdowns, including a 68-yarder to Frier, and rushed for eighty-four yards and one touchdown on nine carries. He was FSU's leading rusher and accounted for 369 total yards. Even with the five turnovers, he still provided more than enough firepower and moxie to beat Duke, 48-21.

While his long-term future was as bright as ever, the five turnovers led some people to wonder if the stress of the moment got to Charlie and whether or not he could handle the stage as the lights got brighter throughout the season. These were concerns people had been raising to Charlie the entire preseason.

Are you nervous? Are you ready? Are you scared?

All summer Charlie had been insisting that he wasn't feeling any pressure. Despite having not been a starting quarterback in three years, and despite being the first black quarterback at Florida State, he remained unbothered. When it came to the latter issue, he had a response ready for anyone who asked about it: "To me, it's a non-factor now. Who was the first white quarterback here?" he asked an interviewer. "If you can tell me that, then put my name in the books as the first black quarterback. When they put me in the books, it's not going to say 'first black quarterback.' It'll just say 'quarterback.'"

Privately, while Charlie remained unworried, his family members knew that there were still people who were uncomfortable with the idea of Florida State having a black quarterback, and it concerned them.

"Our society still had some race barriers to overcome," Willard said.

"There were some people saying nasty things and there were some death threats," Leta Ward said. "That part wasn't good. Our grandmothers were very spiritual women and they prayed for him and his safety and had prayer groups about it. That kept him uplifted and covered."

No credible threats emerged and no serious attempts were ever made to harm Charlie as he went about his business, so he was able to put the issue in the back of his mind. Eventually, reporters and fans and family members didn't bring it up anymore. What they wanted to talk about instead was pressure; and nerves; and, was Charlie worried about the responsibility of living up to his hype; and, was he ready to take over the offense of a top five ranked team in the country? None of it, Charlie contended, got to him.

"I'm not nervous," he said in a preseason interview. "If you're nervous it means you're lacking confidence. I'm the kind of person that can adjust to a lot of things. I'm hoping we surprise a lot of people, just like we did in basketball."

The only problem with that response was that the expectations were so high for Charlie, even winning a national championship in his first season would barely qualify as a surprise. The praise that was being heaped on him was almost impossible to live up to.

"Charlie is a special talent," offensive tackle Robert Stevenson said. "For anybody to play basketball and football at the level he has, they have to have something special going for them."

"I was fortunate to have been around Deion [Sanders]," Wayne McDuffie said from his new job at Georgia. "He was the best athlete I've ever seen. But Charlie is not far behind."

"Star, star, star," Coach Bowden said. "In everything Charlie has done, he's been a star. He's a coach's dream."

"What most people believe to be special," Coach Richt said. "Charlie believes is ordinary."

And those quotes were all said before he had a single meaningful start.

To Charlie, the compliments, the talk of him being 'special,' the occasional looks of awe and wonder—they were all other people's perceptions and were not why he played. In his mind, they were just a byproduct of his effort and love for the sport. He couldn't control how he made people feel or what they said. What he could control was how hard he worked. That was why none of the praise ever went to his head.

"Personally, I don't have an ego; maybe if I did I'd see it that way," he said. "I just go out and perform. That's the way I approach sports and everything in life."

So, fine, he wasn't nervous about anything and he didn't feel pressure.

"Then why the five turnovers in your first start?" reporters asked.

"I don't think there was any pressure involved," he said. "I just wasn't on. In high school, it was the same way: I would throw some interceptions but I would make it up somehow."

Bobby Bowden said he wasn't too concerned about how Charlie played against Duke. "He had his good moments, he had his bad moments," he said. "All he really needs now is some experience. I give him credit as being an experienced football player and he is not. This was his first game as a starter… Sometimes I forget he isn't Superman."

Charlie, for his part, didn't sugarcoat it.

"I'd give my performance a C-minus," he said. "I really don't think I played well at all."

• • •

Seven days later, the Seminoles traveled to Frank Howard Field at Clemson Memorial Stadium to take on the #15 ranked Tigers. Also known as "Death Valley," the stadium was built at the bottom of a hill overlooked by the university's cemetery. In the late 1940s, Lonnie McMillian, the football coach at Presbyterian University, told sports writers before a game that he had to "take his team up to Clemson and play in Death Valley," referring to the cemetery and the fact that whenever his team played there, hopes of bringing home a win would die. Hence, a memorable and macabre nickname was born, intimidating visiting teams for generations to come. The Tigers historically won over 70% of their games at home, and heading into their match-up against Florida State they'd won sixteen straight on their own turf.

So, on this field, with its history of futility for visiting teams, Charlie Ward Jr. would make the second start of his college career. Kickoff took place just before sunset, giving the helmet-to-cleat orange-clad Clemson Tigers an ethereal appearance as darkness fell and the stadium lights took over. Clemson received the opening kickoff, but the Seminoles' defense forced a quick turnover and gave Charlie his first chance to put the spotty Duke performance behind him. On the second play of the series, Charlie set up in shotgun formation and proceeded to fumble the snap, which he tried to pick up, fumbled again, and then was lucky enough to fall on with a lineman to maintain possession. On third down, Charlie was back in shotgun. This time he successfully caught the snap and rolled out to his right. As he searched the field, he sprinted forward and, just before he got to the line of scrimmage, cocked his arm and launched a ball downfield that was picked off by Clemson's Norris Brown, giving Charlie five interceptions on the young season. Then things got worse. After leading the Seminoles to a touchdown and a field goal in the first half, Charlie's start to the third quarter would be absolutely disastrous—he threw two more interceptions. The first would lead to a field goal and the second was returned by Clemson's James Trapp to give the Tigers a 13-10 lead.

Bobby Bowden had seen enough.

His starting quarterback had now thrown seven interceptions in barely six quarters of football (compared to eight for Casey Weldon the entire previous season).

It was time for Charlie to be benched.

"We had people open but Charlie couldn't get it to them," Bowden said. "He was inaccurate all game and it was driving me crazy."

The Seminoles brought in back-up Danny Kanell to start the next series and considered leaving him in. While on the sideline, Charlie never lost confidence.

"I never doubted my abilities. It was just a matter of getting my mind together. I knew if I could get one more shot, I could at least do something with the ball," he said.

He'd get that shot, and with it the football legend of Charlie Ward Jr. at Florida State would officially begin. Here are the specifics: September 12, 1992, with five minutes and twenty-three seconds left on the clock, on the road, in Death Valley, his team trailing 20-17 against one that hadn't lost at home in two years.

The drive began on Florida State's own twenty-three yard line with a hand-off to McMillon for five yards. On second and five Charlie hit Shannon Baker on a quick route to gain a first down. He followed that up with a five-step drop and a beautiful, deep lob to the left side of the field to Kevin Knox to bring them to Clemson's 42-yard line.

The Clemson faithful shouted and stomped and screamed to try to disrupt Charlie as he lined up for the next play. The defense, feeding off the Death Valley drumbeat, collapsed the pocket and brought Charlie down for no gain. Bowden paced the sidelines, adjusting his headset, his hat, his waistband, his shirt—anything to try to get comfortable with having to rely on an erratic, young quarterback facing one of the most hostile crowds in college football. The clock continued to tick as he discussed the play call with his coaches in the booth. All game they had wanted to exploit the middle of the field, but with Charlie's inaccuracy it was a risk. A fifth interception on the night would end the game and possibly the Seminoles' title hopes. Bowden went with his gut.

The next play was a crossing route to Kez McCorvey, which Charlie threw perfectly for a twelve-yard gain to the dead middle of the field. The crowd could feel him getting in a rhythm, and with every completion they dialed up the noise, trying to rattle the first-year starter. Following the McCorvey catch, Charlie tucked the ball for an eight-yard run to bring up a first down on Clemson's twenty-two with less than three minutes to go.

The Seminoles were now in field goal range and could theoretically attempt to tie it up, although that wasn't Bowden's style. His options were to either go conservative and call a series of runs to protect the attempt at three points and not chance a mistake by Charlie, or to keep rolling the dice with his young QB's arm. He kept rolling the dice. The next call was a drop-back pass, and as Charlie rolled to his right, he stopped on a dime and leapt in front of a would-be tackler and slid over to the sideline, hitting tight end Lonnie Johnson with a touch pass for thirteen yards. It was now first and goal on the nine for FSU.

With their backs against the wall and the game on the line, Clemson's defensive front plowed through FSU's line on the ensuing play, collapsing the pocket immediately. Charlie backpedaled to buy time. His left tackle got beat by Clemson's Wayne Simmons, who barreled toward him. A split second before Simmons lowered the boom facemask to facemask, Charlie managed to get loose a perfect dart, threading the needle through two safeties to Knox for the touchdown and the lead.

Charlie pulled himself off the ground and limped to the sideline, his first heroic drive and comeback for the Seminoles in the books. He had preserved the game, the season, and his starting role, despite throwing four interceptions. Yet again, in his personal analysis, he pulled no punches.

"My interceptions kept them in the game," he said. "The wide receivers and the line did a great job all night; it was me who was messing up. But the coaches always talk about what it takes to be a great quarterback. You have to come in for key situations and perform. On that last drive, I just said 'the heck with it' and fired the ball like I know how. John Elway does it all the time. That was my Elway drive. We knew we had openings and we just did what we had to do."

William Floyd was ecstatic. He had been talking Charlie up all preseason to anyone who would listen. The way he led the team in practice and the things he had seen him do blew Floyd's mind. Now the rest of the football world could catch up.

"That was the poised Charlie Ward that we've been talking about," he said about the drive. "He is the most poised player I have ever seen. He doesn't get uptight, he just does what he has to do."

Florida State's offensive coordinator was also obsessed with Charlie's poise after the game.

"Charlie showed a lot of poise," he said. "He made some outstanding plays. He struggled at one point, but he made the good choices in the end.

The Seminoles' defensive line coach, Chuck Amato, resorted to a basketball analogy: that final drive was like a basketball team down by one point and their star player steps to the foul line and hits both shots on a one-and-one. "That was pressure," he concluded.

And what about Coach Bowden, who was furious over the inconsistent passes and the missed receivers and the poor defensive reads?

"That last drive really tells you a lot about Charlie Ward," he said. "And that last drive was great."

• • •

It was no surprise that Charlie Ward brought up John Elway when talking about his final drive in the Clemson game. Elway was the architect of a drive so legendary it became known simply as "The Drive" in the annals of the National Football League. Elway marched his Denver Broncos ninety-eight yards down the field for a game-tying touchdown against the Cleveland Browns in the 1987 AFC Championship Game. It's not hard to picture the Wards sitting in their family room in Thomasville watching that game and dreaming of the possibilities. Charlie would have just finished his first season as the starting quarterback at Central High School, and in Elway he would have watched a kindred spirit at the position.

Like Charlie, Elway was a dual-threat quarterback capable of leading his team in rushing and passing in the same game; like Charlie, Elway seemed completely and totally averse to pressure; and like Charlie, Elway excelled at multiple sports at an elite level, ultimately playing both football and baseball at Stanford University (he hit .361 with 50 RBIs and nine home runs his sophomore year). And here's some bonus trivia: both Elway and Ward were drafted by the New York Yankees to play baseball. Elway even sounds like Ward when talking about which sport he likes to play best.

"It's a seasonal thing," Elway said. "I enjoy football in football season and baseball in baseball season."

By the time Charlie played Clemson, Elway had made a name for himself as a "Comeback King" in the NFL, capable of raising his teams from the dead in the fourth quarter practically all by himself. That Charlie brought up Elway in several interviews across several media outlets following the Clemson game shows just how much "The Drive" and Elway's style of play affected him.

"It [the drive] was the type of character builder any good team needs, especially early in the season," he said. "I've seen John Elway do it many times. I just prayed to the good lord and he answered my prayer."

The Elway-level confidence would become a theme with Charlie as the season progressed. Though naturally poised and with the utmost belief in his abilities, he always made sure to mention that he and/or the team never lost confidence when something went wrong.

Case in point: Charlie started the very next game against North Carolina State by missing on his first five throws—but he settled down and ended up throwing for 275 yards and three touchdowns with only one interception. The Seminoles would easily win the game, 34-13. Afterward, he said, "We made some mistakes early. It was just a matter of bouncing back. We never lose confidence. We know we can make a big play at any time."

After NC State the Seminoles beat up on Wake Forest, 35-7. Charlie would not throw a single interception for the first time all season. "I'm settling in and getting more comfortable with the reads," he said. "It's like second nature now. It was just a matter of time before I came around."

That was his perspective. The coaches would say he came around just in time. The #2 ranked Miami Hurricanes were next on the schedule.

• • •

The stage for this game must be set properly: #2 ranked Miami and #3 ranked Florida State were both undefeated. Miami had won six of the previous seven games between the schools, and in four of the previous five years, the Hurricanes' win directly prevented Florida State from playing for a national championship. Florida State had lost by a single point three times to Miami since 1983. The 1991 game was decided by a missed field goal and was the toughest loss for Bowden in his career to that point. In short, whenever FSU wanted to throw a victory parade, Miami would unleash a torrential downpour of defeat on it.

This time, the game would be set in Miami's famous Orange Bowl. Bowden summed up the face-off this way: "The team that wins it has a good chance of taking home the number one prize. The team that doesn't won't have a chance, I don't think."

Revenge was on the minds of every Florida State Seminole as they headed down to Coral Gables.

"We feel like they're wearing our ring," running back Sean Jackson said. "If it weren't for a missed field goal by a couple of inches we would be national champions. We're going down there to get what's ours."

As the sun kissed the waters of Biscayne Bay in the early morning hours of October 2, 1992, a light rain began to fall over Little Havana, home of the Orange Bowl. The field sat about six miles northeast of Miami's campus, and that morning the temperature was already in the high eighties by 6 am. By 8 am the rain would stop, but the sauna that was the southern tip of Florida would keep churning. By kickoff, the heat index would reach a searing 101.5 degrees. A layer of clouds hovered over the field, as did the tangible feeling that the ghosts of games past were present that day. A majority of the media coverage leading up to the game focused on that heartbreaking loss for Bowden and FSU in 1991. The undercard stories involved

Florida State's defense, Miami's offense, and the first match-up between Charlie and Miami's Heisman Trophy-favorite quarterback, Gino Torretta.

The star of the first quarter, however, was Florida State's fighter-jet fast receiver, Tamarick Vanover, who fielded the opening kickoff, weaved through traffic, then broke to the outside and scorched Miami's entire team on the way to a 94-yard touchdown. It was his second 90-yard-plus kick return for a touchdown in as many games. Both teams would have field goals blocked and the first quarter ended with FSU up 7-0. The next two quarters were a defensive slugfest, with both teams suffocating each other's offense while trying to avoid being suffocated by the humidity. ABC sideline reporter Jack Arute witnessed several Florida State defensive players visiting the locker room to escape the heat and get fluids. With less than ten minutes left in the game, Florida State held a 16-10 lead on two second-half field goals. After the second one, Torretta decisively drove his offense downfield, contributing a third-and-twelve scramble for a first down and several key throws. He capped the drive with a 33-yard touchdown pass to Lamar Thomas. The point after would give the Hurricanes a 17-16 lead.

A few minutes later, Florida State punt returner Corey Sawyer would make a decision so baffling to the FSU staff that it brought Bobby Bowden to his knees on the sideline. After fielding a punt in the end zone, Sawyer slowly jogged to the side as if he were going to take a knee, and then at the last second, as he was swarmed by Florida State tacklers, he began sprinting and shoveled the ball out of the end zone as he was brought down. At first it appeared that the blunder had given Miami a touchdown. As the officials huddled, Bowden crouched to the turf, hat on the ground, face in his hands, defeated. The referees ruled that the illegal forward pass took place in the end zone, so it was a safety. Florida State was still breathing. But the best—and the worst—was yet to come.

The Seminoles' defense stepped up after the safety and held Torretta in check, forcing another punt. This time, it was fielded properly and Florida State had life. Barely.

Charlie took the field on his own 19-yard line with 1:35 on the clock and one time out against a Miami team that had won twenty-one games in a row and forty-seven straight in the Orange Bowl.

He was thinking of another legendary drive.

He was thinking about his confidence.

He was thinking once again of John Elway.

The first play of the drive was a slow-developing roll out to the right that resulted in a 40-yard pass attempt that fell incomplete. On second down, with 1:26 left, Charlie hit Matt Frier for a quick three-yard pass. Nearly twenty seconds ran off the clock while the Seminoles decided the play call, and when the ball was finally snapped Charlie was sacked by 6'4", 250-pound Darren Krein with less than a minute left. Bowden was forced to call a timeout. It was now fourth and twelve.

"That sack hurt us," Charlie said. "But we still had a lot of time on the clock and I knew we had the timeout. I was confident we could get the first down."

While FSU huddled on the sideline, the small portion of the 70,000 plus fans in attendance who were rooting for the Seminoles tried as hard as they could to drown out the Miami band, which was playing "The Imperial March" (Darth Vader's theme) from *Stars Wars* practically on a loop. The FSU fans rained the War Chant and the Chop down onto the field of the Orange Bowl, providing the rare mash-up of famous Hollywood composer John Williams and a made-up American Indian war cry. A few Florida State players motioned for their fans to get louder as the timeout ended.

Charlie stood five yards behind his center and surveyed the field. There was fifty-seven seconds left in the game, and he needed at least thirteen yards on this play or the game and their title hopes were done. After checking his pre-snap reads, he kicked up his right leg, stomped and took the snap. The Hurricanes' ends rushed hard. Charlie felt the pressure, stepped up into the pocket and unloaded a missile 40 yards downfield that was caught by Kez McCorvey to keep the Seminoles' chances alive.

With no time outs and less than fifty seconds remaining, Charlie took the next snap, saw an opening and sprinted straight up the middle for a fourteen-yard run and another first down. There was now thirty-two seconds left and the ball was on Miami's 42-yard line. It was happening. Again.

The Seminoles could feel it. They'd seen Charlie finish a drive against Clemson and they were in the midst of another legendary, clutch performance. The fans, the guys in the huddle, the coaches—they all believed.

"We really had a rhythm going," Ward said. "Our line gave me time and our receivers were getting open. All I had to do was deliver the ball."

The next play was also out of the shotgun. Frier ran an out-and-up along the sideline and Charlie found him for a seventeen-yard gain. Frier was 5'11"; the pass was perfect for someone about 6'4". As Frier cleared his defender, he leapt, laid out with every single inch and cell of his body and made an incredible catch to give the Seminoles the ball on the 25-yard line with twenty-two seconds left. There was nobody open on the following play and Charlie was forced to run out of bounds with only thirteen seconds remaining.

On the sideline, FSU field goal kicker Dan Mowrey paced back and forth. He was 3-for-5 on the day, with one kick blocked. His three conversions were from 22, 38 and 41 yards. On the field, the Seminoles tried one more play but the ball skipped off of Shannon Baker's hands, stopping the clock.

Mowrey walked calmly onto the field with barely any time left on the clock, facing a 39-yard try. The Hurricane fans booed him with no remorse as he got set behind Danny Kanell, his placeholder. The snap was good… But the kick… Was not.

It was wide right.

Again.

Legendary announcer Keith Jackson called it this way for ABC:

> "It's a thirty-nine yarder. Mowrey hit it. It's far enough! He missed it to the right! The game is over! And Bobby Bowden wonders, 'Why, Lord, me?'"

The Seminoles were in shock.

"Why did it have to be right?" Mowrey said afterward.

Other players, like Robert Stevenson, were a mixture of angry and frustrated. "I had no doubts we were going to win," he said. "I thought this was our day. This happens every…year."

Some players blamed themselves. Others blamed the game plan. Others blamed fate or even faith.

"They [the Hurricanes] have been praying so much, it kind of makes you wonder whose side the Big Man is on," Florida State receiver Omar Ellison said.

Emotions were running high and guys were swearing at each other and yelling to nobody in particular about what they felt went wrong. It didn't help that Miami players were gloating, saying how they knew Florida State would choke because they always do and that Miami had more heart. Overall, it was another classic, devastating loss for the Seminoles, who were going to need an emotional anchor to help pick them back up. That man would have to be Charlie.

"We had big plays, we just didn't convert them all," he said. "It was one of those things that didn't happen. We're still living. We'll try to win the rest of our games."

It was the kind of calm, matter-of-fact response that teammates and fans would come to expect from Charlie. In essence, he personified the line in Rudyard Kipling's poem "If—"

If you can keep your head when all about you are losing theirs and blaming it on you...

Charlie kept his wits about him because, well, he just always did. Logically, he knew it was a long season and the Miami game was only one loss. Yes, it was a brutal loss, but it was still only one. They were still front-runners to win the ACC title and, if things broke right, a possible national championship.

• • •

Florida State bounced back the following week and handled North Carolina, 36-13. However, there was a philosophical debate brewing amongst the coaches about the offense. The issue wasn't whether or not Charlie was improving week-to-week (the staff believed he was), the issue was that occasionally he looked like the best player in the country and other times in the same game the offense would stall completely.

In the aftermath of the Miami game, Bowden noticed something on film that reminded him of a conversation he had with his sons in Panama City on a family vacation. Terry Bowden was a football coach at Samford and Tommy Bowden was coaching at Alabama at the time.

Terry tells the story this way in his dad's book, *Tales from the Seminoles Sideline*: "I remember sitting at the beach at Panama City, and Dad talking about it [the shotgun] before the '92 season. Dad ran that split-back, West Coast offense in the mid-'80s up to the early '90s. We're sitting there together in Panama City, and he said, 'you know what I want to do, I want to take the two-minute offense and run it the entire game.

"If I could do that, I think I can beat anybody and everybody. We got eight plays or eight pass plays and have them all memorized so you're signaling 'em, and we get two deep at every position and run it 60 minutes non-stop."

Cut to a few months later when Coach Bowden is watching the tape of the gut-wrenching loss to Miami, a game now referred to as "Wide Right II." Bowden explains what happened next in his book:

"I begin to think, 'Well, hold on now.' We go out and play Miami 60 minutes and can't move the ball worth a darn. We score once, but I don't know how. But right before the half Charlie takes us right down and scores, and then at the end of the game he gives us that chance to tie.

"Why don't we use the two-minute offense the whole game—that was my thinking. I might have mentioned it to some other coaches after the game, but I know it was going through my head.

"That [Miami game] is where I saw the light—Charlie Ward is better in the shotgun. I first thought Charlie would be much better up under center because he could run better out of it. But when he took the ball out from under center and came back to pass, he would be turning his back to the defense. He couldn't see what was happening down there. But when he's sitting in that shotgun and took the snap, he could see everything. And if a big hole opened right there, boom, he was gone. He couldn't see that coming out of center. Those thoughts began to add up."

At the same time Coach Bowden was having these thoughts, his offensive coordinator Brad Scott, his quarterbacks coach Mark Richt, and even Coach Richt's wife were thinking the same thing.

"I remember one night I was talking to my wife about Charlie and how well he was doing out of the shotgun under pressure, and she just said, 'why don't you just do that? Charlie seems to do well when you do that,'" Richt said. "And she was right. We had been thinking about it for a while."

The two-minute drill, shotgun-style attack coming into form in the minds of Richt, Scott and Bowden would soon become known as the nearly unstoppable "Fast Break Offense," a name playing off of Charlie's basketball skills. Still, they had yet to pull the trigger on it for a large portion of a game, so the college football world had nothing to fear. Yet.

"After Miami we played North Carolina and we won it big and probably didn't have to get in the shotgun," he wrote. "But now we go up to Georgia Tech the next week. We're playing conventional offense and the game gets out of control. I might have said, 'Let's get in the shotgun and air it out. It is the only chance we have.'"

Georgia Tech was ranked #16 when Florida State traveled to Atlanta for their mid-October match-up. For Charlie, the game had several layers of importance. It was the first time he would be putting on a helmet and pads in his home state of Georgia since his Central High School days; it was the first time he'd be playing against a school that he was heavily recruited by; and as fate would have it, the starting quarterback at Georgia Tech was his childhood best friend Shawn Jones.

"It's going to be the battle of the Thomasville quarterbacks," Georgia Tech coach Bill Lewis said. "It will be very interesting to see how this story plays itself out as to how one town can produce two quarterbacks of such caliber at two of the finer football programs in the country."

Thomasville was on cloud nine. For the city to have two of its favorite sons on a national stage playing quarterback for two top-sixteen teams was a dream from which the community wished it would never wake up.

"They are the kind of people any town would be glad to have representing them," Karl Abrams, from Thomasville's YMCA, said.

"It was a very proud moment for us, as parents, but also for Thomasville," Willard Ward said. "Our boys were out there putting our names and our town on the map. And our two families had so much history. It was like having our family on display. It was wonderful."

The irony of the match-up is that the old "Thomasville Twins" chose their schools so they wouldn't have to play each other. At the time when Jones chose Georgia Tech, they were in the ACC while Florida State was not.

"They knew what schools they were going to long before anyone else," Willard said. Once FSU joined the ACC, however, their clash at the college level was inevitable.

"I didn't expect it to happen after high school," Jones said. "But I'm looking forward to it more than anything because they're consistently ranked in the top five. If we lose it's hard to say I'll mind because I know we will have lost to some people who can perform. It's Florida State and Georgia Tech and we are just two of many players who will decide the game."

True, but they were certainly the most important.

Heading into the game, Jones was having a strong year, completing 96 of 171 passes with nine touchdowns and only two interceptions. He had already led the team to a national championship a few years earlier and was now in his last season as a Yellow Jacket. In high school, he had lost three of four games against Charlie. He was determined to put an exclamation point on his college career with a signature win against his old buddy who, despite only one loss, was still a candidate to be benched if he wasn't playing well, as had happened the previous week.

"I won't go in there with a plan that says if he does this, then I'll take him out," Bowden said. "I don't think a quarterback can operate knowing he'll be jerked at any minute. The only way I'll put Danny [Kanell] in there is if Charlie is really struggling."

Sure enough, Charlie and the Florida State offense got off to a horrible start in Atlanta. After throwing a touchdown to William Floyd with nine minutes left in the first quarter, Charlie had little success throwing the ball the rest of the half and even threw another interception. At halftime Florida State led 7-6, and other than the initial TD, the Seminoles could barely move the ball. The third quarter opened with a Georgia Tech touchdown on a 41-yard pass from Jones to Bobby Rodriguez. Charlie later threw a second interception and found himself on the bench for a series with his team behind 21-7.

Charlie was forced to watch as freshman quarterback Kanell bounced his first pass off the turf and fired the next ball eight feet over the receiver's head. Charlie's helmet was off and his face was stone. He shuffled slightly from one foot to the other, lightly rolling his lower lip into his mouth, betraying a small amount of nervous energy. His eyes glanced from the field to the scoreboard and back again, almost as if he was calculating whether there would be enough time left for his heroics when he got back on the field. Kanell then failed to convert on a third and twenty-seven, handing the ball back over to Jones and the Yellow Jackets.

"We had gotten into a pattern that, when he got into trouble, we'd take him out of the game and put Kanell in," Bowden said of Charlie. "Danny was no more ready to play than the man on the moon. He was a pure freshman, and no way was he ready."

The Seminoles now found themselves down fourteen points—on the road—with just less than fifteen minutes left in the game.

"We were getting beat so bad, we just told Charlie to get in the shotgun," Bowden said.

Over the next eleven plays and three minutes of game time, Charlie cut through the Georgia Tech defense with his arm and his legs, including a game-saving fifteen-yard run on third and two. The drive was capped with a Floyd one-yard touchdown run—the only yardage on the drive Charlie was not a part of. Georgia Tech led 21-14.

"*Boy*, I thought to myself, *that Charlie was something out of that shotgun,*" Bowden said.

Georgia Tech would answer the drive with a field goal at the 5:24 mark of the fourth quarter to go up 24-14. Despite having a double-digit lead, Jones felt like he had seen this movie before and he warned all of his teammates on defense as Charlie took the field

"I told them to watch out," Jones said. "He beat our team enough in high school when we led, so I know what can happen."

Within two minutes, Jones' teammates knew exactly what he was talking about. Whether throwing or running, Charlie led the Seminoles right down the field, making big play after big play. As the clock wound down and the pressure ratcheted up, the Florida State players began to believe that Charlie was impervious to nerves. He talked calmly. He walked confidently. He made every single play that needed to be made, including a fourth-and-four conversion to Omar Ellison and a five-yard touchdown run with 3:20 remaining. He had sixty-five yards throwing the ball and twenty-five yards rushing on the drive.

Bowden made the call to go for an onside kick following the touchdown. Corey Sawyer recovered it, giving the Seminoles the ball on Georgia Tech's 40-yard line with three minutes left, down 24-20.

By this point, Charlie was almost unstoppable. He played exclusively out of the shotgun for the entire quarter and there was nothing Georgia Tech could do to counter it. One down after another, he moved the ball.

Four-yard completion.

Nineteen-yard run.

Four-yard run.

In no time, Ward had the Seminoles deep into Georgia Tech territory. After a few stops by the Yellow Jackets, the Seminoles found themselves faced with fourth and five on Tech's 17-yard line. During the ensuing timeout, Bowden, who had by this point in his career handed over the play calling to his offensive assistants, got heavily involved. While the crowd roared into a tornado of noise and the seconds ticked down, Bowden recalled a play from 1991 against Florida where Kez McCorvey was wide open but Casey Weldon didn't see him. The old coach was 100% confident that the play would work against Tech and he called it.

Charlie, for the first time in the quarter, called the play under center, dropped back and hit McCorvey in stride on the 5-yard line. McCorvey juked his man and ran into the end zone, giving FSU a 27-24 lead that once felt improbable.

"Coach Bowden knew it would work, he convinced us," receivers coach John Eason said. "Charlie had the option of going to the other side to Tamarick Vanover, but Kez has always been a clutch receiver for us and he responded again."

"We ran maximum protection to keep from getting a sack," Ward said.

"They left Kez, our best receiver, one-on-one and he always makes the kind of great moves that great receivers make."

Florida State would ice the game with a safety and win 29-24. It was, by all accounts, one of the greatest comebacks in Seminoles history and left players struggling to find the right words to describe their quarterback, who was responsible for 207 of the 208 yards gained on the game's final three drives.

"Charlie is a winner," McCorvey said. "It's definitely the most exciting game I've ever been in."

"Charlie—well," Bowden said, searching for words. "Well, that's unbelievable. Charlie just started making plays."

Once again, his heroics would come at the expense of his friend Shawn Jones, who played a solid game with 173 passing yards and no interceptions.

"It was just like those old high school games," Charlie said. "It was a matter of which one of us had the ball last."

In the locker room after the game, reporters mobbed Charlie. He had now engineered three remarkable fourth-quarter drives and comebacks that, if not for the missed field goal against Miami, could be considered among the most clutch comeback winning streaks of all time. Whenever he could, he passed around the credit, even mentioning his basketball team.

"Everyone did their job," he said. "The comeback was the same as when we played Louisville in basketball."

After so much back and forth about running the shotgun and maybe sitting Charlie and using the two-minute drill for a whole game, all Coach Bowden could do was make light of the situation as the celebration and emotions wound down.

"Next week I think I'll sit him down for the first two minutes," Bowden joked. "Every time he's gone back in he's done well."

• • •

In many ways, the Georgia Tech game was Charlie's coming out party to a national audience—a culmination of the buzz that had been building after the Clemson comeback and the Miami almost-comeback. The heroic win in Atlanta aired on ESPN in prime time. It led all the highlight shows that night and stole all the headlines the next morning. Suddenly, the name Charlie Ward was synonymous with late-game magic and Florida State football, two things he had been working a long time toward.

The next week FSU beat the University of Virginia in a rainy, miserable game on Halloween that saw a combined fifteen punts. Neither team could run its offense properly in the wet conditions. Virginia was the #23 ranked team in the nation, and an upset would not only put them in the top ten but it would keep Florida State from clinching the ACC Championship in its very first year in the league. It was not to be. The Cavaliers managed only three points, losing to the Seminoles 13-3. Despite the win, there were Seminole die-hards and college football analysts who questioned the up-and-down FSU offense and wondered if it would ever reach the consistent heights it had under Casey Weldon and Peter Tom Willis.

Coach Richt, Coach Scott and Coach Bowden weren't immune from the critics. They tweaked and analyzed the Fast Break Offense after the Tech win, but due to the awful weather they were not able to implement many of the changes they wanted to against UVA. That meant the true unveiling of the offense from kickoff to the clock reading 0:00 would have to be the following week against the University of Maryland.

Poor Maryland.

They were 3-7 heading into the game, and from the second Charlie took his first snap the Terrapins looked like a fighter taking punches from an opponent with rolls of quarters in his fists. Florida State scored on every possession in the first half, racking up forty-two points and 450 yards of offense in two quarters. And they wouldn't let up after the break, adding another twenty-seven points and 400 yards of offense in the second half. The numbers for the game would make Neil deGrasse Tyson's head hurt.

Florida State tallied 858 yards of total offense in only 28:57 of possession. Charlie alone ran for 111 yards and threw for 395. In the end, eleven school records and six ACC marks were broken. And so was Charlie's Buster Keaton-esque stone-faced disposition. After the game, he admitted that the constant questions about the state of the Seminoles' offense were bothering him a little. It was a first for Charlie, who had up to that point acted as if no matter what was said or written about him, he'd keep his hands in his pockets and whistle along like he didn't have a care in the world. His brief moment of opening up after the demoralization of the Terrapins revealed a desire—even in the always measured Charlie—for vindication against his critics.

"Everywhere you turned, people were saying the offense wasn't what it had been the past few years," Charlie said. "I'm not the kind of guy who gets mad, but all the questions about the offense did aggravate me a little. It's not possible to play like this every game, but we should gain a lot of confidence from the way we played. With so many people questioning our production, there had to be some doubts in our minds. After today, we know we can do it. We know when we have it going, it's hard to stop us. We showed today that we can be as good as any offense Florida State has had."

Tamarick Vanover echoed Charlie's statement about the critics. "It's hard to feel good about yourself when others are constantly running you down and saying what you do wrong," he said.

Receivers coach John Eason said the team had planned on starting in the Fast Break and seeing how it went, but they weren't thinking of using it exclusively. Once it got going, however, there was no reason to stop it. Why would they? The receiving corps had been dying for this kind of opportunity.

"We needed a game like this to show people we have as much ability as any offense that has played here," Kez McCorvey said.

In many respects, Charlie needed this game too. While his cool exterior, icy veins and clutch performances belied a man with total confidence in himself and his abilities, the inescapable truth was that all of his late-game heroics were built on a foundation of early-game futility. If Charlie was going to be as great as it looked like he could be, he should be able to have his team in the driver's seat from the outset, rather than having to scramble to come back. This was that first real opportunity. He sensed it and he grabbed it.

"After the first couple of possessions, you could see it in Charlie's eyes," receiver Kevin Knox said. "The man could feel it. He was just hot, and he gained confidence with every completion. The man was in a zone."

Even Maryland coach Mark Duffner acknowledged it, searching out Charlie after the game to compliment him on his performance. The beating was so bad it affected Florida State's conditioning—the receivers did so much running that they had to dial back plays to give themselves a break.

"We hated to get out of the shotgun when it was clicking so well," Richt said. "But at some point, you have to give the receivers a chance to catch their breath."

All thanks to the breathless play of Charlie Ward.

Incredibly, the offense would score more points the following week, beating Tulane 70-7. Charlie threw three touchdowns in the first quarter and the game was 35-0 and effectively over in the first fifteen minutes. Still, there were critics.

But those high scores were against a weak Maryland team and a totally outgunned Tulane team. What about a quality opponent? Could the Fast Break hold up against a ranked team for a full game?

In short, yes.

The last game of the regular season was against #6 ranked University of Florida, led by Coach Steve Spurrier and his gunslinger of a quarterback, Shane Matthews. Most people expected it to be a close game between the team at the top of the ACC and the team at the top of the SEC. Most people were wrong. John Romano, who covered the match-up for the *Tampa Bay Times*, wrote about the opening of the game this way: "For the game's first thirty minutes, Ward passed and ran like he had a date with a bronze statue at the Downtown Athletic Club next month. By halftime, he had accounted for nearly 250 yards of offense and had gotten UF coach Steve Spurrier to very nearly concede."

"By that point, we had total belief in what we were capable of," Charlie said. "I knew they were going to try to get me out of a rhythm after the games against Maryland and Tulane, but we set the tempo."

It was a tempo that left the Gators' defense, and Spurrier himself, unable to keep pace. "He needs a red cape and a big 'S' on his chest," Gators defensive tackle Bill Gunter said about Charlie.

Gunter and his fellow defensive linemen spent the day chasing Charlie all over the field with exactly zero success. Despite dropping back to pass more than four dozen times, Charlie was never taken down behind the line of scrimmage.

"He's obviously a guy you can't sack," Spurrier said. "Or at least we can't sack. Our best defense was a bad throw or a drop or a penalty."

Charlie again tallied more than 400 yards of total offense, and in doing so broke a school record for total offense in a season with 3,151 yards, passing Peter Tom Willis' mark of 3,004 yards set in 1989. The Seminoles beat the Gators that day 45-24, and the outcome added an unexpected wrinkle to the in-state rivalry: Despite the loss the Gators were scheduled to face Alabama in the SEC Championship game, and the way the rankings and bowl games were decided, Florida State needed Florida to beat #2 ranked Alabama to make their win over the Gators look even better. The way the polls would shake out, a Gators win would jump the Seminoles over Alabama in the Associated Press rankings and give them a rematch against #1 Miami on New Year's Day.

Florida quarterback Matthews exemplified the quandary and confusion of his team's position. "It did sound funny hearing Florida State people yelling for us to beat Alabama," he said. "I'm really looking forward to next Saturday in Birmingham, but we're not going up there to win anything for FSU, we're going to win for ourselves."

That statement was most definitely true, but in this rare instance, a win for the Gators was a win for the Seminoles. Unfortunately for both teams, however, the Crimson Tide won the game the following week, 28-21, giving Alabama the match-up with Miami, who they would ultimately beat to win the National Championship. Florida State ended up in the Orange Bowl against Nebraska with nothing on the line but pride.

"Do I think about not playing for a national championship?" Bowden responded to a reporter. "I don't think so much of that as I do Miami being there instead of us. Other than a couple of wide rights we'd be in New Orleans [for the Sugar Bowl]."

Nebraska was a ten-point underdog heading into the game. With the national championship out of the picture, the FSU coaches focused on keeping the team's seven-game win streak alive and giving themselves momentum to carry into the 1993 season. Not to mention, they could use the game as a nice recruiting tool for a haul of five-star athletes. It would also give Charlie and other returning starters some bowl-game experience they believed they'd need, should the team be in a position to play for the national championship the next year.

The game was never close.

Florida State went up 7-0 in the first quarter and led 20-7 at halftime before scoring in the third to jump to a 27-7 lead. Nebraska scored a late TD in the fourth once the game was put away for a final score of 27-14. In his first start in a bowl game, Charlie threw for 187 yards and two touchdowns and rushed for twenty-three yards, winning the Orange Bowl MVP Award.

Florida State's nemesis, Gino Torretta, went on to win the Heisman Trophy, while Charlie's otherworldly finish to the season landed him sixth in the voting behind Marshall Faulk, Garrison Hearst, Marvin Jones and Reggie Brooks.

"That was not something I expected," Charlie said. "But it was an honor to be included with those guys. The main thing from that season was that I knew we were set up really well to make a run at a championship the next year. I've never been into the personal awards, so from the minute that game against Nebraska ended at the Orange Bowl, I was thinking about how we could win it all in '93."

Charlie had finally arrived.

Or, as his center Robbie Baker said: "He will lead us to a national championship. This ain't Florida State anymore. It's Charlie Ward's team. He's remarkable."

But first, he had a basketball season to finish.

Chapter 18

Charlie Ward 2.0

This time the transition back to basketball was different. Charlie was no longer the point guard who punted for the football team. He also wasn't the back-up red-shirt quarterback taking the year off to play hoops. He was, as legendary sportswriter Bob Ryan would put it, a capital S.T.A.R. football player joining the basketball team.

This was a top-six Heisman vote-getter, an Orange Bowl MVP, and the most prolific single-season offensive player in the history of Florida State trading in his cleats for high tops. Rather than make the transition between sports in obscurity as he had the previous two years, this time he was in the national spotlight with the biggest names in sports paying attention. In fact, *the* biggest name in sports.

A few nights before the Seminoles played Nebraska in the 1992 Orange Bowl, Charlie was asked to attend the Miami Heat basketball game against the Chicago Bulls. As the game wound down, a team representative from Chicago approached Charlie.

"Mr. Jordan has invited you to visit with him in the locker room after the game," the team representative said. "Do you have time to say hello?"

"Mr. Jordan? You mean, *Michael* Jordan? *The* Michael Jordan?" Charlie asked.

"Yes, that one," the team representative said.

"Uh, yes," he said. "I have time."

It turned out that Jordan had been following Charlie's basketball career since he led FSU to their big win against Jordan's alma mater North Carolina, and he became enamored with his recent football comebacks. Astonishingly, Michael Jordan was, to use his word, a "fan" of Charlie Ward.

"That was not something I ever thought I'd hear," Charlie said. "Michael Jordan was a fan of mine?"

The two talked in the Bulls' locker room for a while and Jordan wished him luck in the Orange Bowl. "It was exciting," Charlie said. "Obviously I need a lot more luck to be successful than he does with his ability."

A good rule of thumb to determine whether someone was a true superstar in the 1990s: If Michael Jordan went out of his way to meet someone after a Bulls game, it's safe to say he was.

• • •

Even though Florida State had owned Nebraska in their game, Charlie and the Seminoles took a physical beating. After the game, Charlie put off celebrating and spending time with his teammates for some quality time with the whirlpool in the locker room. Other than the game against Miami, that game was the hardest he had been consistently hit. He hid the effects of the pummeling during the game by bouncing off the turf immediately after getting taken down, never letting the Cornhuskers know they were hurting him. But now that his helmet and pads were off, his body throbbed and he needed some relief. He didn't have an entire off-season to recuperate and get ready for spring practice like his teammates did. He had a basketball game against the University of Virginia to play in five days.

Of course, there had been two-sport stars before in college football. Florida State alone claimed two of them: Deion Sanders (football, baseball and track) and Brad Johnson (basketball and football).

Historically, the two-sport combination of football and baseball was the most popular among high-level college athletes. From Sammy Baugh at Texas Christian University in the 1930s to Bo Jackson at Auburn in the 1980s, and modern-day athletes like Russell Wilson at NC State and Wisconsin, Jeff Samardzija at Notre Dame, and Florida State's most recent dual threat, Jameis Winston, the transition from the gridiron to the baseball diamond was a fairly common one. Several football stars also ran track, like Ed Reed at Miami and Denard Robinson at Michigan. Jim Brown was the country's best lacrosse player while at Syracuse.

In terms of the football-basketball college combo, there have been plenty of men who have pulled it off. Tony Dungy played basketball for a year at the University of Minnesota before becoming the team's starting quarterback. And NFL Pro Bowler Julius Peppers walked on to the North Carolina basketball team while he played football for the Tar Heels. He was a role player and got minutes as a forward in the 2000 Final Four, but he left the following year to focus on football. Future NFL Hall of Famer Tony Gonzalez played basketball for three years at the University of California while playing tight end on the football team. He averaged six points and four rebounds for his career.

The closest comparison to Charlie would probably be Terry Baker of Oregon State, who won the Heisman Trophy in 1962 as the team's quarterback and helped the Beavers get to the Final Four as the point guard. But unlike Charlie, Baker wouldn't win a National Championship or play professional basketball.

There were others who went from pigskin to parquet to be sure, but in terms of visibility and media attention, Charlie was in uncharted waters. Also, considering that Bobby Bowden and Florida State had yet to win a national championship and the basketball team was now competing in the toughest conference in the sport, the level of difficulty for him to achieve immortality as a college athlete was extremely high. But that was the path he continued to choose. Nobody was forcing him to play basketball. If he had decided after the Orange Bowl to focus on football, most people would have considered it a reasonable decision. But like John Elway, his love of each sport was unconditional and seasonal. As long as he could physically play both sports, in his mind, there was no decision to be made; he'd play both sports.

That's why immediately after leading one set of teammates to a bowl win he began preparing his body to lead another set of teammates to the NCAA Tournament.

In Charlie's absence, the basketball team had gotten off to an 8-4 start and was ranked #19 in the AP Poll. They were about to get into the meat of their ACC schedule with games against Virginia, Maryland, Wake Forest, NC State, Clemson, Duke, North Carolina and Georgia Tech. Duke, UNC and Georgia Tech were top-twenty teams with some of the conference's most legendary players in their primes. Duke had Bobby Hurley, Thomas Hill and Grant Hill, all averaging over fifteen points a game; North Carolina was led by Eric Montross, George Lynch and sophomore star Donald Williams; Georgia Tech had future NBA guards Travis Best and Jon Barry on the floor at the same time. And although not in the top 20, Wake Forest boasted Randolph Childress, All-American Rodney Rogers and freshman phenom Tim Duncan.

Florida State was also in the midst of its golden era. Bobby Sura was averaging twenty points and seven assists a game. Sam Cassell was averaging eighteen points a game and led the team in steals. Doug Edwards was a beast, scoring eighteen points and grabbing ten boards a game. Rodney Dobard was on his way to 111 blocks. All they were missing was what Coach Kennedy called their "emotional anchor."

Finally, he was back.

Charlie's first game in the line-up was against Virginia. He was rusty. His shot was off. He still played twenty-three minutes in the four-point loss.

"I thought I was going to get more tired," he said. "I'm hungry. I want to be out there. I thought I played well. I think this year football has helped me. I'm ailing, but that's part of it. I'll fight through it."

Gone were the days when Charlie would spend his first few weeks back with the basketball team clutching the bottom of his shorts and sucking wind. As the first-string quarterback he took all of the team's reps in practice, and once Bowden committed to the Fast Break Offense, he got in loads of running work and conditioning. It paid off.

His second game back was an overtime win against Wake Forest. He played forty-three minutes, the most on the team. He scored only four points, but had five assists, three steals and two rebounds.

"He is remarkable," Coach Kennedy said. "To play forty-three minutes...that's just incredible for him. But he does so many things. He frees up Sam and Bobby. He gets our press going. He puts pressure on the ball. And he's been doing it for two years. He drives guys nuts."

Games three and four on the season were blowout wins against Maryland and North Carolina State. All was going according to plan, but one thing was off: Charlie was passing up shots so often that even his mom noticed.

"We'd talk on the phone after those games and I'd say, 'Junior, you're not shooting the ball,'" Willard said. "He was so concerned about coming over as the star football player and drawing attention away from his teammates that he was taking his responsibilities to set up his teammates a little too literally."

The team was winning, which was all that mattered to Charlie, but he knew his mom had a point. Passing up open looks could be just as detrimental as not making the extra pass. After not hitting double digits in his first four games back, he scored nineteen in a win against Clemson.

• • •

Off the court, Charlie was equally conscious of his newfound stardom and made efforts to not let it affect his classmates or his routine. He was often spotted sliding quietly into a classroom just as it was supposed to start and then slipping out the moment it ended so as not to disrupt the teacher, leaving his classmates to whisper, "Was that Charlie Ward?"

Just as he did on the football field, he seemed to appear and then quickly disappear. He was polite to those who asked for autographs or pictures, but he made a point of keeping his head down and not making waves. In order to juggle his responsibilities as a sports star, a student body vice president, a student and a man of faith, he maintained a fairly regimented schedule, splitting his time between schoolbooks, playbooks and the bible—all thoroughly annotated, highlighted and littered with Post-It notes throughout.

His weeks consisted of following his class schedule, his football and basketball schedules, attending bible study groups for the Fellowship of Christian Athletes (every Thursday night), and a few other responsibilities that once he committed to he never veered from.

"Some people like to party, some people like to play basketball," he said. "I just like to keep busy so I don't have time to do anything that might not be in my best interest."

He also fell asleep on his couch. A lot. Be it while watching SportsCenter or a west coast NBA game, once all his work was done and he settled into his favorite seat, it wouldn't be long before Charlie was out like a grandfather in his favorite recliner. When he did have free time, he often reached out and offered support in unexpected ways to people—even his coaches.

"One off-day I'm home with my wife and kids and we hear a knock on the door," Coach Kennedy said. "It was Charlie. Normally, when a kid comes to your house he's got a problem. With Charlie, I had a feeling it wasn't the case, but I still didn't know why he was there. Well, the background to this is that my third child was a preemie baby and had spent a lot of time in the incubation area. It had obviously taken a great toll on my wife and me, and we had just brought my daughter home from the hospital a few days before. Charlie is standing at my door, all of maybe twenty-one years old with the world at his fingertips, and he said he wanted to see how my wife and baby were doing. I couldn't believe it. I let Charlie in and he sat with my newborn daughter and my wife for over an hour. It was so special to my family. My wife remembers it clear as a bell and still talks about it to this day."

This sensitive side to Charlie was also paying off in his personal life, as a girl he'd known since childhood was slowly moving away from the "family friend" zone to something much deeper.

• • •

Breakfast played a critical role in the relationship between Tonja Harding and Charlie Ward. The first time they saw each other as something other than additions to their parents' long-standing friendship was over eggs and pancakes after a Magnolia High School reunion they attended with their parents. The Hardings had kept missing the Wards the whole trip, and the only time it appeared they'd be able to catch up was for breakfast. Charlie was about to enter community college and Tonja was a freshman at Spelman College in Atlanta. They had run into each other at events like this throughout their lives, but to say they were friends at that point would have been a stretch. As they approached the table, Charlie noticed Tonja's bright eyes and large smile and had one of those moments when someone you've known for a while suddenly looks like a new person. She wasn't the Hardings' daughter so much as a pretty girl his own age with whom he had a lot in common. For the moment, he was just tagging along with his mom before going school shopping, so while she and Mrs. Harding caught up, he and Tonja engaged in some small talk.

"We talked about school, our parents, whatever we were up to," Tonja said. "We exchanged addresses and for the next few years we became pen pals. We probably wrote each other every couple of months."

In addition to the letters, Charlie made a habit of including an updated team or individual photo in the envelope. He sent his posed football photo, shots from the basketball team—anything to keep Tonja in the loop on what he was up to. But Tonja? She was in pre-law. She played it cool.

"It was a pre-selfie way of sending me pictures," she said, laughing. "But I never sent him pictures back. I always thought he was this sweet country boy and I went to school in the city, so I was all about trying to meet a city man."

Their letters passed in the mail between Tallahassee and Atlanta off and on for the next few years, but they each made an effort to stay in touch. They'd write about their lives, their class work—regular college kid stuff. In the spring of 1992, Tonja wrote Charlie to tell him she was about to start law school at the University of Miami. Charlie didn't write back. She wrote him again later in the summer and he didn't write back. Again. She put it out of her head for a few months until October when Florida State was coming to town to play Miami. Then she reached out one last time.

"My friends knew that I had a friend who went to Florida State, and since grad students didn't get tickets to the game, I called him," she said. "And once again I didn't hear back, so my friends and I scheduled a watch party at someone's house. The day before the game, Mrs. Ward called me and said she had tickets to the game and asked if I wanted to go. I wasn't going to ditch my friends to watch another friend who didn't call me back, so I turned down the tickets. I didn't hear from him after that for almost another six or eight months."

What Tonja didn't know but would later find out, was that Charlie had a girlfriend at that time who wasn't comfortable with him having friendships with other girls. Out of respect for her, he stopped writing Tonja and cut out a few other friendships he had with women as well. Over time, Charlie realized that with his high-profile position on campus and the uncertainty of where a professional athletic career might take him, it would be difficult to be with someone who was insecure about him when he was on the road, so that relationship didn't work out. Very soon after it ended, Charlie's mind wandered back to the cute girl from breakfast and he called her parents' house. He spoke to her sister and left a message. She didn't call back. Now the shoe was on the other foot and he followed up with another call, this time talking to Tonja's sister for a long time and convincing her to insist Tonja call him back.

"I talked to my sister and she said, 'Tonja, you have to call him back,'" Tonja said. "I called him when I was back in Miami and he caught me up on his girlfriend situation. We spent a lot of time talking about how important trust is in a relationship and about what we both valued in other people. I joke about it with him now about how he wouldn't call me, but at the time, the fact that he respected his girlfriend enough to not continue relationships she wasn't comfortable with was a big plus in my book. It showed the kind of integrity he had."

Over the next few months their calls and letters became more frequent, and soon Tonja began to see Charlie in a different light.

"I stopped thinking of him as this country boy and began to realize he's kinda cute and he's such a nice guy," she said. "And I had heard about how quiet he was, but he talked my ear off! I fell asleep some nights when he'd still be talking."

For Charlie, it was nice to talk to someone who didn't care whether he was the quarterback at Florida State or the point guard at Florida State or the top fire extinguisher salesman east of the Mississippi. With her, he could open up and let his mind relax, which was something he needed to do as the pressure ratcheted up on the basketball season.

Chapter 19

Being Elite

The temperature had plummeted into the high thirties on Friday night, but the warning from Mother Nature went unnoticed. On Saturday night and early Sunday morning, Florida State students brought tents, sleeping bags, blankets, coffee, sweatpants and sweatshirts as they set up shop in line for the general admission booth at the Leon County Civic Center in Tallahassee. Their goal was to score tickets to the biggest basketball game in Florida State hoops history: their Seminoles versus the #3 ranked defending national champion Duke Blue Devils. The game was the marquee event on ABC's national television Sunday line-up, and Florida State was going to introduce their football team at halftime and present Charlie Ward his Most Valuable Player award. If ever there was a night when his twin passions collided, it would be this one. To top it off, Duke was coming off a 92-56 throttling of NC State and the Seminoles had won four in a row.

"There seems to be a greater anticipation for this game than any other," Coach Kennedy said. "Hopefully it will be the best game we've ever had at Florida State. It's going to be a great atmosphere. We are approaching them like they're the best team in the country. I think they are capable of winning the whole thing again."

Kennedy's concern leading up to the 3:45 pm tipoff was one of focus. There was no way for his players to avoid the local media attention the game was being given, and it certainly wasn't lost on them that their fellow students were camping out in front of the arena and that scalpers were roaming campus trying to buy student tickets or flip what they had. For an emotional team with scorers like Cassell who fed off the energy, the coach worried they might burn out early or come out with too much excitement. He was going to have to rely on Charlie more than ever to keep an even keel in the over-hyped atmosphere.

As for the opposition, Duke Head Coach Mike Krzyzewski was thinking about Florida State's football player. "It would be a great win for us to win at Florida State," he said. "I think they're really good. They're accustomed to playing with Charlie Ward now."

As the athletes took the floor, eight future NBA players were among them: Bobby Hurley, Grant Hill, Cherokee Parks, Antonio Lang, Sam Cassell, Bobby Sura, Doug Edwards and Charlie. The Bobby Hurley vs. Charlie Ward storyline was among the main talking points of the day, along with whether Grant Hill would guard Cassell or Sura.

Thirteen thousand three hundred and thirty-three people were able to squeeze into the Civic Center to watch a back-and-forth game that became a classic with just a few minutes left. After a career night with twenty-one points and twelve rebounds, Doug Edwards fouled out late and Florida State was forced to bring in senior Byron Wells off the bench. With the game tied at eighty and five seconds left on the clock, Duke had one final chance to end it in regulation. They put the ball in Grant Hill's hands and he calmly brought it to the top of the key to take measure of FSU's defense. With three seconds to go he jabbed left, then drove right to the basket. As he passed the foul line, Ward darted from the elbow and stripped the ball, which bounced off Hill's foot toward the sideline. Ward switched directions, laid out on the floor and pushed the ball out of Duke's reach with no time on the clock to preserve the tie and send the game into overtime.

Dick Vitale described it like this in his post-game analysis: "Now watch him [Charlie] defensively. He's gonna make a strip late in the game. Duke could win at the end of the game but Charlie says no—he's like a linebacker, diving for the loose ball!"

The game went into overtime and remained tight until the very end. The fans at the Civic Center who braved the chilly nights in cheap tents were being treated to the greatest game ever on campus. With less than ten seconds left and FSU down 88-86, Coach Kennedy drew up a play for Sam Cassell to either shoot or pass. As Cassell dribbled out the clock, he spotted Wells in the corner and fired him the ball. Wells rose up and sunk a three with 2.7 seconds left to put the Seminoles up 89-88.

"It's something I'll be able to tell my grandkids about," Wells said later. "I knew I had to take the shot."

Duke had one more chance to win the game, but once again Charlie wasn't having any of it. They set up an inbounds play from under their basket and, well, let's let Dickie V take it from here: "In the overtime, Duke is down one. They try to throw the miracle pass like they did against Kentucky… Then the interception from Mr. Ward. I'll tell you what, he better play defense, Bobby Bowden!!!"

It was a game for the ages in front of a national audience. Aside from Wells' huge shot, Charlie had two of the most important plays of the game, both on defense. Afterward, Cassell talked about Charlie's timing in almost mystical terms.

"I don't know," he said. "He iced that game for us. He could just see it before it happened. His sense of anticipation was awesome."

Charlie spread the credit around.

"I was trying to anticipate what they'd do in both those situations and I was able to guess right," he said. "Byron hit two incredible shots and even had a big steal. Before Doug fouled out he was having a really big game. It was a team win."

That it was, but in the end, Dickie V was raving about one PTPer (prime-time player) in particular: Charlie Ward.

• • •

The Seminoles lost only three games the rest of the season with Charlie in the starting lineup. At one point they rose to #6 in the AP poll before dropping three of their last four games leading up to the NCAA tournament. One loss was to UNC, one was to Duke and the third was to Clemson in the first round of the ACC tournament.

They finished the year 22-9 and earned a #3 seed in the Southeast Regional bracket of March Madness, their first game against the Evansville Purple Aces. Injuries (Charlie's dislocated shoulder), a three-point shooting slump (18% over the last four games) and questions about inconsistency hovered over the team before the game.

Charlie claimed that his shoulder was fine and fought back against the attacks claiming the team had been erratic. "When we won thirteen out of fourteen nobody said anything. But since we lost two out of our last three, people say we're inconsistent," he said. "Teams are better prepared later on in the season, and there is nothing you can do about that. All we can do is play hard and hope for the best."

The game against Evansville took place in the old Orlando Arena, known for its intimate atmosphere and 50/50 split between the upper and lower bowls circling the court. It was home to the Orlando Magic and their rookie center Shaquille O'Neal. Shaq was in the middle of averaging nearly twenty-four points and fourteen rebounds a game when the Seminoles borrowed the floor for a few nights to go on their tournament run.

Purple Aces coach Jim Crews had spent the week trying to figure out how his squad could match-up against the Seminoles. His forwards, Parrish Casebier and Andy Elkins, handled a bulk of their scoring while guards Scott Shreffler and Todd Cochenour combined for eight assists a game. Athletically, they didn't fare well against Florida State. No matter how many times he drew up the Xs and Os, he came up short in devising a strategy to stop Sura, Cassell and Ward, while also containing Doug Edwards and Rodney Dobard. He ultimately landed on the unconventional strategy of double-teaming everyone on the team and leaving Charlie open to shoot. On paper, it probably seemed like a good idea. After all, Charlie didn't even think of himself as a shooter, and with so many other scorers on the team there was no reason he had to extend himself in that area. What Crews didn't realize was that just because Charlie *didn't* shoot a lot, it didn't mean he *couldn't* shoot.

Evansville wasn't very far into the game before Crews realized he had made a mistake. While Cassell and Edwards fought off double teams, they kicked the ball out to Charlie, who knocked down shot after shot, at one point sparking an eighteen-point run. By halftime Florida State was up 41-27. They were ahead by double digits most of the second half as the entire team got hot, shooting 53.7% from the three-point line. Charlie was

3-for-4 from downtown and 6-11 overall, scoring fifteen points while adding four assists and five steals. Cassell scored eighteen and Doug Edwards added fourteen points and twelve boards.

"Ward really did a great job of hitting some shots," Crews said after the game. "We were gambling he wasn't going to hit those."

The gamble backfired. Coach Kennedy said it was the team's best ball movement all year. "This looks like the club that moved through the NCAA Tournament last year," he said. "All the little things coming into this game that we were concerned about got squared away. The guys got their confidence back, we made threes and played good defense."

The star of their second-round tournament game against Tulane was easily Cassell. He had a shooting night that gunners dream about, going 7-for-7 from downtown (then a tournament record) on his way to thirty-one points. Edwards added another twenty-two and Charlie led the team in assists. The Seminoles led the game the entire way, leaving no doubt that they were going to the Sweet Sixteen again.

Unlike the previous two years when they faced a powerful Indiana team led by Bobby Knight, the Seminoles were matched up against that year's "Cinderella Story," #7 seeded Western Kentucky from the Sun Belt Conference. The Hilltoppers were a solid team that had gone 26-6 in the regular season, so Coach Kennedy refused to refer to them as underdogs.

"They are not a Cinderella team," he said. "They had wins at New Orleans and at Louisville. They're deep and use a lot of schemes, more like a Cincinnati even than a Kentucky."

The game was in Charlotte, North Carolina. The Seminoles had spent enough time watching tape before the match-up to know that if they didn't control the pace of the game they'd be in for a fight. All five starting Hilltoppers could handle the ball well, and when they crossed half court they made a point of taking it right to their opponent's defense, hoping for a collapse and either a kick out or an easy lay-up. Starting 5'8" senior point guard Mark Bell was the driving force behind their offense, and the responsibility of stopping him went to Charlie.

"Bell likes to try to beat you with the dribble," Charlie said before the game. "That's how they get into your defense. It all starts with Mark Bell."

Kennedy warned Charlie and Cassell that their breaks would be few and far between in the game. Of course, that was music to Cassell's ears—the more time on the court the better. Charlie maintained his 'whatever needs to be done' demeanor, and the rest of the players felt the same way. The bottom line was that Florida State had not been past the round of sixteen in the tournament in more than twenty years, and with the lineup of future NBAers they put on the floor, they were all thinking one thing: Final Four or bust.

The Hilltoppers had the same thought.

The game was a track meet from tipoff, with every player for both teams hopped up on a cocktail of adrenaline and desire. Before the telecast even reached its first TV timeout the score was 16-13, with Dobard leading the way for the Seminoles with seven quick points. Sura and Cassell then traded buckets, sparking a run to put FSU up 26-15 before Western Kentucky gained their footing and went on an 11-2 run. After that it was one Seminole bucket, one Hilltopper bucket, one Seminole bucket, one Hilltopper bucket, all the way to a 40-40 tie at halftime.

In the locker room, the players caught their breath from the torrid pace of the game. Cassell, Ward and Dobard barely sat. They slugged water and 10-K (Florida State refused to drink Gatorade and had a contract with their then-competitor) and rested their legs. They were now roughly twenty minutes from where no Seminoles team had been in two decades, and Kennedy told them he planned to keep pushing the tempo.

Unfortunately, while the pace stayed up in the second half, none of their shots from the free-throw line were going down. Doug Edwards and Bobby Sura hustled on offense and harassed Western Kentucky on defense, but the Seminoles' abysmal foul shooting (13 of 29) kept the Hilltoppers in the game and led to a 69-69 tie at the end of regulation.

Early in overtime Florida State found their shooting touch from the floor, and a lay-up by Edwards followed by a three-pointer each from Cassell and Sura put them up 78-74 with just over two minutes left. Then they went ice cold again. In fact, they didn't hit another field goal the rest of the game. It was maddening to Coach Kennedy. After the season they had been through and the scorers they had on the floor, to watch his offense stall like that was baffling. A full minute passed with no scoring and then Charlie gave them a little breathing room.

With just under a minute left, Charlie established position in front of Mark Bell and drew a charging foul, which was Bell's fifth, meaning he'd have to leave the game. It was exactly the kind of smart, heads up play the Seminoles had relied on Charlie for the whole season. Not only did the play take Western Kentucky's leader off the floor for the remainder of the game, it gave Charlie a chance at two free throws. He calmly sank both, giving Florida State an 80-76 lead.

Western Kentucky made a basket to cut it to 80-78 and then Rodney Dobard was called for traveling, giving the Hilltoppers the ball. Coach Kennedy was apoplectic. His team could not make two positive plays in a row. Michael Fraliex then threw the ball out of bounds with 7.5 seconds remaining. When the Seminoles got the ball back, Derrick Carroll was fouled and made one free throw, putting them up 81-78. Cypheus Bunton of Western Kentucky launched a three with no time remaining that bounced off the rim twice before not going in the basket.

Florida State held on to win by three.

They were going to the Elite Eight.

And they all knew they were lucky to escape.

"It went our way," Cassell said, after a dismal 3-for-12 night shooting. "To be successful in this tournament you have to have some type of luck, and we got it tonight."

"To make the final eight is just a fabulous accomplishment for this team," Coach Kennedy said afterward. "I'm just so proud of these kids. Everything they've been through…it's nice to have some good luck."

Even Charlie got in on the act when talking about the charge he drew on Bell that led to his crucial foul shots. "He came down the lane and I just wanted to play smart," he said. "I stepped up and took the charge and they (the officials) called it. I just came up lucky."

Lucky or not, they won.

• • •

The Kentucky Wildcats were a juggernaut in the 1993 NCAA Tournament. They beat Rider in the opening round 96-52. Then they beat #19 ranked Utah 83-62. Following that they smoked #16 ranked Wake Forest 103-69. Rick Pitino's team, led by All-American Jamal Mashburn, won its first three games by a combined 99 points. Despite Florida State's talent, few people not wearing garnet and gold gave them a chance, which was fine by Cassell.

"I hope everybody counts us out," he said. "That's fine. Put Kentucky right into the Final Four. Our guys know what we're in for. We're a bunch of overachievers who play our hardest when the chips are down."

For a brief moment before the game at the Charlotte Coliseum, the Seminoles thought maybe they had intimidated the Wildcats into not showing up. Alas, the UK bus was stuck in traffic. It didn't faze Charlie.

"We've put together some great games," he said. "We put together one more, and you never know."

The Seminoles did their best early on to hang with Kentucky, beating their famous press as no team had all year. Cassell opened the game by hitting Sura with three straight passes to tie the score at 6-6. They continued to push against the press and stay strong on defense, with two straight steals (one by Cassell and one by Charlie) that were converted to buckets to give them a 27-26 lead halfway through the first half.

"We can beat 'em," Cassell told his teammates over and over. "We can beat 'em."

The Seminoles largely kept pace as the game went to halftime with Kentucky up by eight points. The feeling in the Seminoles' locker room was that they had weathered the storm. They grabbed a lead, lost it, and now it was time to get it back. What they didn't know was that they had really just weathered the outer bands of the storm. As the second half got going, they bore witness to the full force of talent that Coach Pitino had at his disposal. After a 20-6 run, Kentucky was up by twenty points with six minutes remaining, and the Seminoles were helpless to stop them. They were gassed. The 106-81 final score was the second worst loss Kennedy had at Florida State. Still, they had earned Pitino's respect.

"Give a lot of credit to Florida State," he said. "That was the best anybody has attacked our press in a long time. Their defense forced us to have someone other than Travis [Ford] or Jamal step up."

The sense on the Seminoles sideline was that they had a few chances, but in the end they just couldn't keep up with the Wildcats.

"We took the season as far as we could and we finally hit a wall," Florida State assistant coach Tom Carlson said. "We just didn't have any juice left. We missed our jumpers and couldn't even hit layups. It was all gone."

As the reality hit the team that their run was over, they began congratulating each other on getting as far as they did. Sometimes, they told each other, you just run into a buzz saw. Doug Edwards and Sam Cassell were headed to the NBA. Others were looking forward to a long off-season to recuperate and rest. Charlie was contemplating surgery.

Ever since he had reinjured his shoulder in late January against Georgia Tech, he had been playing with a brace and fighting through the pain. With the season over, it was time to address the issue and get his body healthy for the 1993 college football season. He was, after all, the leading candidate to win the Heisman on a team set to compete for a championship.

Charlie had stayed mostly quiet about his injury during the season and didn't have much to say about it following the loss to Kentucky. He spoke more about how special this team was and how far they had gotten. He let Florida State's team trainer comment on his health.

"We're going to give him some time to catch his breath," Sam Lunt said. "But we want to do it [the surgery] as quickly as we can. He'll be able to fully rehab it before football starts."

Those were the only words Florida State football fans wanted to hear.

Chapter 20

Superstardom

The question he'd been asked wasn't hard to answer but he found himself squirming on the couch anyway. He rolled his lower lip under his top teeth. He leaned forward and readjusted the pillow behind him, wondering why it was so bunched up. He sat back again and crossed his leg over his knee. Then switched legs. He draped one arm across the back of the couch and then put it in his lap. He stared at the little Sony tape recorder on the coffee table.

"Well?" his interviewer asked, impatiently.

Charlie stared into the ceiling lights. He looked for a moment too long and blinked, bringing a racing green dot across his vision as he turned away.

"Do you want me to ask the question again?" the interviewer said.

"No," Charlie said.

"Then answer it, please," the interviewer said.

Charlie leaned forward and put his hands on his knees. He took a deep breath, opened his mouth and… Nothing. No words came out. He collapsed back into the couch.

"C'mon, Mom," Charlie said.

"Junior!" his mom said, leaning forward to click off the tape recorder. "I'm not Mom, I'm from *USA Today* and I traveled all the way here to do a story on Heisman candidate Charlie Ward and I'd like some well-thought out answers."

"Okay," Charlie said. "Let's start over."

And so they began again, Willard asking Charlie questions that a reporter might ask and Charlie working on answers that were longer than one word and had some depth to them. This was Willard Ward Media Training 101, with a class size of one. What Willard recognized early that summer was that the visibility of Charlie's Elite Eight appearance, coming on the heels of the Orange Bowl, was a mere appetizer to the upcoming media main course. Come September, Charlie would be the face of college football as the leading Heisman Trophy candidate and quarterback of a top-five team. The problem was that his impending megawatt stardom stood in stark contrast to his low-voltage introverted personality.

"I was a very quiet person all the way through college, so I put myself in Junior's shoes," Willard said. "I called it the 'quiet gene.' I thought, *what would I have needed to prepare for the cameras and the questions and the spotlight if I were put in his position?*"

By this time, Charlie was used to being interviewed about a particular game or about an important play or teammate. What he wasn't comfortable with was answering personal questions. For those, he often used single-word answers as if he was being fined $50 per letter.

"I said, 'Junior, your answers can't just be *yes* or *no* or *sure*. If someone asks you if you're excited about being a Heisman candidate you can't just say *yes* and leave it at that. They want to learn about you,'" Willard said.

With this in mind, she began reaching out to media members for help, eventually finding a few journalists who were willing to send her some sample questions that might come up once the football season got underway. She put them on a list and then role played with Charlie, posing as the interviewer. She'd also leave the tape recorder out so he could play it back and hear how his answers sounded to someone else.

Her next step was to give him a notepad and pen to write down whatever thoughts came to his head following a question. From those notes, he could form a well thought out answer. Then he'd rehearse the answer until it sounded natural and off the cuff. That was part one.

"Once he could compose his answers, the next part was to make sure he didn't sound like a robot," she said. "These were all his words and his thoughts, but now he had to add what I'd call animation. It wasn't as if he couldn't do it. In the course of normal conversation with me or other family and friends he had expression; he'd just get very low-energy during an interview. Over the course of that summer, I was finally able to pull some of his true personality out of him."

Tonja also talked to Charlie about the attention he would soon be getting and how he could manage it.

"We had a lot of conversations about how he was so quiet to the outside world and how he just had to develop his voice," she said. "He was kind of a walking oxymoron, because he was blessed with the athletic skills that couldn't help but draw everyone's attention, but personality-wise he didn't like attention on himself. Mama Ward was really great about helping him work through it."

By the end of the summer, Willard had removed roughly 60% of Charlie's "uhs" and "ahs" and "ums" and replaced them with seamless transitions. She had also helped fill his head with an inventory of answers to a variety of questions reporters might ask about his love of football, his family, his teammates, his motivation, what the Heisman would mean and on and on. In short, Charlie was ready for his close-up off the field.

• • •

As for on the field, Coach Richt and Coach Scott had spent the winter and spring doing a deep dive on the Fast Break Offense and experimenting with permutations and variations of the shotgun. With four or five receivers spread out in the Fast Break, the concern was that all it would take would be one missed block or unaccounted for blitzing defensive player and Charlie could get blindsided and blown up.

"I can make one guy miss," Charlie told his coaches. "But I might have trouble with two."

Richt and Scott traveled to visit the Tampa Bay Buccaneers and the Buffalo Bills, both well versed in the shotgun on the professional level, to study new blocking schemes for protecting their quarterback. Bowden, ever curious, pored over their findings. To close observers, there seemed to be a sense of urgency in this particular off-season to make 1993 the year the Seminoles finally cashed in on their talent and won a championship.

The fact that Charlie was the most potent offensive weapon in college football raised the stakes even higher.

If Bowden couldn't win one with Ward, when would he win one?

The coach himself was so certain that Charlie was going to win the Heisman Trophy that he told sports information director Rob Wilson to not bother launching a campaign for him. "We'll just mess it up," he said. "Charlie is going to win the thing on his own."

Craig Barnes of the *Fort Lauderdale Sun Sentinel* did a wide-ranging interview with Bowden before the season and asked him explicitly about his feelings on having not yet won a national championship.

"If I left the game tomorrow it would be something that is missing from my résumé," Bowden said. "But my faith tells me there are things in life more important than a national championship. I'd like to have it for Florida State, for all the boys who have played for me, and for all the people who have supported our program through the years. I'm aware the near misses have been more frustrating to others than to me, but they shouldn't think I don't want it. Naturally, I want it, and our intensity to pursue it won't be reduced until we get it."

Part of that pursuit involved surrounding Charlie with as much talent as possible, and in 1993, that meant pairing him with someone equally explosive on offense who would turn out to be his roommate and closest friend on the team.

• • •

On January 7, 1993, less than a week after Florida State won the Orange Bowl, Betty Smothers, an off-duty police officer working a security job on the side to save money for a house, was ambushed and killed outside of a bank by armed robbers in Louisiana. Her son, Warrick Dunn, a star football player who had committed to playing at Florida State, was devastated. His mother was also his best friend—his world had been turned upside down. To make matters worse, it was just a few days after his 18th birthday. The tragedy was nearly unbearable for the young man, and as the time came closer for him to attend Florida State, Charlie asked if they could room together. It was rare for a senior and freshman to live together, especially a senior of Charlie's status, but he had hosted Dunn on his official visit and the two got along well. Considering everything Dunn had been through, Charlie figured the least he could do was be there for him to talk, or not talk, if he needed it.

"We were very compatible. Almost made for each other," Charlie said. "On his recruiting trip he didn't want to do much and that was fine by me because I didn't like doing much, but we were able to connect. We were very similar. At that time in his life he needed someone like me who didn't talk much because he needed someone to be able to listen when he felt like talking. We were both quiet guys."

For Dunn, the immediate comfort level he had with Charlie was the most important thing. After all he'd been through prior to arriving on campus, he had to live with someone who would allow him to be himself and work through whatever was in his head.

"Sometimes I have learned that God puts people in your life for a reason," Dunn said. "With Charlie, I was able to go to him and talk about a lot of my issues. I just observed. He didn't give direction, but he was a sounding board. Being able to open up and express myself was huge and vital for me. He was an outlet I needed at that time and he was there for me in ways I could have never imagined."

While the roommate pairing had a serious foundation, the atmosphere was not a somber one. They ate fast food. They watched TV. They argued about sports. They had fun. They even became the butt of a running joke amongst teammates who would wonder what happens when you put the two quietest guys in Tallahassee in the same room. Was it a never-ending game of "whoever talks first loses?"

"We played along with the jokes, but while we were naturally quiet we were very vocal with each other," Dunn said.

Another factor to consider was that Charlie was a fifth-year senior with only a few classes left to complete. Dunn was a freshman with a full course load and a new playbook to learn. In fact, he basically had two playbooks, offense and defense, because he was recruited by Bobby Bowden to play cornerback. Only after extensive negotiation did Dunn, an eventual three-time First-Team All ACC running back and three-time NFL Pro Bowler, get to play running back for Florida State.

"We recruited Warrick out of Baton Rouge, Louisiana for defensive purposes," Bowden explains in *Tales from the Seminoles Sideline*. "We already got [Rock] Preston out of Miami, and we were only looking for one running back. We didn't have any more offensive scholarships to give. Mickey [FSU's Defensive Coordinator] had one left, and he said, 'We'll offer it to that Dunn boy.' We told him, 'We are offering you a scholarship, but it is a defensive back scholarship. Are you willing to play defensive back?' 'Yes, I'd be willing to play defensive back,' was his reply. 'That will be all right, but would you give me a chance to play tailback?'

"Yeah, I'll give you a shot at it. But I just want you to know, if we need you at corner, that's where we'll play you.

"So he comes in, and we had three tailbacks returning. So it looks like he's going to play corner. Then Tiger McMillon got hurt, and you had Sean Jackson and Marquette Smith. That's not enough tailbacks, so now we had to move one of the freshmen up. Rock Preston is the guy...but he sprained his ankle and we had to bring Dunn up. He got in a couple of scrimmages and it was obvious this guy needs the ball under his arm."

Standing 5'9" and weighing 190 pounds with fire hydrant legs and a low center of gravity, Dunn was impossible to tackle that day. The defense noticed. The offense noticed. The coaches noticed. It would be the last day he would ever practice with the defense. From that moment on he was a running back, which made sense since he truly had world-class speed. In addition to football, Dunn was a two-sport star like Charlie, except his other sport was track. He was a sprinter who would become an AP All-American as part of Florida State's 4x100 relay team. His top time in the hundred was a scorching 10.3 seconds.

When it came to Dunn's relationship with Charlie, it's important to note that Dunn had watched almost all of Charlie's games when he was a senior in high school, so he was a fan before he was a friend. Even though they hit it off and became close, he'd occasionally forget that the general public and most of the kids on campus still looked at Charlie the way Dunn used to. Which is to say, they treated him like a celebrity.

"After that Georgia Tech game, which I remember watching, he was all over SportsCenter," Dunn remembers. "Then every week he was on TV for another highlight. I couldn't appreciate how great he was and what he meant on campus until I saw it every day in person. People idolized him. It was crazy. But to me he was just Charlie and we stayed focused on the task at hand, which was winning a championship."

• • •

The expectations for 1993 were the highest in Bobby Bowden's tenure at Florida State. The Seminoles began the year as the #1 ranked team in the country. Charlie Ward was the front-runner for the Heisman Trophy. Derrick Alexander, Derrick Brooks and Corey Sawyer were primed to be All-Americans on defense. There were no more excuses to be had. Ninety-three should be the year Bowden finally wins it all.

The season began with Florida State taking a flamethrower to their schedule, torching every single opponent in their path with no remorse. The super-charged Fast Break Offense shattered defenses like a cannonball through a greenhouse. The Seminoles' defense might as well have been security around Fort Knox. Through five games, which included tilts with two Top-25 teams, the offense outscored their opponents 228-14.

Yes, 228-14.

The defense allowed only two touchdowns in twenty quarters of football.

"Charlie was so focused one time that he threw me a pass when he wasn't even looking at me and I dropped it," Dunn said. "When you can read a defense and read a coverage and not even have to look where you need to throw, it is...there aren't words. How does this dude throw a pinpoint pass without seeing me?"

In the fifth game of the season—facing Georgia Tech, the team against whom the Fast Break Offense was born one year earlier—the Seminoles showed no mercy in embarrassing the Yellow Jackets 51-0. Whereas a year earlier at that point it seemed as though Charlie had thrown a hundred interceptions and been benched a dozen times, this year he'd thrown one only pick and never came off the field. He was leading a juggernaut of an offense that was supported by a six-inch steel wall of a defense.

The five-game numbers were staggering.

Charlie Ward led his backs and receivers to 2,868 yards of total offense in barely half a season. The defense had three shutouts in five games while the offense averaged forty-five points per game. But none of it would matter if in the sixth game of the season they lost to the University of Miami. Again.

Bobby Bowden had become so paranoid about facing Miami that he once joked his tombstone would say: AT LEAST HE PLAYED MIAMI. And there was still one more mind game left before the 1993 match-up on October 9. After all the stomach-punch losses and Wide Rights and championship opportunities ripped away in the closing seconds, he would be facing Miami with his most talented team ever as an overwhelming favorite, not only putting pressure on him to finally win, but to win big.

The headline in the *Palm Beach Post* before the game said it all:

Bowden's Nightmare: FSU a 14-Point Favorite Over UM

Then came his reaction to the point spread.

"Why do they do this to me?" he said during his news conference. "What did I do to deserve this? Why me? That will be to their psychological advantage. Every coach wants to walk in before a game and say, 'Look what they say about us.' When you're a 14-point favorite, you can't say that. Miami can. I haven't beaten them. I can understand saying 'Hey, you're at home so I'll give them three points.' But not two touchdowns."

Bowden had a point. Lifetime he was 5-12 against the Hurricanes and they had ripped his heart out several times over the last few years alone. And it wasn't as if Miami was having a down year. They were coming into the game undefeated as the #3 ranked team in the country. A one-touchdown spread or less would have felt more appropriate. Las Vegas didn't care. They'd seen the Seminoles in action and they believed they'd win handily. Bowden wasn't so sure.

"Charlie may have to calm us coaches down," Bowden said the day before the game. "I wish I could adopt his demeanor for this game, but I keep thinking about what Miami has done to us in the past. We seem to match up well, but this is Miami."

• • •

Cautious excitement would be the best way to describe the atmosphere in the locker room heading into the noon kickoff in Tallahassee. In the stands, however, it was bedlam. In a tongue-in-cheek stat, the *Tallahassee Democrat* rated the hype before the game "Six Game-of-the-Century labels out of five." One visiting Hurricanes fan mockingly held up a poster reading: TIME IS RIGHT, TITLE IN SIGHT, ANOTHER...WIDE RIGHT! The War Chant thundered through the stadium on an endless loop while the Hurricanes fans in attendance tried to counter with their own chant, "*It's great, to be, a Mi-ami Hurr-icane!*"

For Charlie, there was one particular Hurricanes fan in attendance that he paid some attention to. After months and months of phone calls and letters, and after ignoring a request for tickets a year earlier, he finally invited Tonja to the game against her alma mater to watch him play in person for the first time.

"He called me and invited me up to stay with his sister," she said. "I took off work and we got to spend some quality time together the day before the game. It was fantastic."

"I was excited about that, and it helped me relax," Charlie added. "Coach Richt was great and let her sit in on a quarterback meeting so she could see what it was like. I also got to show her around. It felt good."

Unfortunately, Tonja was the only Canes fan in attendance that day that wanted Charlie to do well. The rest would have liked to see their defense pound him into the ground with an endless barrage of tackles and takedowns. When the teams matched up in 1992, Miami sacked Charlie seven times. They believed they'd have to come close to equaling that number in '93 to slow down the Seminoles' offense.

• • •

Miami took the opening drive to the Seminoles' 40-yard line before Florida State's defense held strong on a third and six and forced a botched pooch punt attempt that went out the back of the end zone. After a full year to think about the hits, the missed field goal and the loss, Charlie brought the offense out on their own 20-yard line to get to work.

On the sideline, Bowden paced back and forth in quick bursts of about five feet, like he was trying to parallel park a car but just didn't have the room. He wore a white FSU baseball cap with a pair of large, dark aviators tucked under the bill. He fidgeted with the rims, he touched his face, he rubbed his eyes under the lenses—he needed something to relieve the stress. The first play didn't do it. The coaches tried to get cute and had Charlie line up in the Fast Break shotgun offense, only to put him back under center for the snap for a handoff. The Hurricanes' wrecking ball of a defensive lineman, Warren Sapp, plowed through the offensive line and stopped running back Sean Jackson in his tracks.

The next play Charlie was back in the shotgun and found Kez McCorvey for a twenty-yard pass over the middle and a first down. On the third play of the drive, Jackson took the handoff, bounced outside and ran sixty-nine yards for a touchdown, providing a much-needed boost for Coach Bowden. For the moment, he stopped pacing.

The Seminoles' offense chased down the field after Jackson, celebrating a little harder than they would for the first touchdown of a regular-season game. But everyone knew this wasn't a "regular" regular season game. If they were going to once and for all exorcise their demons against the Hurricanes, game-breaking plays were going to be necessary against a defense that featured Sapp, Ray Lewis, Darren Krein and Dwayne "Not Yet The Rock" Johnson.

Frank Costa fumbled a snap on the Hurricanes' ensuing drive, but Florida State couldn't capitalize and was forced to punt it back. The Canes answered with a six-yard touchdown pass to Donnell Bennett, putting the score at 7-7. After the great start for FSU the momentum had swung back in Miami's favor, and to many it felt like the first seeds of the big gray cloud that hung over Bowden were starting to form. Then, Charlie happened.

It was third and ten on Florida State's 28, and Charlie took the ball out of a shotgun set. He barely got a beat to survey the field when his pocket collapsed, sending him racing back and to his right. He was almost in a full sprint when he crossed the right hash and cleared the defense for his first look down field. He slowed ever so slightly as he neared the line of scrimmage because he saw something: receiver Matt Frier getting over the top of the defense. With what looked like a tiny flick of his wrist, Charlie threw the ball on a line thirty yards to hit Frier at full speed and send him racing seventy-two yards to the end zone.

Keith Jackson's legendary call on the play was simple, but said it all: "That's what Ward will do to you."

Later in the second quarter, the Seminoles lined up Warrick Dunn right next to Charlie on a third-down play and caught Miami off guard by snapping it directly to Dunn, who picked up the important first down. A few plays later, Charlie made a two-yard touchdown run to give FSU a 21-7 lead going into halftime.

After two quarters, Bowden's pre-game worrying was proving to have been unfounded, and the Vegas odds makers were being proven right. In the locker room, the defense that had allowed only two touchdowns all year now had a two-touchdown lead. As the players rested and the coaches schemed, the players looked at each other with sheer determination in their eyes. *We got this.*

The Miami Hurricanes managed only 100 yards of total offense in the second half against the Seminoles' defensive onslaught, which included an interception return for a touchdown that put Florida State up 28-7. A late, meaningless field goal by Miami made the final score 28-10.

The Seminoles had finally beaten the Hurricanes—and they beat the spread to boot.

The fans at Doak Campbell gave the team a standing ovation, and the players, after hearing all week and all year that they were snake-bitten against the school from Dade County, soaked in every moment and celebrated. Even Charlie.

Dave Hyde covered the game for the *Sun Sentinel* and described how rare it was to watch Charlie give in to the emotion of the moment. "This is the Charlie you never see: Running around the field alone after a victory, football held high, leading delighted Seminoles fans in postgame cheers," he wrote in his post-game column. "Ward is typically as emotionless as a computer chip, as cool as a December morning. But here the FSU quarterback was after Saturday's 28-10 victory against Miami, doing what would be expected by anyone else, jumping around the field basking in fans' approval."

"I usually don't do that," Charlie said later in the piece. "I was pretty much the last player to leave the field, and the crowd still wanted to cheer…so I cheered along with them."

This time, it was Bowden who seemed to keep his feet on the ground while everyone around him was jumping for joy. He shook Miami Head Coach Dennis Erickson's hand and left the field without much incident. In the post-game press conference, he spoke briefly about getting the proverbial Miami monkey off his back, but when he spoke to his players afterward, he was already putting the win in perspective, telling them that, "You don't win a national championship in the middle of the year."

The winning continued for Charlie long after the game was over because he was able to celebrate with Tonja in person. Their relationship was based largely on phone calls and letters, so sharing a big moment with her in real time, rather than writing about it later or recapping the event on the phone, felt very special.

The next morning, he picked Tonja up from his sister's place and took her to breakfast at the Village Inn.

"It was our first real date," she said. "I had some pretty clear goals that I wanted to achieve in my life after law school, but while we were eating I saw some real potential there for us."

Shortly after Tonja returned to Miami, Charlie did what all young guys in the '90s did to let a girl know how he feels about her: he sent her a cassette tape. In this case, it was Regina Belle's "Do You Wanna Get Serious?"

Tonja replied with a simple but effective answer that would make the ever-taciturn Charlie proud: Yes.

• • •

40-14. 54-0. 49-20. Those were the scores of Florida State's games against Virginia, Wake Forest and Maryland following their win against Miami. Next up was a road game against the #2 ranked team in the country, Notre Dame. The Seminoles were once again favored in what Lenny Del Genio, the sports book director for Bally's, called "the largest college football game ever bet on in the state of Nevada." The lines opened with Florida State as an eight-point favorite.

To show team unity (and to tweak Notre Dame), the Seminoles flew to Indiana on Friday wearing green baseball caps with gold shamrocks stitched into them. Every guy on the team wore his hat into Notre Dame stadium for the walk-through as a sign that they weren't intimidated.

Bowden, who was in fact good friends with Notre Dame Head Coach Lou Holtz, hadn't been to the field since 1981. The main thing he noticed upon returning there was the grass being shorter than he remembered. For almost all of the players, it was the first time they'd stepped foot on the hallowed ground of Knute Rockne and Joe Montana and Alan Page. Charlie, as usual, was nonplussed. "It's Notre Dame and they have a lot of tradition," he said. "I understand that. But it's no different than going to the Orange Bowl or Florida Field. It's an away game...and we're going there to play a game, not sight-see."

It might have been "just an away game" to Charlie, but it was to be the Seminoles' second "Game of the Century" in about a month and what many considered the only serious challenge on their schedule before an inevitable championship game on New Year's Day. ESPN brought their Game Day crew, and Notre Dame's sports information director issued more than 750 press credentials for the impending battle.

The Seminoles got off their bus in garnet-and–gold, classic early '90s warm-up track suits. Notre Dame attended mass at Sacred Heart Basilica in suits and ties and then walked right to the stadium. One team looked like a cool Starter jacket commercial; the other, like a law firm. It was also unseasonably warm for late November in Indiana, with a game-time temperature of fifty-nine degrees and a 15-25 mile per hour wind blowing.

• • •

The game opened easily enough, with Charlie marching the Seminoles down the field on an 89-yard, ten-play drive that ended with a touchdown pass to Kevin Knox. They didn't score the rest of the first quarter. They didn't score in the second quarter. They didn't score to open the third quarter.

With ten minutes left in the third quarter, the Seminoles found themselves stuck in a bad dream: They were down 24-7 and could not move the ball.

"At that point, we needed something to hang our hat on," Charlie said. "We had to put points on the board."

They did just that, with a nice drive and a touchdown pass from Charlie to Warrick Dunn. The score was now 24-14. On the Seminoles' next possession, Charlie hit McCorvey four times to put kicker Scott Bentley in position to hit a 24-yard field goal and cut Notre Dame's lead to a touchdown.

The Irish then fired back with a clock-eating, comeback-dream-killing, nine-play, eighty-yard drive and score of their own. Four minutes and five seconds remained and Florida State was now down 31-17. The ever-cool Charlie summoned his inner Joe Montana and led his team down the field, all the way to the 5-yard line before several penalties backed them into no man's land: fourth and goal from the 20-yard line.

A field goal would be useless with so little time left. They needed a touchdown or their season was over. Charlie fielded the snap out of the shotgun with two minutes and five seconds left in the game. He took two quick steps back to settle himself, cocked his arm and then ripped a missile of a pass through the heart of the Fighting Irish defense towards McCorvey. Somehow, he didn't see Notre Dame safety Brian Magee, who tipped the ball in the air. McCorvey stayed zeroed in on the pass and miraculously caught the tipped ball in the back of the end zone. The extra point was good. Score: 31-24.

The onside kick failed, but Florida State's defense bore down and forced a three-and-out, giving them possession on their own 37-yard line with fifty-one seconds left. With so many comebacks under his belt, the Seminoles' coaching staff had total faith in Charlie and they put together a play sequence that would theoretically drive them right down the field.

Play number one was a scramble and easy pass to McCorvey for nine yards. Play number two was a short throw to Dunn. Play number three was a cross-field throw to McCorvey for eighteen yards, but it took far too much time to develop. Florida State had a new set of downs but only seventeen seconds left. Play number four was a laser over the middle to McCorvey, again for eighteen yards, giving FSU the ball on Notre Dame's 14-yard line with ten seconds left.

The Notre Dame crowd was deafening as Charlie took the snap and dropped back, eyeing the end zone. He had a man open and he fired, but the pass was blocked and driven behind the line of scrimmage, stopping the clock with three seconds left. On the final play, Charlie scrambled to buy time, only to have his pass to Dunn batted down by Shawn Wooden. The game was over and, seemingly, their title hopes were too. Charlie stood quietly on the 20-yard line as Notre Dame fans rushed the field, surrounding him on all sides like human confetti.

"If I had the chance to have that last play redone, I would like to have thrown the ball to Matt Frier," Ward said after the game. "He was open but I didn't see him."

The team, the coaches and the fans were devastated. After finally slaying the Hurricanes, they themselves were slayed by Notre Dame. The locker room was despondent, so Charlie decided it was up to him to set the tone. The season was far from over and a lot could still happen.

"We go back to work this week," he said, talking as much to the reporters as his teammates. "And if things work out, we'll get another chance at Notre Dame. Let the coaches or writers or whoever votes match us up again. That would be fine with us."

And then, to address those on the verge of a meltdown, including some FSU players, he said this to provide some perspective amidst the pain: "I'm not taking this too hard. Football is not life. We haven't gotten killed. No one is dead. Football is not a game of life and death. The fans are down, but I know that tomorrow the sun will come up on a new day."

• • •

There were a few scattered clouds in the sky covering Tallahassee on November 20, and the magma-level heat and humidity from the summer had passed. The temperature was a very reasonable eighty degrees late in the afternoon as the Doak Campbell stadium staff prepared for that night's home game. The field was being tended to. The cups were being stacked. The hot dogs were being cooked. All was on schedule for the 7:30 pm kickoff against North Carolina State except one tiny detail.

The Florida State football team hadn't arrived yet.

"We were watching the game," Charlie said.

"The game" was Boston College versus Notre Dame, aka the Holy War.

After Florida State's crushing loss to the Irish, they dropped to #2 in the Associated Press poll, #3 in the *USA Today/CNN* poll and, most important, #2 in the bowl coalition poll. All of this meant that they still had a path to the national championship game, but it was a tricky one. If they blasted NC State, the voters could be justified in setting up a rematch against Notre Dame, considering the first match-up was #1 versus #2 and decided by only a touchdown. However, Nebraska was also undefeated and had a game left against Oklahoma. If all three teams won out, the voters could make the case that the championship game should be Notre Dame versus Nebraska since both teams would be undefeated and FSU had one loss.

If Notre Dame lost to Boston College, Florida State was back in the driver's seat with a direct road to the national title game.

"We all knew the implications of the game," Dunn said. "We couldn't take our eyes off it."

Practically the entire team was glued to the TV set that Saturday afternoon as Boston College seemed to be on the verge of a monumental upset. In fact, for much of the afternoon, a Boston College victory seemed likely. Notre Dame was clearly suffering an emotional letdown after beating the Seminoles and was throttled by BC for three quarters. With 11:13 left to play in the game, the Irish were down 38-17. Then the ghosts of the four horsemen seemed to emerge on the field and the offense woke up, leading an improbable comeback. Notre Dame scored twenty-two points in nine minutes and had a 39-38 lead with only a few minutes left.

"For most of that game it felt like everything was going BC's way, which meant it was going our way," Charlie said. "Then in about a half-hour, Notre Dame kind of killed our chances for a second time with that rally."

In the end, the game rested on the foot of David Gordon, Boston College's placekicker. As his 41-yard field goal went through the uprights, ensuring a victory for the Eagles and a de facto win for the Seminoles, the Florida State players went berserk.

"It was mayhem!" Charlie said. "Everyone came out of their rooms whooping and hollering. It was like we had just won the championship. We knew the opportunity we had just been given."

Bobby Bowden no longer concerned himself with giving a pep talk before the NC State game—they had all the motivation they needed. Even NC State Head Coach Mike O'Cain commented on the deluge his team was about to face. "People have said they [FSU] have to come out and score fifty to sixty points. If they have to do that to impress the voters, so be it. If we're not ready, we could be embarrassed."

They weren't ready and they were embarrassed, losing 62-3.

The next morning Florida State was back to #1 in the AP poll. Nebraska was #1 in the CNN/*USA Today* coaches' poll.

"I was elated," Bowden said. "We only had to play Florida to go to the national championship."

Only.

The University of Florida had not lost at home under head coach Steve Spurrier since he took the job in 1990. Heading into their game with FSU, that streak was at twenty-three games. The Gators' offense was averaging forty-two points a game on the season, and freshman quarterback Danny Wuerffel threw twenty-one touchdown passes to set a record for first-year college QBs. There was absolutely nothing the Old Ball Coach would like more than to shatter the Seminoles' title hopes on his home field, furthering his team's feeling of invincibility when playing at The Swamp.

"The night before we played the Gators, I did not tell my players what was at stake. They knew if we beat the Gators there was a very good chance we were going to play Nebraska in the Orange Bowl in Miami for the National Championship. 'Can we beat them in the Swamp?' I asked my boys. 'No one thinks we can. But everyone in this room knows we're going to do it.'"

It was the biggest game the intrastate rivalry had ever seen, and a record number of people turned out to see it—the 85,507 fans made up the largest crowd in Florida football history. But what they ended up witnessing was more akin to a track meet.

Charlie threw to eight different receivers for 446 yards and four touchdowns. He also ran for thirty yards. The Seminoles went into halftime up 13-7 and scored fourteen unanswered points in the third quarter to go up 27-7 heading into the fourth.

But the Gators would not go down without one last attempt at a death roll. They scored two touchdowns in the fourth to cut the lead to 27-21 and sucked every last ounce of momentum from the Seminoles. After the Gators' last score, FSU's drive stalled and the game hinged on a pivotal third-and-ten play from Florida State's own 21-yard line.

"That was without a doubt the loudest crowd I ever heard in my life," Charlie said. "We couldn't hear ourselves at all. It was like the fans were nonexistent until that moment. They sensed that if they stopped us we'd punt, and with our defense on its heels they had plenty of time to score, and probably would have."

Calling the play in the huddle was like trying to have a conversation on an airport tarmac. Charlie harnessed every bit of lung power he had to cut through the sound and relay the call. He stood under center, once again with the season on the line, assessed the defense, and took the snap with five seconds on the play clock. What happened next was one of the most famous plays in Seminoles history.

"The play call was three 44 verticals," Charlie said. "I'm always looking for the Y on a bender route. If the Y wasn't there, I'd normally hit the check down. I got pressure up the middle and I was able to escape. While I was dodging defenders I had to make a tough throw going to my left as a right-handed quarterback with a guy chasing me down. It was one of those flips that hit Warrick out of the backfield as the check down man. We got a great block on the defensive back and Warrick used his incredible speed and took it all the way up the sideline to seal the deal for us."

Final score:

Florida State 33

Florida 21

The Seminoles were finally going to play for the national championship.

Chapter 21

The Heisman Trophy

The 1993 Heisman Trophy ceremony had about as much suspense regarding the ending as the movie *Titanic.* Yes, Heath Shuler, the stud quarterback from the University of Tennessee technically had a shot to win. And, yes, Alabama running back David Palmer had a mathematical chance, and San Diego State's Marshall Faulk hypothetically was in the running, but in reality, the limousine drivers who brought them to the Downtown Athletic Club had the same odds of leaving with the hardware.

The award had been Charlie's to lose since the Orange Bowl eleven months earlier, and all he did since was exceed every single expectation people had for him. If it were up to his teammates, there wouldn't even be a vote.

"Playing with Charlie Ward is like going to Disney World," Tamarick Vanover said. "He's a magical person."

"When they made the Heisman Trophy years ago and looked into the future—and this was before Charlie was ever conceived—he was just what a Heisman winner was supposed to be," Florida State linebacker Ken Alexander said. "If he can't represent what the Heisman is supposed to be, no one can. He's definitely the best player in the country, and he's also one of the best gentlemen."

"By the middle of the season CW was playing so well he was like a senior playing against a bunch of ninth-graders out there," William Floyd said. "Charlie was the real-life Heisman."

Even ESPN's Lee Corso, who wasn't a teammate but a Florida State alumnus, heaped praise on Ward. "He's the best quarterback I've seen since Roger Staubach," he said at the time. "He takes the game and plays it at another level."

The Heisman voters agreed.

Charlie received 91% of the first-place votes. It was the largest margin of victory in the history of the trophy, at that time. He was also the first Florida State player to win, which, even at the ceremony, took a backseat to Charlie's ultimate goal.

"I'm very appreciative of the award and I know it's a prestigious honor to receive," Charlie said after winning. "This is something I'll cherish more in ten years. It's not as important to me right now as a national championship. I'll feel much better about being the first FSU quarterback to win a national championship than the Heisman."

Bowden, naturally, echoed that sentiment.

"It's thrilling as heck for me," he said. "I've always been envious of coaches and schools who had a Heisman winner. It's not quite as important to the university and players as a national championship, but it has to be up there, way up there."

This isn't to say that Charlie and his record-breaking entourage of eighteen family members who accompanied him to the week's festivities in New York City didn't have fun. They had the time of their lives. The memories from that week are as vivid today as they were nearly thirty years ago.

• • •

Sitting in his house on Heisman Way in Thomasville, Georgia, Charlie Sr. let his mind wander back to December of 1993 and the week's events surrounding the Heisman ceremony. He looked up at the ceiling, took a deep breath, exhaled and said, "It was heaven on earth. Heaven. On. Earth. We were treated like football royalty."

He wined and dined with the football players he had watched his whole life and dreamed of competing against as a young man. Johnny Rodgers and Archie Griffin and Tony Dorsett and Earl Campbell. He rubbed elbows with all of them. Campbell even treated his kids to lunch. After watching the ceremony on television every year, mingling among the legends was like an out of body experience. And that was just at the football events.

Willard, sitting next to him, listed all the things they did.

"We went to the Statue of Liberty and Chinatown, and we saw the Rockettes and opened the New York Stock Exchange and just…so many things," she said. "We saw them light the Christmas tree in Rockefeller Center. We went to Spike Lee's studio. It was a whirlwind of memories."

The younger members of the Ward family remember that trip to Spike Lee's studio for two very different reasons. The first was that they got to see footage of the movie *Crooklyn* long before it came out, which in the pre-internet days was something that almost never happened. The second was that they got to witness their mom, a nice lady from a small Georgia town, ask Oscar-nominated and iconic Hollywood director Spike Lee why he had to use so much profanity in his movies. The best part, the kids say, is that it wasn't as if she was a mega *Do The Right Thing* fan. She had never actually seen one of his movies. She had just heard they were filled with swears.

"Well, he gave me an answer," Willard said. "He told me that was what people wanted to see. He said that if he did a documentary or something, people wouldn't go see it and he wouldn't get the audience he wanted. He said he was in show business and he had to give the people what they want. And that was fine with me. He was very nice. But those scenes from *Crooklyn* are still the only scenes of his movies I've ever seen, by the way."

In addition to sight seeing, they all ate. A ton.

They went to steakhouses and pizza places and then more steakhouses. Everyone wanted to take them out to dinner. It was a never-ending parade of invites.

"They gave everyone in the family these cards that we could use to eat anywhere in the hotel and at the Downtown Athletic Club, and the kids tried everything," she said. "I was yelling at them because they'd just take a bite of one thing and order something else, but it was all so overwhelming for them. For all of us."

"We got to experience New York City in a way very few people get to experience it," Leta Ward, Charlie's sister, said. "We usually lived vicariously through Charlie, but that week we did everything he did."

They went backstage at the *Today* show. They watched him tape the *Bob Hope Christmas Special.* And they even watched him turn down several offers to fly to Los Angeles to appear on Jay Leno's *The Tonight Show* because he was too busy.

When the New York City trip finally wound down, the celebration (and work) simply moved south. The Wednesday following the award ceremony was Charlie Ward Day in Tallahassee, with a fan event at Doak Campbell Stadium that attracted 25,000 people. On Thursday, Charlie was honored at a banquet as the Fellowship of Christian Athletes' Athlete of the Year for the state. He also took the final exam in his public speaking course, as if giving an acceptance speech for the most prestigious award in college sports in front of the New York media didn't automatically give him an A+ in the subject.

On Saturday, he officially graduated from Florida State, and then on Sunday he went home to Thomasville for a parade and ceremony at Thomas County Central High, where they retired his football and basketball jerseys. Thousands of people showed up.

In addition to the Heisman, he won the Johnny Unitas Golden Arm and Davey O'Brien quarterback awards, and was named the Walter Camp Player of the Year and the Toyota Leader of the Year. He won several other awards from the ACC and other media outlets and each of them came with their own media responsibilities. None of them, however, would get in the way of his preparation for the biggest game of his life: the National Championship game.

Chapter 22

National Champions

A scratchy throat. A slight fever. Random chills. Body aches. A throbbing head.

Charlie listed his symptoms to Florida State trainer Randy Oravetz like he was reading a NyQuil bottle. It was the Wednesday night before the national championship game in Miami, and the newly minted Heisman-winning quarterback was in rough shape. He'd spent the day with city and state politicians, posing for photographs, signing autographs and shaking hands. Somehow, the general public was able to do what few defensive linemen could: slow him down.

Everywhere he went in Miami, traveling FSU alumni and college football fans swarmed around him. Like it or not, the man who hated being the center of attention found himself at the epicenter of the sports universe. Earlier in the week, he commissioned William Floyd and FSU tight end Lonnie Johnson as his official media partners. While Charlie got endless accolades, and the receivers and running backs often shared in the glory during the season, he wanted to share the championship week attention with two of the unsung heroes of the Fast Break offense.

"In that offense we didn't get a whole lot of reps," Floyd said. "A lot of time we were used to set up plays or block or just hang in to give Charlie more time. He was always sharing the spotlight, and that week he was really cool. Wherever he went he made sure his fullback and his tight end were there and he showed us so much love."

As the week unfolded, the kind gesture led to a new responsibility that Floyd and Johnson had perfected on the field: bodyguard.

"He had so many people around him at all times," Floyd said. "We never saw anything like it."

Eventually, Miami officials realized they had a potential safety problem on their hands with how in-demand Charlie was at events, so they assigned police officer Brian Calloway to be his bodyguard. Charlie was thrilled.

"I really, really appreciate what he's done for me," he said that week when asked about Calloway. "At times, there just seems to be so many people around."

Per doctor's orders, Charlie tried to get a good night's sleep Wednesday evening, but when he showed up for practice on Thursday morning his problems had compounded. Now his shoulder felt tired and his elbow was sore. In addition to his litany of other woes, medically speaking, he had a dead arm.

"We worked pretty hard early in the week, throwing a lot, and we had been off a couple of days," Coach Richt said. "He just had a little bit of a dead arm, but a couple days off would help."

The coaching staff sent Ward home to relax.

"Preparation isn't our worry with Charlie," Bowden said. "The rest will probably do him as much good as anything. At this point, I have no reason to be concerned."

Following Charlie's departure from practice, Bowden ran his team through its normal routine, attended a luncheon and fulfilled the rest of his media obligations before retiring to his room to wind down. He hadn't heard from his quarterback all day, but figured he'd been napping and taking it easy.

He flipped through TV channels for a while and then settled into the 11 o'clock local news for its sports coverage. The Orlando Magic were in town playing the Miami Heat that night, and the newscaster talked over Shaq highlights before mentioning a few celebrities in the crowd. Madonna, at the height of her fame, had just moved to Miami and was at the game drawing the requisite amount of attention. Then the camera panned over from the Material Girl to the last person Bowden expected to see: Charlie Ward.

"I was surprised," Bowden said. "I didn't know until I saw him on television. I asked the doctor, 'You told him what he could do?' and he said he did. I guess that was the proper rest."

"I felt better after taking the afternoon off so I went," Charlie said. "After that night, it was time to get dialed in. We had two days until kickoff."

• • •

The hype surrounding the game in South Beach swelled on Friday like a fast-filling water balloon. It was part circus, part football game, part media frenzy. Ken Hambleton of the *Lincoln Journal* chronicled the week's events for his hometown Cornhusker fans by pointing out absurdity after absurdity.

"Omaha television newscasters are riding in Florida State Patrol cars," he wrote. "*USA Today* columnist Bryan Burwell said he would take a bath in a bowl of creamed corn if Nebraska beats Florida State… Television reporters are touring the year-old wreckage of hurricane Andrew… The *Miami Herald* newspaper has a staff of 10 writers working on the game until Saturday. Then, as many as 22 writers will be involved in covering the game, the halftime performance, the crowd and the neighborhood around the Orange Bowl stadium… More than 700 credentials, not including the 135 passes for NBC television, have been issued for the most-covered Orange Bowl ever."

Burwell tracked down Lisa Franson, director of communications for the Orange Bowl, and she was fairly blunt in her assessment of how the week had gone. "It's a mess, and it's getting crazier every day," she said. "This is more than two times as many press people as we had a year ago and more than ever before."

Reporters even interviewed Charlie Sr. about his son and the game. Senior being Senior, he happily gave sports journalists a history lesson on the Orange Bowl, including the key fact that he had played for a small conference football championship in that very stadium as a student at Florida A&M just a few decades prior.

"Look it up," he said, laughing. "Charlie Ward already played in a game like this. This is part two."

The contrast between the game he played in, which was a match-up of two historically black colleges, and this game was striking. He didn't mention that if not for segregation he likely would've played in a game of this magnitude, but he was no doubt thinking about it somewhere in his mind. Junior, in his own way, was giving the Ward family name the recognition on the gridiron it had long deserved.

The Las Vegas betting line for the game had Florida State at minus seventeen, making the undefeated Nebraska team an underdog by more than two touchdowns. Tom Osborne, Nebraska's legendary coach, was in a similar position to Bowden: He had been an elite coach in college football for several decades, having won 208 games in his twenty years at the school; and he also had yet to win a national title. Where the two coaches differed, however, was in their bowl results. Bowden's teams often fared very well in bowl games and Osborne's did not. Starting in 1987, the Cornhuskers lost the the Orange Bowl three times, the Fiesta Bowl twice, and the Citrus bowl once for a six-game bowl losing streak heading into their rematch with Florida State.

"I was always very fond of Tom Osborne," Bowden said in his book, *Called to Coach*. "One of us was finally going to win a championship ring, and the other coach would begin the quest for a title again the next season."

The night before the game was New Year's Eve. As was tradition, Bowden gathered his players at the hotel for a talk. His theme that night focused on having peace of mind as they went to bed that night. He wanted to make sure "his boys," as he often called them, wiped everything else from their minds and concentrated solely on Nebraska. He even quoted scripture, Philippians 4:13 from the New International Version: *I can do everything through him who gives me strength.*

Charlie absorbed Bowden's words and married them with his own thoughts on the game. He was aware that Florida State had come up short in the past. He heard all week that Heisman winners often didn't perform well in bowl games (2-10 since 1980). He ignored it all. "We had won all of our bowl games while I'd been at Florida State, and even more before I got there," he said. "Our pattern was that if we got in a bowl game we'd win it. That was my mindset, and all of our mindsets. If we prepared the same way we did in the other bowls then the results would be the same. We had just prepared for, and beat, Nebraska the year before, so even though we didn't expect them to come out the same exact way, we were ready. There was just a bigger piece of hardware on the line."

• • •

A cameraman walked alongside Charlie as he strode to the Orange Bowl field like he was Stone Cold Steve Austin strutting into the ring at Wrestlemania. He was wearing gold game pants with his white home jersey. An 'ACC 40th' [anniversary] patch was sewn into the left shoulder pad and the Orange Bowl logo was sewn into the right shoulder pad. He had elbow wraps on but his signature towel was not yet hanging from his belt. He clutched his helmet in his right hand, and with the first roar of the crowd at about the 5-yard line, he raised it above his head and pumped his arm up and down. The camera continued to follow him as he made his way to the Seminoles' sideline. His head was held high. His eyes looked straight ahead. He was stoic and serious and ready to go.

At about the 50-yard line, Osceola sprinted out of the tunnel with his burning spear atop Renegade, his Appaloosa horse. The Florida State mascots led the rest of the team from the tunnel in a whirlwind of white and garnet and gold. The South Florida crowd looked and sounded to be about 75% in favor of the Seminoles. Possibly more. When Nebraska ran out of the tunnel moments later, the boos mostly drowned out what little crowd support the Cornhuskers had.

Unless there were punting enthusiasts in the stands, neither team's fan base had much to cheer about in the first quarter. The teams combined for five punts and a missed field goal in the first fifteen minutes of play. Nebraska's plan on defense was to clog Charlie's passing lanes and keep him from breaking off big runs. If they could do that without having to pull a defensive player away from their main responsibility, they'd have a chance.

"The key is that you have to be aware of Charlie Ward at all times, " Nebraska Coach Tom Osborne said. "You can't put somebody on him as a shadow, because that will leave somebody open."

The other thing the Cornhuskers wanted to do was hit Charlie early, hard and often. "I'm going to try to hit him as hard as I can, but I really respect Charlie Ward," said Nebraska linebacker Trev Alberts. "I think it's obvious he has a good head on his shoulders and he handles pressure the right way."

"I'd say the best way to stop Charlie Ward," Nebraska defensive coordinator Charlie McBride said, "is to get him out of the game."

They didn't get him out of the game, but they did get him out of rhythm. Despite driving his team sixty-three yards to set up a Scott Bentley field goal for the first score of the game, Charlie was only able to lead the team to one more field goal before halftime. After two quarters, his team was down 7-6. This was only the second time all season the Seminoles were behind at the half. The other was against Notre Dame.

After the wild success of the Fast Break offense all season, the FSU coaching staff for some reason decided to put Charlie in the I-formation under center for much of the first half. It was a complete disaster. Charlie had no time, he was taking hits, and the offense had no flow. Alberts, the 6'4", 250-pound Butkus Award winner, was leading the effort to wreak havoc on the Seminoles' offense. The Nebraska defenders were collapsing pockets, covering receivers and filling passing lanes better than they had all year. Bobby Bowden was interviewed at halftime and admitted that their first-half game plan was a colossal mistake.

"We just didn't have any continuity offensively. It's a case of trying to get the I-formation running game going, but we can't protect Charlie from the 'I,'" he said. "I think we're gonna have to get in the darned shotgun and just go after it. For some reason we get sacked out of the 'I' and we're established better out of the gun. We're getting hurt. We thought maybe we could mix the run and the pass from the 'I' but they're killing us. We're going to have to go to the shotgun it looks like."

On the sideline, Charlie could be seen wincing ever so slightly as he made his warm-up throws. Despite the constant pressure and a few hard hits, he threw the ball well in the first half. Arm pain didn't seem to be the problem.

"I took some hits but I was fine," he said. "We just needed to find a way to move the ball down the field. Our defense was playing great. It was the offense's responsibility to play like we had all year."

The first play of the second half was a pass out of the shotgun that was knocked down. The second play was also a pass out of the gun to Vanover for eleven yards. The next play was a twenty-yard rocket that went right through Kevin Knox's hands. It was also out of the gun. The Seminoles' coaches were getting back to what had worked all year. Charlie then hit another eleven-yard pass to Frier on second and ten and followed that up with the pass of the game, a forty-yard streak to Knox that dropped right over his outside shoulder and into his hands before he went out of bounds at the 5-yard line.

Charlie handed the ball to Floyd on the next play and he plowed into the end zone. Or so everyone in Seminoles nation thought. The officials ruled the play dead at the 1-yard line.

"I couldn't believe it," Floyd said. "I said, 'Give it right back I'm getting in.'"

The Seminoles got in the huddle and called a handoff to Floyd, who promptly dove into the end zone. Just after he allegedly crossed the plane, he lost the ball. Nebraska thought it had a fumble and recovery in the end zone, and a reverse-angle replay added additional doubt about the ball crossing the goal line. But the touchdown ultimately stood and Bowden chose to go for two. The conversion failed and the Seminoles were up 12-7. They controlled the clock for most of the quarter, and despite a few more sacks on Charlie, he led them on another drive to a field goal. Nebraska's option quarterback, Tommie Frazier, had a drive of his own going when the third quarter expired.

Florida State was ahead 15-7 with fifteen minutes left.

On the first play of the fourth quarter, Frazier handed off to freshman Lawrence Phillips for a run right up the middle of the field and a twelve-yard touchdown. Osborne chose to go for the two-point conversion. Frazier faked the end-around and rolled left. He had a man open in the end zone but didn't see him and was knocked out at the 1-yard line by Ken Alexander.

Bobby Bowden's "boys" were up 15-13.

Florida State's next drive flopped. Then the FSU defense bent and bent and bent as Nebraska drove down the field. It looked as if the Seminoles were about to be broken for a touchdown when Richard Coes intercepted Frazier at the FSU 9-yard line.

"That felt like a game-saving interception," Ward said. "All we had to do was score and eat up some time."

They did neither, giving Nebraska the ball with 4:39 left in the game.

Starting on his own 20-yard line, Frazier reeled off chunks of yardage at a time, including a 32-yard run. The Cornhuskers weren't able to put the ball in the end zone, but they kicked a field goal to take a 16-15 lead with 1:16 left to play.

Seventy-six seconds was all that stood between Tom Osborne's first national championship and another tragic loss for Bowden.

Close to a half-dozen times that year, Charlie had taken the field in need of a scoring drive to keep the team's national championship dreams alive. The only time he failed was in the Notre Dame game. He was determined to not do so again. What very few fans realized was that Charlie had injured his left shoulder in the third quarter and it had been tightening up ever since, affecting his throwing motion. During the entirety of Nebraska's final drive he played catch on the sideline, trying to keep his body loose for one last chance at victory. When he took the field, the injury and the pain were the last things on his mind.

"It's my job to win the game," he said. "That's it."

Nebraska's kickoff went out of bounds, giving Charlie the ball on his own 35-yard line to start the drive. He had already thrown an Orange Bowl record twenty-two completions. It was times like these when his teammates were happy that Charlie was "Cooler than Kool-Aid," as Matt Frier liked to say.

On first down he had to throw the ball away but Alberts still took him to the ground. Again. Alberts had three sacks on the night and spent so much time in Charlie's passing pocket he could have been charged rent.

A quick pass on second down to Warrick Dunn brought up third and two with a minute left to play. After a missed throw, Floyd again came up huge with a two-yard run for the first down. On the next play Charlie hit

Dunn for a 21-yard pass, and they also benefited from a 15-yard late-hit penalty on the Huskers.

Charlie then threw incomplete to McCorvey in the middle of the field to stop the clock with forty-one seconds left. On the next play, Nebraska was called for pass interference in the end zone, advancing the Seminoles to the 5-yard line.

Of course the game had to come down to a field goal. As visions of *Wide Right I* and *Wide Right II* weaved their way through Bowden's brain, he sent Scott Bentley on the field for a 22-yard kick.

As it sailed through the uprights, the ghosts of kicks past sailed out of the stadium. FSU was ahead, 18-16. Bowden and the Florida State sideline went bonkers. Bowden pumped his fist and then immediately regained his senses, waving his celebrating players off the field to avoid a penalty—but he was too late. The team got a fifteen-yarder. He was furious, but all the Seminoles had to do was hold Nebraska for twenty-one more seconds and the title was theirs.

Nebraska took the kickoff to the 44-yard line.

The Huskers missed a big throw on first down, but on the next play Frazier hit Trumane Bell for twenty-nine yards over the middle as the clock wound down… 3… he ran… 2… defenders grabbed him… 1… they brought Bell down as time expired.

The Seminoles won! The Seminoles won! The Seminoles won!

The Florida State sideline erupted in joy. After Bowden received a Gatorade bath (with 10-K) he walked across the field to meet Tom Osborne with his team flooding the field around him to celebrate.

Only, as he shook Osborne's hand, the officials were trying desperately to tell him something: There was one second left on the clock.

Florida State hadn't won.

And not only that, Nebraska was in field goal range.

The officials scrambled to clear the field and give Nebraska the chance for their last kick. Bowden and his team could not believe it. This was a nightmare. It didn't feel like it could really be happening. *They made their comeback. They made their kick. The game was over!!!*

But the clock said otherwise. It was complete chaos.

It took a few minutes to get the situation squared away, but eventually the playing field was emptied and Nebraska's kicker, Byron Bennett, stood over a 45-yard attempt. Bowden, Ward, Dunn, Floyd... they all had been celebrating a moment ago and now were stuck on the sideline, watching to see if their dreams would turn into disaster once again. Bowden was actually toweling himself off after the 10-K shower and didn't even put his glasses on to watch the kick.

After so many wide rights killed them, a wide left saved them.

Bennett missed.

Florida State, Bobby Bowden and Charlie Ward were finally, finally, finally, national champions.

"It's the greatest feeling you can have in sports," Charlie said. "There aren't words. A team of individuals coming together and overcoming adversity to become champions is something beyond special. It's a hard-earned gift to each other."

Chapter 23

The NFL or the NBA?

After he'd received so many handoffs and swing passes and screen passes from Charlie, the least Warrick Dunn figured he could do to help his roommate get ready for hoops was play a little "21" in the basketball gym. *It can't be that much of a mismatch. It'll be fun. We'll get a good sweat.* Wrong. He didn't realize he was signing up to be a Washington General to Charlie's Globetrotter. He tried to dribble and the ball was stolen. He tried to shoot and it was blocked. He tried to stay in front of Charlie and he was crossed over, left guarding air.

Bill Vizzini was the Seminoles' basketball team manager at the time and he opened the gym for Charlie and Dunn. A few hours earlier, they were in attendance for Florida State's humiliating home loss to Tim Duncan and Wake Forest. Charlie was watching the game in street clothes, having just finished a week off to rest after football. He wasn't going to enter a basketball game for six days, but watching his team be embarrassed gave him the urge to ball. He had to play and he had to play soon. Toward the end of the 24-point beatdown, Charlie signaled to Vizzini and asked if he would open the gym for him.

"He said, 'Can you open the gym?'" Vizzini said. "He wanted to do some shooting. I told him I had to take care of some things, and said let's make it 6:15 pm. He was there when I got there."

Vizzini stuck around to watch Charlie and Dunn and another football player shoot around and then finally play 21.

"He literally wore Warrick Dunn into the ground," Vizzini said. "He won every game. He could do whatever he wanted. If he wanted to steal the ball from the other guys, he'd do it. If he wanted to guard them as they're moving down the lane, he'd let them drive. He is ready to play. He wants to get back on the court."

In his absence, the basketball team had gotten off to an average start. They were 7-4 but had lost all three of their ACC games. To be fair, the team was missing more than just Charlie. Two of their best players from the Elite Eight run a year earlier were now in the NBA—Sam Cassell was on the Houston Rockets and Doug Edwards was an Atlanta Hawk. That meant Bobby Sura and Chuck Graham were being asked to replace Cassell and Edwards' combined thirty-seven points per game. Charlie's return wasn't going to help the offensive firepower, but it was much needed in almost every other area.

"We've had a horrible assist-turnover ratio, and we've just made bad decisions with the basketball. It's one of the major things Charlie will assist us with on this team," Coach Kennedy said before Charlie's return. "He won't have his full basketball timing, but by Sunday he'll have his basketball conditioning. He never loses his hand-eye coordination, and he's got quickness. I think he'll be 100% (except for) his timing."

Kennedy was right.

Charlie played thirty-four minutes in his first game back, a loss to NC State. He didn't shoot well from the floor, but he had five steals to put him just five short of Florida State's career record. He played thirty-eight minutes in the team's next game, a win against Clemson, but a long winning streak didn't follow. There were too many new faces, too much erratic play.

"When you don't do things consistently, you're kind of fishing for anything that works," Kennedy said.

Nothing worked. The team won a few, then lost a few, and on and on. There were no signature wins, only frustrating losses. Not even Charlie's senior leadership, defensive pressure and steady hand could help. They simply couldn't overcome their talent deficit and the ACC powerhouses they had to face in the middle of their season (Duke and North Carolina were both in and out of the top five in the AP poll and Georgia Tech was in the top 25 for much of the year).

Florida State hovered around .500 for most of February before dropping three in a row to Florida, Duke and North Carolina—teams that were all ranked in the top ten. A few weeks later, the Tar Heels blasted the Seminoles by fourteen in the first round of the ACC tournament to put an end to a maddening season. They were 1-7 against top 25 teams, played terribly on the road and finished the season 13-14—certainly not the Final Four run to back up a national championship that Charlie would have liked. He left the team as its career leader in steals with 236, was the record holder for most steals in one game with nine, and was fifth all-time in assists with 396. His legacy with the program, and with his coach, was set in stone.

"I'm not saying this to slight any of the other guys," Coach Kennedy said. "And I've had twenty-five guys play in the NBA and fifty overseas… But Charlie was the finest person and finest student athlete that I ever had the honor to coach. I really, really mean that."

• • •

I think Charlie Ward should play pro football because he was really good for Florida State. I don't know how good he is with basketball, but he needs to stick with football, I think he'll have a better career —Joshua Krieg, Pensacola

I think Charlie Ward should play in the NFL because he would be much better in the NFL. —Clayton Barnes, Molino

Charlie Ward is a much better NFL player, so he should play in the NFL. —John Orvis, Pensacola

I think Charlie should play in both sports because he's a great athlete in both sports. —Patrick Elebash, Pensacola

I think Charlie Ward should play in the NFL because he has the ability to throw the ball, he's a good quarterback, and basketball is just not his sport. —Amos Watts, Pensacola.

These responses were from a FAN LINE survey conducted by the *Pensacola News Journal* and published on Sunday, April 24, the day of the 1994 NFL Draft. Other papers around the country ran similar surveys, including Florida State's home paper, the *Tallahassee Democrat,* which ran a contest titled, "I Think Charlie Ward Should…," in which readers wrote in with what they thought Charlie should do regarding his decision to play in the NFL or NBA. More than 100 people responded. The answers were split fairly even between basketball and football, but many football readers said he should go to the Canadian Football League.

Everyone had an opinion, from second-grade students at Kate Sullivan Elementary School outside of Tallahassee—a majority of whom thought Charlie should play in the NBA—to his head football coach Bobby Bowden, who went on the record in the *Tallahassee Democrat* saying, "If I were giving advice, everything being equal, I'd say go basketball," Bowden said. "The money, and simply because of the physical nature of football, the pounding, the knees.

The *Orlando Sentinel* took the inquiries a step further, asking Coach Kennedy to write a special column in the paper making the case for Charlie to play in the NBA, and asking Coach Richt to write a column discussing why he should play football. They're worth reading in full:

Ward Can Play in the NBA, With Full Commitment
By Pat Kennedy – Special to the *Sentinel*

> I would like to think, and I could be wrong in my assessment, that Charlie is going to be more secure and have more impact as a professional athlete than everyone is giving him a chance to.
>
> I hear all the NFL stuff, about this and that, what he can and can't do.
>
> There is no doubt that he can become a classic, back-up point guard to start out his career in the NBA. With a 12-month-a-year commitment to basketball, he could really play in that league.
>
> Take the Orlando Magic. You've got Anfernee Hardaway, whom they're grooming, I guess, as a point guard. He's on his way. You've got Shaquille, the big franchise. I guess they're trying to trade for Horace Grant, so you put Charlie in there with Shaquille and Grant and Nick Anderson, can you imagine that? I think he would fit in perfectly in getting those guys the ball when Hardaway needs to come out for a rest or foul trouble.
>
> I think there have got to be general managers out there who can see that Charlie could fill that void for several teams in the league. The X-factor is the time. If Charlie had 12 months a year dedicated to basketball, he could be out of this world. I keep thinking back to the

game against North Carolina in 1992 when we beat Carolina in our first game in the Atlantic Coast Conference. Charlie played great and after the game Dean Smith grabbed him and said, "I really love the way you play. Play basketball."

That was the same year that Jim Valvano came and saw us play, and after a game here, he grabbed Charlie and said, "Hey, stick to basketball. You'll be great."

Those are two people who know the game telling a young man what they see. Now, obviously, anything could happen, but what does that say about Charlie's basketball skills?

Well, since then, he has played football most of the time. So there's that question. As limited exposure as he has had to basketball the last two years—I don't know how good he can be.

The liability right now is you don't know. People will talk about shooting the ball and size and all that stuff, but I wouldn't question too much about him. I would think if you have a need, you could rely on him. I think he can easily make a living in that league.

Accuracy, Mobility Keys to Ward's Game
By Mark Richt – Special to the *Sentinel*

To start off, I think Charlie Ward can play in the NFL.

The NFL is looking for guys who are accurate, and Charlie is a very accurate passer.

They're looking for guys who have a quick release, and Charlie has a quick release.

They want someone with a lot of arm strength, and his arm strength is more than adequate. He may not have a John Elway arm, but his arm strength is underrated. How many times do you really launch it? And how far does a take-off route travel—maybe 55 yards? Not many balls travel farther than that, so his arm strength is fine.

I think he's one of the better decision makers I've ever had. In that league, you have to make a quick decision a lot of times, quicker than in college, and he's very capable of doing that.

He understands fronts and coverages. He knows how to handle the blitz. His first year as a starter here he had trouble throwing the ball where he shouldn't at times, but even when he had all those intercep-

> tions, I think a lot of it was because of adrenaline. Once he settled in he didn't have that problem any more.
>
> At first, he didn't do a great job protecting the ball. I think he learned a great deal about how important it is to protect the ball in football. In basketball if he turned it over, he just stole it right back.
>
> The last thing I mention is his mobility, and I mention that last because I think even without mobility he would still be one of the better passers and decision-makers I've ever had. I rate that mobility as a bonus more than something he has to be successful.
>
> Casey Weldon had good mobility, but not like Charlie did. Casey didn't cross the line a whole lot. Peter Tom Willis never crossed the line of scrimmage, but he did other things well.
>
> For some reason—whatever it was—Charlie was the most dominating player in college football last year, maybe the most dominating that college football has seen in a while. He didn't just go out there and play really good, he dominated a lot of ball games.
>
> If it ever got to the end of a ballgame and something good had to happen, he made it happen. Some guys faint in that situation. We may not have won every game, but we were in position to win or tie every game at the end that he was in.
>
> Charlie, he's a winner. And you're not out of ballgames if he's in there at the end and you have time to score.

Lost in all of the "NBA or NFL" debate was the staggering uniqueness of an individual athlete gifted enough to be in the position to legitimately play those two sports professionally. As recently as John Elway and Bo Jackson and Deion Sanders, the American sports landscape had seen a handful of athletes with a high enough skill level to choose between the NFL and Major League Baseball—or actually play each.*

But pro football or pro basketball? This was uncharted territory. And it wasn't as if Charlie was a 6'8", 260-pound tight end/power forward who used his natural physicality to get an edge in both sports. He wasn't the Incredible Hulk. He was a 6', 180-pound quarterback and point guard, the two most important positions on each team. Every play ran through him.

Super Bowl-winning coach Tony Dungy played basketball and football at the University of Minnesota, and that experience gave him a unique perspective on Charlie. He was also the defensive coordinator for the Minnesota Vikings under Dennis Green in 1994.

"Think about the amount of time you need to put in to succeed not only in those sports at that high level, but in those positions in particular," he said. "To be able to lead your team to a bowl game win one week and then play in the ACC against Duke and UNC and win and get to an Elite Eight a few months later is phenomenal. The mental approach and time commitment needed to excel at either position is hard enough. But to be quarterback all season, then miss the basketball off-season and step in to play point guard and be a leader on the team, that is truly special."

Dungy was so impressed with Ward that he walked into Coach Green's office during their draft planning and expressed how high he was on Charlie. Green had a reputation for being a quarterback guru, and even though Dungy was on the defensive side of the ball he felt he needed to make the case for Charlie from his standpoint.

"At the time, Steve Young had just begun playing for Bill Walsh and they were ahead of the curve," Dungy said. "Walsh was of the mind that you tailor an offense around the talents that you have, so in Charlie's case I was thinking about the kind of offense you could run with his athletic ability and decision making. He had that cool personality and great presence and charisma that Joe Montana had. I knew the headaches he could cause a defense in the NFL."

So Dungy's pitch to Green was that Charlie might be a combination of the best traits of Joe Montana and Steve Young. Not bad.

"He could have been Russell Wilson twenty years before Russell Wilson," Dungy said recently.

Coach Green agreed completely about Charlie's talent level and with Dungy's assessment, but he was in the same predicament as every other NFL head coach and front office executive. Nobody knew which sport Charlie was going to play—and draft picks were far too valuable to use on someone who might commit to a different sport a few months later. It was an issue that Charlie was happy to let sort itself out.

"I want to keep my options open to play either sport," Charlie said. "I'll work out for everyone in both sports and it's up to the teams if they want to draft me. I'll pursue whatever is the best opportunity after both drafts."

In truth, by saying he was keeping his options open he was actually limiting them. In the weeks leading up to the draft, NFL teams who were questioned about Charlie consistently said two things: They raved about his leadership and work ethic and talent, and then simultaneously stated they needed a commitment to playing football to draft him.

"The thought was that if we didn't draft him very high he might go play in the NBA, and ultimately, that risk was the reason Dennis decided not to draft him," Dungy said. "I knew in my heart what Charlie could do in an NFL uniform, but we couldn't afford to lose a draft pick if he chose basketball."

To make matters more complicated for NFL teams, Charlie was lighting up his workouts both on the court and on the field. About three weeks after his college basketball season ended, he was named Most Valuable Player of the National Association of Basketball Coach's All-Star game at the Final Four, then impressed upward of seventy NFL representatives at his pro day, quickly and accurately working through a passing route tree to former teammates Kevin Knox, Matt Frier, Lonnie Johnson and Sean Jackson. He threw in the pocket and on the run and from under center and shotgun.

"My impression is he had a good workout," Tampa Bay Buccaneers head coach Sam Wyche said. "I would liked to have seen him run [40-yard dashes] and throw into the wind some, but you can tell he's a very special athlete."

Charlie was happy with his performance as well.

"I felt great about that workout, and the NFL or NBA will make my decision for me," he said. "They're the ones doing the drafting."

And yet, "they" could not get past his indecision.

The Bucs in particular were sensitive to Charlie's situation. In 1986 they drafted Heisman Trophy winner Bo Jackson with the number one overall pick, only to watch Jackson play baseball with the Kansas City Royals. Jackson later signed on to play football for the Los Angeles Raiders.

Other teams did not have direct experience with being spurned by a draft pick, but they were equally wary.

"The football or basketball decision is an important item," Green Bay Packers General Manager Ron Wolfe said after watching Charlie work out. "We have to know what that's going to be. He has had ample opportunity to explore it, and he has to reach his decision before teams draft."

"Basketball is the concern," said James Harris, a former NFL quarterback and scout for the New York Jets. "There's no question he has the talent to play. He really has special skills in awareness and peripheral vision. He throws the ball well in the pocket and makes plays in tough situations."

And no draft evaluation would be complete without Mel Kiper Jr. weighing in.

"There's really no way to project which round he's going to go," Kiper said. "It would be ridiculous for me to say 'third round' if he has not said publicly which sport he's going to play. As far as the NFL is concerned, he's got a lot to do."

Despite rumored interest from teams like Green Bay, Cincinnati, Minnesota and Kansas City, Kiper believed that there were really only two teams that made sense, and they both ran run-and-shoot offenses.

"He's only suited for Houston and Atlanta," he said. "He's got to learn to take the snap from center, take a five- to seven-step drop, read a defense and accurately deliver the football. If he focused on football, he could go as high as the third round."

At that point, however, the decision could easily come down to a financial one. While the average first-round pick made roughly $1 million and second-rounders made $400,000, the average third-rounder salary in the NFL Draft in 1994 was about $260,000. It dropped to $135,000 in the sixth round.

Compare those to the four-year, $750,000 per year contract a late first-round NBA pick would earn and the money would likely make Charlie's decision easy. Neither of these scenarios took into account the interest that was being expressed by the Winnipeg Blue Bombers, who had Charlie's rights in the Canadian Football League. There were rumors of a $2 million total package being put together by the Bombers. And there was also the added bonus that the season ran from July to November, leaving open the possibility for Charlie to play both sports at the professional level.

On the NBA side, Charlie's performance at the NABC All-Star Game, at individual practices and at the Nike Desert Classic had turned a few doubters into believers.

"He can play in the NBA," Marty Blake, the NBA director of college scouting said. "I remember when Magic (Johnson) came out he couldn't even make a layup. I don't worry about his scoring."

• • •

Two days after leaving Phoenix at the close of the Nike Desert Classic at America West Arena, Ward sat in his parents' house surrounded by family and close friends. He invited a select group of people over on Sunday, April 24 to celebrate a very special day: his parents' 30th wedding anniversary.

"It was our day first," Charlie Sr. said, laughing. "The draft just happened to be scheduled for the same day."

No national media or television cameras or local journalists were included in the party, so there would be no cutaways to the Ward House during the ceremony in New York City.

"We put the draft on the television," Charlie said. "But I wasn't going to sit down and go crazy over every pick."

Good thing.

The Washington Redskins took Heath Shuler with the third overall pick, and then the Bucs took Trent Dilfer with the sixth overall pick. The first round closed with no other quarterbacks selected, and no team selected a quarterback in the second round. The draft continued the following day, and so did the trend of teams ignoring Charlie. No quarterbacks were selected in the third round, but in the fourth, the Falcons took Perry Klein of C.W. Post and the Saints picked Doug Nussmeier from Idaho. Jim Miller from Michigan State was picked in the sixth round by the Steelers; then the Patriots selected Jay Walker with the 198th overall pick; the Chiefs took Steve Matthews with the 199th overall pick; and the Jets took Glenn Foley with the 208th overall pick.

And that was it.

The 1994 NFL Draft concluded with Charlie Ward Jr., the reigning

Heisman Trophy winner and national champion, going undrafted. Though NFL teams may have felt justified in selecting the likes of Doug Nussmeier and Perry Klein over Charlie, his college buddy William Floyd summed up most people's feelings the best:

"How does the Heisman trophy winner not get drafted?!" William Floyd wondered. Others, like Warren Moon, believed there was a racial component and bias against black quarterbacks in the NFL. Warrick Dunn believed that might have played a part in teams passing on him as well. Deion Sanders also came to Charlie's defense.

"He should have definitely been a first-rounder," Sanders said. "But that's what happens when you're black and have a lot of ability at the quarterback position. He didn't just win the Heisman trophy. He won quarterback awards. How can you not draft somebody like that? It's ridiculous. It's a race thing, and it's a position thing."

Following the draft, however, the teams that liked Charlie all stated that it was his indecision about whether or not he would play football that kept them away.

"If he said football was what he'd have wanted to do, he'd have been drafted in the first two rounds," Dennis Green said. "He was a great college player."

"It's a situation he has presented himself," Wolf said. "No one is really sure how important football is to him."

"I would have picked Charlie in a minute if he had just made up his mind," John Becker, director of player personnel for the Rams said. "I loved his mobility and athleticism. What killed him was his inability to make a decision."

Charlie took the news in stride. He believed he had done everything he could to be drafted by an NFL team and that his not being selected was just part of his options being narrowed.

"The Lord is going to guide me in the right direction. The NFL has given me the first step to see what my options are. Now the NBA draft is coming up and I have the chance to prove myself in that sport," he said.

By this time, the notion of playing two sports professionally was gone.

He was going to pick one sport and focus on that sport as his career. It was time to simplify things a bit.

• • •

Sam Cassell was never one to mince words. By June of 1994 he was playing in his second NBA Finals in only his second season with the Houston Rockets, and he was getting tired of so-called NBA experts questioning Charlie Ward's ability to play at the next level. In the midst of a heated NBA Finals against the New York Knicks, he took a moment to address the issue with any reporter within earshot.

"He's going to play in this league," Cassell said. "There are questions, but there were questions about me too. He'll be a leader, like Maurice Cheeks used to be. He'll know who to get the ball to and in which situations. That's what he does best."

In many ways, the two months following Charlie's NFL Draft snub were turning out exactly as coaches Kennedy, Smith and Valvano believed they would if Charlie committed himself to basketball. The more he played, the more he impressed, both as an athlete and as a point guard.

At the Phoenix Desert Classic pre-draft camp, he had the highest vertical leap of any player in attendance. And the leadership ability he'd always displayed on the football field wowed NBA executives who were watching him in person for the first time. Even hardened NBA front office vets like the Indiana Pacers' Donnie Walsh took notice, saying, "He has a presence about him you just can't teach."

Unlike with the NFL draft where executives and coaches were asking if Charlie would commit to football, the question their NBA counterparts were asking was, "Now that he's committed to basketball, how good can he be?"

In interviews, Charlie was comparing himself to Phoenix Suns star Kevin Johnson, who was a sub off the bench before becoming a scoring machine and an all-star point guard. Without the burden and/or pressure of gearing back up for football after basketball, Charlie was seeing the results of focusing on just one discipline—and his confidence was soaring.

"Once you practice, you can do whatever you want," he said. "You can do anything. I'm a person who loves challenges. Whatever I put my mind to do, I can do."

In early June, Charlie joined the Jacksonville Hooters of the United States Basketball League to get in some reps against stiffer competition. He led the team to three wins in four games and put up numbers that scouts couldn't ignore, including seventeen points, nine assists and five steals a game, nearly doubling all of his game averages from his time at Florida State.

After his stint with Jacksonville, he played on a college all-star team in Europe for a short trip and then participated in the pre-draft camp in Chicago, where he continued his upward rise with scouts. With each game, he seemed to excel in an area scouts had labeled as a weakness, as if he was checking off boxes one by one.

Can't shoot outside? Here's a string of three-pointers in a row.

Can't guard one-on-one? Check out this dazzling foot speed.

Has an inconsistent jump shot? Watch this knock-down jumper on a fast break.

"He's raised the attention level of a lot of people here, more so than any other player," an NBA insider said during the Chicago camp. "The big question mark with a lot of people was his outside shooting, but he's shooting it a lot better now."

Charlie was also being helped by something beyond his control: a shallow pool of point guards available in the draft. Jason Kidd was the clear-cut number one, but after that there was a steady drop-off that led Seattle Supersonics scout Yvan Kelly to say that Charlie could be the third-best point guard in the draft.

Slowly but surely, other NBA teams were coming to that conclusion as well. In the two weeks leading up the June 29 NBA Draft, he worked out for six teams: The Orlando Magic (27th and 31st picks), the Denver Nuggets (13th pick), the Chicago Bulls (21st pick), the San Antonio Spurs (22nd pick), the New York Knicks (24th and 26th picks) and the Atlanta Hawks (25th pick).

In one of his final workouts for the Orlando Magic, he was pitted one-on-one against all-star Anfernee Hardaway. Hardaway was an elite NBA point guard who towered over Charlie by eight inches, was a much purer shooter and had an incredible wing span. Still, Charlie impressed.

"I knew he was good, but I didn't know he was this good," Hardaway said after they played.

"Those of us who were there looking for leadership and intelligence, poise and potential, Charlie has that nice little portfolio," John Gabriel, the Magic's vice president of basketball operations, said.

Most mock drafts had Charlie going to either the Knicks or the Orlando Magic in the first round. The Magic made sense as, in addition to their private workouts, they had probably seen more of Charlie in person than any other team in the draft because of their proximity to Tallahassee. Their only concern was that Charlie might not last long enough for them to draft him.

Amazingly, after having played only fifteen games of college basketball in the past year, it was a valid concern.

On the night of the draft, things went about as expected. Glenn Robinson went number one overall to the Milwaukee Bucks, followed by Jason Kidd to the Dallas Mavericks and Grant Hill to the Detroit Pistons. The next point guard to go was Khalid Reeves out of Arizona, who was taken by the Miami Heat. B.J. Tyler, a point guard out of Texas, was picked 20th overall by the 76ers, and then, with the 26th pick in the first round of the 1994 NBA Draft, the New York Knicks selected Charlie Ward.

"We couldn't pass on his leadership skills. He is a natural floor leader, whose passing abilities will make his teammates better," the Knicks' statement read.

"It's funny, but only the Lord has a series of events like this," Ward said during his introductory press conference at the Doral Tuscany Hotel in Manhattan. "I'm going to accept it and adjust to all the different lifestyles. I'm just very happy to be here."

**Charlie was actually drafted by the New York Yankees in the 18th round of the 1994 Major League Baseball draft as well, even though he hadn't played baseball since college. The Milwaukee Brewers had drafted him in the 59th round in 1993. As far as sports trivia questions go, this is a good one: "Which of the three major professional sports did Heisman Trophy-winning quarterback Charlie Ward NOT get drafted in?" Answer: football.*

Chapter 24

Welcome to New York

Six-foot eight-inch, two hundred and forty-pound Charles Oakley snorted like a bull trying to bust out of his chute. Six-foot seven-inch, two hundred and fifty-pound Anthony Mason flexed and grinned and dug in his high tops. The industrial lights high on the gym ceiling reflected off the sweat and muscles and jerseys of Mason, Oakley and another fifteen hundred pounds of angry Knicks lined up for their favorite rookie initiation ritual: the gauntlet.

On one side stood 7' all-star Patrick Ewing with 6'10" 250-pound back-up center Herb Williams. On the other stood Charles Smith and Doc Rivers and Anthony Bonner.

Four months earlier, the 1993-94 New York Knicks lost a soul-crushing game seven in the NBA Finals to Hakeem Olajuwon, Kenny Smith, Sam Cassell and the Houston Rockets. It was their 25th game of that post-season, at the time an NBA record.

After beating the New Jersey Nets in four games in the first round, it took them seven games to get past the Chicago Bulls (without Michael Jordan, who was playing baseball) and another seven games to fight their way through Reggie Miller and the Indiana Pacers in the Eastern Conference Finals. In that series, they jumped out to a 2-0 lead, only to lose the next three games and put themselves in must-win contests the rest of the way. The Knicks then won two in a row to earn the right to face the Houston Rockets.

The NBA Finals was a defensive battle that reflected Knicks Coach Pat Riley's bruising style of mid-1990s basketball, for which his philosophy seemed to be 'you'll get to 90 points over our dead bodies.' It was excruciating to play in, and at times, even more excruciating to watch—especially for Knicks fans. New York was up in the series 3-2 as it headed to Houston for the final two games. They were one win away from bringing the first basketball championship to New York City since the 1973 team with Walt Frazier and Earl "the Pearl" Monroe. They lost game six, 86-84, and then dropped game seven, 90-84.

With most of their team back, healthy and angry, the Knicks viewed the 1994-95 season as a revenge tour, with their eyes dead set on another Finals appearance. Pat Riley in particular, and the veterans in general, were not to be trifled with. They had no time to waste easing rookies into their system, even if one of them won the Heisman Trophy eight months earlier. Their other rookie, taken two spots ahead of Charlie in the first round, was Monty Williams, a 6'8" small forward out of Notre Dame. The veterans didn't have patience for him either. They determined that it was going to be trial by fire for the young bucks, and the gauntlet was the furnace. Jeff Van Gundy, Riley's assistant coach at the time, remembers what happened after that vividly.

"Those veterans were tough and not impressed by much, but I'll never forget that day," Van Gundy said. "Today you'd be fired, and rightfully so, but Coach Riley liked the gauntlet, which was one step below hazing. Once the veterans were lined up, the rookies were supposed to run through and the vets could hit them with forearms and stuff. Well, Monty was big and strong and went through first. He was getting banged around like a ping-pong ball. I felt bad for him. Now I'm looking at Charlie, who's six-foot, maybe one hundred and eighty pounds, and I'm wondering if he's going to make it through. But he did this high knees thing and you saw just incredible balance. The guys were hitting him but he didn't even feel it. He ran through and his facial expression never changed. He was like, *'Is that it? That's all you got?'* They respected him right away after that. He had a physical toughness from football you could not deny. He had great humility and you had to respect what he accomplished off the court."

In the months leading up to the gauntlet and the official start of camp, Charlie and Williams played in an endless parade of summer league and pick-up games. Monty was getting his professional sea legs under him and

Charlie was trying to establish a baseline of NBA-level ability that he could build off. He was, game-wise, several seasons behind his counterparts.

"It's going to take Charlie some time," Knicks vice president and general manager Ernie Grunfeld said. "We will be patient with him. I think he realizes that he's going to need some time because he is behind the other first-round picks. He hasn't put as much time into it as they have."

Charlie was aware of this, and whenever he was asked about his overall basketball experience compared to other rookies, he owned it. "My job is to come in, practice hard and do what the coaches want," he said. "Being patient is something a lot of players miss. When the opportunity happens, you have to be ready to step in and perform."

In addition to a lack of high-quality hoops reps, Charlie was in a logjam of Knicks point guards battling for a roster spot, including Greg Anthony, Derek Harper, Doc Rivers and Corey Gaines, all of whom were playing behind John Starks. Drafting Charlie was a vote of confidence, to be sure, but it guaranteed him nothing.

His journey toward becoming a full-time member of the Knicks officially began on July 11, 1994 with a series of two-a-day practice sessions with Monty Williams, run by Van Gundy. The workouts were designed to push, prod and pressure cook the rookies to prepare them for practices in Pat Riley's world, should they make the team. They were built around the Doral Arrowwood New York Summer League, which played its games at the Westchester County Center in White Plains, New York.

"It's been tough," Williams said. "They expect perfection, 110 percent each way."

Charlie replied to how difficult the practices had been with an answer that was short for even him. "Brutal," was all he'd say.

In his first summer league game Charlie scored eleven points in a win against the Philadelphia 76ers' equally young and inexperienced team. New York sports writers were constantly trying to get him to comment on the status of the other guards, or whom he thought he would beat out for a roster spot, but he never bit.

"The only thing I can do is come in and do the things I'm capable of doing: running the team, breaking down defenses, playing good defense," he said after his first game. "My job is to learn the system and play hard. That's not my job to sit down and think what they're going to do with the other guards."

Coach Van Gundy was tasked with bringing Charlie up to speed and he knew he had a major reconstruction project on his hands. "His basketball skills at that time lagged behind," Van Gundy said. "He couldn't handle with his left very well or finish left well. As a coach, you knew a lot of this was the fact that football had been his primary sport and basketball was his hobby. But you knew he had this competitive instinct. As a quarterback he had a huge advantage because of how much content he could absorb. Tom Thibodeau always said this about Charlie: 'He may be outplayed, but never outcompeted.'"

That mentality served Charlie well in the early days of the summer league when he had to rely on instincts and raw talent more than reps and fine-tuning. One night, he'd be off and shoot 1-for-8 from the floor like he did against the Celtics; another night, he'd hit a game-winning three-pointer like he did against the Milwaukee Bucks.

And amazingly, when the summer league wrapped, Charlie managed to outshine players who had done nothing but play basketball since they were eighteen years old by winning the Most Valuable Player award, averaging 12.8 points and 6.8 assists for the Knicks.

The harder he worked, the better he got, and the more potential Van Gundy and the coaching staff saw. His efforts paid off on September 28, when the Knicks offered him a five-year, $4.6 million contract just ahead of the official start of training camp. It was the culmination of a four-month basketball frenzy.

"I played everywhere," Charlie said. "I've been working on my whole game, not just one individual thing. I want to be able to knock down the open jump shots, and I've tried to improve that part of my game this summer. In my position, I'm just very happy to be on the team."

His professional debut under contract came in a pre-season game a few weeks later in Charleston, South Carolina against the 76ers. His first points came on a reverse layup, and though he started off slow he finished with ten points and five assists.

"I feel good," he said after the game. "To get the first one out for a rookie is satisfying. Also, to go out and do well."

His new head coach, Pat Riley, agreed.

"With what we're doing in balancing the floor and pushing the ball, he's got the ability to break defenses down," Riley said.

The compliment was a rare one from Riley, who Charlie took a good amount of time getting used to. During his time in Tallahassee, he had become accustomed to the informal, down-home, baseball hat-wearing southern charm of Bobby Bowden. Riley, with his suits and slick hair and mind games, was an acquired taste for the young point guard.

"I remember as a rookie he gave me a leadership book that he wanted me to read, and I thought to myself, *I'm already a leader, I don't have to read this book,*" Charlie said. "I was young and I didn't realize what it takes to keep men motivated, and that philosophy played a role. He told stories to fire guys up and he was just tough-minded. I understood after the fact what he was trying to do."

Still, in the moment, Charlie struggled. He was working harder than he ever had, but when the season started he barely played. Even his fellow rookie, Monty Williams, saw some action as the calendar turned to December and then to January 1995. During his rookie campaign, when the Knicks went 55-27, Charlie played in only ten games for a couple minutes per outing. Then, as if to remind him of how little the team needed him at the moment, he was left off the 1995 Knicks playoffs roster. There would be no run to the Finals that year, as the Knicks lost to the Pacers in the Eastern Conference Semi-Finals.

Unlike his pal Sam Cassell, he wouldn't wrap up his rookie year with a championship ring. Instead, he'd do so with a slightly more important one: a wedding ring.

• • •

Aside from the on-court adjustments Charlie had to make in becoming a member of the Knicks, he also had to uproot, rearrange and turn upside down his entire personal life. Thomasville and Tallahassee were geographically, demographically—and almost any other *-aphically* you can think of—polar opposites. All the fish-out-of-water, country-boy-in-a-big-city clichés that applied to young New York athletes as far back as Mickey Mantle were in play. If the pace of life in Thomasville was slow as molasses, New York City was a Class VI rapid that never stopped.

Fortunately for Charlie, his faith, his family foundation and his disposition steeled him against many of the distractions that other young athletes who found themselves rich and living in the Big Apple couldn't resist. In addition, he wasn't single. His relationship with Tonja had grown in the past year and Charlie was ready to commit to her for the long haul. In fact, once he got to New York, he couldn't wait.

Tonja was busy studying and working at a law firm so she wasn't able to visit him in New York until it was close to Christmas. When she finally went, he had a speech prepared and a rose to give her as part of his proposal. As he had a hundred times on the football field, he composed himself and began to deliver a game-winning performance, expressing his love and desire to spend the rest of his life with her. Somewhere in the middle of his speech, the ring, which was hidden in the rose, fell out, and Mr. Ice Cold, Mr. Never Rattled, Mr. Even Keel, was flummoxed. He stammered for a moment before gathering himself and popping the question.

"This was a time where Mr. Cool and his cool points went away for a little while," Tonja said, laughing. "He got it together though."

After the proposal, Charlie took Tonja to the team Christmas party at Pat Riley's house, where the Knicks were waiting to congratulate the couple. They announced that they'd be getting married in the summer of 1995, and then Tonja began planning for her move to New York City.

"It was a big adjustment for me," she said. "My dad was a big sports fan so I grew up a sports fan, and everywhere you'd go you'd be star gazing. All of a sudden, Patrick Ewing is your fiancé's co-worker. Pat Riley is his boss. As an organization, the Knicks did such a great job of getting the families included in the culture. Herb Williams' wife led an initiative for wives and fiancées of the players to get to know each other and have a support group. It was a very welcoming organization and made my transition there much easier."

"That was really important to me, obviously," Charlie said. "I wanted her to be comfortable. It also helped that Monty and I had become good friends and I knew Tonja would get along well with his wife, which she did."

An added element to the move was Tonja's budding law career. Once she was engaged to Charlie, she had to decide between accepting a job offer at a prestigious law firm in Tallahassee (which would mean they'd have a long-distance marriage) or moving to a highly competitive job market in New York City. Ultimately, she chose to be near Charlie in the Big Apple, but this would be the first of many sacrifices she'd make to support and prioritize the family and her future-husband's career.

"I was just completing my final year of law school so I shifted my plans to take the bar in New York that summer," she said. "I passed the bar in July and we got married a month or so later."

Just like that, two kids born in Georgia became a power couple in the biggest city in the United States.

Chapter 25

The Back-Up

It was the fax heard 'round the sports world. On July 16, 1995, Pat Riley left a $3 million per year offer on the table and abruptly quit his job, informing the New York Knicks of this by sending a fax. In the days before Twitter and Facebook and *The Player's Tribune,* quitting by fax was akin to informing your employer via a LinkedIn post. Riley said he wanted more control over decision-making and personnel and all the other things coaches say when they really just have a better offer somewhere else.

In any event, Riley, the biggest obstacle to playing time for Charlie during the 1994-95 season, was out. The Knicks were coming off their most successful four-year stretch in decades with a strong, albeit aging, team mostly in tact. Patrick Ewing, Charles Oakley, John Starks, Derek Harper, Charles Smith and Herb Williams were all over thirty years old. Anthony Mason was twenty-nine. Charlie, Monty Williams and twenty-five-year-old Hubert Davis were the only truly young guys on the team. The Knicks' front office knew they needed to replace Riley with a seasoned coach who had a résumé the elder players would respect. After interviewing several candidates, they signed fifty-five-year-old Don Nelson, who recently resigned after six seasons with the Golden State Warriors and a feud with NBA all-star Chris Webber. Nelson was sixth on the all-time coaching victories list with an 815-604 record. Prior to that, he had been a hall of fame small forward for the Boston Celtics during their run of titles in the '60s and '70s.

Most important to Charlie, Nelson had an open mind about the team he was inheriting. Under Riley for a full season, Charlie had played less than one hour of NBA basketball, finishing the season with forty-four minutes. He spent game after game in a place he had typically only sat during picnics: the bench. It was a hard transition for one of the most recognizable athletes in the country, even though to the general public and the media he was still Charlie Ward, Heisman Trophy winner and national champion. Quite often after games, he'd have more reporters around him than anyone other than Ewing, Starks, Oakley and Mason, even though he likely didn't play in that night's game.

One game, the ratio of playing time to reporters waiting for an interview was so out of whack that Doc Rivers jokingly said from his nearby locker, "Charlie, you need to tell these guys that this isn't the Orange Bowl." Charlie smiled and took it in stride. He was aware of how things looked and he knew the easiest solution was to earn more time on the floor.

"By the middle of my rookie year, I realized that I wasn't going to be playing much under Coach Riley," Charlie said. "As a person, I'm thankful it happened. It allowed me to sit back, look at the whole picture and relax. It's one of the maturation processes I went through in high school and college. I understood and went about the business of learning. I just figured I had to wait three years to start at Florida State, and maybe I'd have to wait three years to make my mark in the NBA."

The arrival of Coach Nelson shortened that timeline considerably once the new coach watched Charlie during a series of pre-season mini-camps he held for rookies and free agents. As usual, the intangibles Charlie demonstrated on the court, especially against other young players, separated him from the pack. His anticipation. His leadership. His defensive pressure and ability to run an offense. Nelson noticed all of these things and liked what he saw.

"Charlie Ward was the most pleasant surprise in our mini-camp," Nelson said. "He has to get more information in his brain. He can only do that by playing and understanding the rigors of game situations. He's got the ability and the mental toughness. He just needs the experience."

As the pre-season wore on, Charlie found himself getting valuable minutes with the starters and running Nelson's offense for considerable stretches. Each minute of quality practice time was a like a megabyte of information he could download and draw upon later in a game. Soon,

Nelson noticed the same thing Coach Richt noticed when he began working with Charlie: you only need to teach him a play once and he'd have it committed to memory. The time on the floor with Ewing and Oakley and Mason, as well as the encouraging comments from Coach Nelson, put a slight hop in Charlie's step.

"Last year I was excited about being here," he said. "This year, I have a grasp on what can happen and what might happen. You can say there's a little excitement."

By late October Nelson all but declared that Charlie Ward had won the back-up point guard job behind starter Derek Harper. There was no official announcement or release, but as the pre-season continued, he was consistently leading the second unit when Harper would come out. He considered it a blessing. "All I can say is I'm thankful," he said. "Most people aren't lucky enough to be paid to play basketball. I have a lot to do to keep the coaches' trust, and a lot to learn."

Nelson was a little more pragmatic. In surveying his roster of veterans with nagging injuries, aching knees and sore hips, he simply said, "I need him this year." In fact, he'd need him in the first game.

Due to a combination of aggressive officiating and a hot-headed John Starks picking up too many fouls, Charlie was a major part of Nelson's seven-man rotation when the Knicks played the Detroit Pistons in their road opener at the Palace of Auburn Hills. In that one game Charlie nearly matched his entire point total from the previous season (16) with fifteen points off the bench to help the Knicks win.

"Charlie played a lot more than I thought he would," Nelson said. "Ward played a beautiful game."

The Knicks won ten of their first twelve games before leveling off in December. Viewing things from outside of the organization, things seemed to be going great. On the inside, there was turmoil.

Nelson was beginning to see what Riley likely did when he chose to leave: the Knicks, while able to compete and aim for 50-plus wins and a playoff berth, were deeply flawed...and old...and maybe had already peaked. Nelson was known for creative thinking and for staying ahead of the game's curve, and he floated an idea to management that they should prepare the team to be buyers in the free agent market following the season. In order to do so, he thought they should attempt a sign-and-trade that involved sending Patrick Ewing to Orlando for Shaquille O'Neal, who was set to be the biggest free agent on the market that summer.

"I had coached Shaq in the world championships in '94 and established a pretty good relationship with him," Nelson said, looking back on his time in New York. "I knew he wanted to go elsewhere and so I brought this up in a meeting with the Garden people. I said, 'He would come to New York. It's going to be Los Angeles or us. And if we give 'em Ewing, it would be the best deal Orlando could make.' Well, somehow that got back to Ewing, and after that I was toast."

In addition to the news that Nelson wanted to get rid of him, Ewing also hated the fast break, up-tempo style the team was now playing. The offense was no longer a slog that worked inside-out from Ewing in the post to the rest of the team. It was free-wheeling, fast and, dare it be said, fun. The team scored 100-plus points in seven of its first twelve games. Somewhere around January, Ewing began rallying the team to his cause, slowing the pace of play and openly defying Nelson. By February the writing was on the wall. The team had topped 100 points only eight times in roughly two months. On March 8, 1996, Don Nelson was forced to resign despite a 34-25 record.

Jeff Van Gundy, the Knicks coach who spent more time with Charlie than anyone, who spent an hour before every practice working with him, who saw his talent, drive and intelligence first-hand on a daily basis, became the head coach. This was another win for the young point guard.

"Coach Van Gundy and I got along really well," Charlie said. "He's a worker and he showed up every day to try to help me get better. He really took care of me when it came to being able to play in the NBA. We started developing that relationship when I was a rookie. He invested a lot of time and energy in my development and I reaped the benefits."

Charlie's playing time settled into about twelve minutes per game while the team muddled through a coaching change, trades, trade rumors and overall upheaval. They would ultimately finish 47-35 and lose to the Chicago Bulls (with Jordan back in the fold) in five games in the Eastern Conference Semi-Finals.

• • •

The running joke in the New York football media throughout most of 1995 and 1996 was that the best quarterback in the Big Apple was playing back-up point guard for the Knicks. And there was a case to be made. The Giants were steamrolled in the opening game of the '95 season by the Dallas Cowboys, 35-0. Starting quarterback Dave Brown looked hapless and hopeless. Things barely improved as the team limped to a 5-11 season. The Jets also were destroyed in their opening game of 1995, losing to the Miami Dolphins, 52-14. Head Coach Rich Kotite was clearly overmatched, and his quarterback, aging and past-his-prime Boomer Esiason, was certainly not the future of the franchise. Neither was back-up Bubby Brister.

It was perfect fodder for the media and for football fans who last saw Charlie in pads hoisting the national championship trophy and posing with his Heisman. Publicly, Charlie stated that he was completely done with football, and for all intents and purposes, he was. But with the Jets and Giants both having awful seasons, the story, and the possibility that maybe, just maybe, Charlie could outplay Brown and Esiason (he couldn't do worse), had legs. Add to that the 1996 NFL Draft was arguably the worst ever for the quarterback position, and two and a half years after his last down of football, people were still asking him if the NFL was an option.

The *Philadelphia Inquirer* ran a piece in June of '96 dedicated to this very subject. The Eagles had Ty Detmer and Rodney Peete on their roster; both were around thirty years old, neither was spectacular. Had there been a quarterback worth taking late in the first round they might have selected him. But neither the Eagles nor any other NFL team chose a quarterback in the first round. Not until the middle of the second round did the St. Louis Rams select Tony Banks. The Eagles finally took Bobby Hoying out of Ohio State in the third. The dearth of QBs had football executives searching for answers, and the trail occasionally led to talk of Charlie.

Dick Daniels, the Eagles' director of football operations, thought highly of Charlie as a prospect. "I think Charlie has ability and is very capable," Daniels said. "He's well thought of by a lot of teams, by any team that runs a West Coast offense. It wouldn't be so much about capabilities as it would be how long you'd expect it to take him to develop and give indications he could play on a higher level."

Asked whether he could still play in the NFL, Charlie's answer was unequivocal: "I know I can play."

Tony Dungy remained a fan as well. After he became head coach of the Tampa Bay Buccaneers he drafted Charlie's old roommate, Warrick Dunn, to be his running back. They invited Charlie to the Bucs' facilities to hang out, and Dungy confessed to Charlie how badly he wanted him.

"I told him about my conversations with Dennis Green, but once he got drafted by the Knicks I stopped fantasizing about what it would be like to watch him run an NFL offense," Dungy said. "But I knew if we put him in a system like Bill Walsh ran, with some out-of-the-box thinking, we could have utilized him right away. He could have been very special. He had all the tools: Poise. Decision Making. Accuracy. And he had such high character and was a natural leader."

Dungy and Charlie hit it off. Their similar athletic backgrounds, as well as their faith, bonded them immediately, and though they've never had a player-coach relationship they've remained close ever since that first in-person meeting.

"I know he would have been a great football player," Dungy said. "But who would want to give up being an NBA point guard on a playoff team for the Knicks?"

Chapter 26

The Veteran

Charlie and Tonja lived in a nice place in Stamford, Connecticut that they never fully moved into because Charlie seemed to be involved in every single trade rumor that passed through New York. The gamble the Knicks had taken on him as a rookie paid off. He was in the league and getting valuable minutes while many players selected ahead of him in the 1994 NBA Draft were playing overseas or were out of the sport entirely. The better Charlie played and the more valuable he became, the more the last few years of his contract looked like a bargain to outside teams seeking to shore up their back court. Perhaps due to his relationship with Van Gundy or the team's continued success (they made the playoffs in each of Charlie's first four seasons) they never actually pulled the trigger on a trade.

It also could have been that Charlie endeared himself to Knicks fans both famous (Spike Lee) and not famous (his jersey could be spotted on middle school and high school kids all over New York and New Jersey). He wasn't a star on the level of Ewing or a local icon like Oakley or Mason, but he had carved out a niche for himself. Somewhere along the line fans began to view him as an NBA point guard first and a Heisman winner second. As he became more comfortable with New York City, he reignited the initiatives he had been so fond of while in college. He sponsored a section at Madison Square Garden for underprivileged kids. He began hosting charity golf tournaments to raise money for his causes. He assembled a bible study group that would meet before games and on the road in his hotel room. Rather than let an NBA career in New York City mold him, he chose to turn the baller lifestyle on its ear and continue to be the same humble man of faith he was before the money and the league and the fame.

That isn't to say he was without controversy while playing under his first pro contract. During the 1997 playoffs, Charlie was the central figure in a now-famous brawl between his Knicks and the Miami Heat, coached by Pat Riley, the man who buried Charlie on the bench.

• • •

The Miami Heat versus New York Knicks series in the late 1990s fell somewhere between a WWE steel cage match and a UFC title fight. There was bad blood between Riley and the Knicks, between Charles Oakley and Alonzo Mourning, between Chris Childs and P.J. Brown, and between Larry Johnson and anyone who looked at him sideways. The hatred between the two teams was real, palpable and bubbled over from game to game and series to series—which says a lot because they faced each other in the playoffs four years in a row.

In May of 2017, *The Ringer* website published an oral history for the twentieth anniversary of the fight. Mike Breen, the WFAN radio play-by-play man, described the Knicks of the late 1990s by saying, "Doing the Knicks at that time I received a lot of boxing play-by-play experience. There were a lot of brawls. Instead of doing play-by-play, you do blow-by-blow."

The signature moment of the melee involved 6'11" P.J. Brown bending down over Charlie's back, grabbing him around the waist, leveraging him against his upper thigh and flipping him 360 degrees, pinwheel style, and sending him head-over-heels into the row of photographers under the basket. To fully understand this sequence of events, the minutes leading up should be explained.

The Knicks were up 3-1 in the series but they were getting beaten badly on the road in game five. Down 86-74 with 1:56 left, Oakley laid out Tim Hardaway on a pick. Alonzo Mourning rushed to defend Hardaway and jawed with Oakley. Referees flew in and Mourning shoved Oakley in the throat to move away, smiling as they were separated. At the same time,

Brown and Childs jawed at each other and had to be separated. While they were being separated, Oakley and Mourning wandered back over to each other, trash talked and antagonized each other until Oakley shoved and then swung at Mourning's face, received a technical foul and was ejected. Whistles were being blown all over the court. The crowd jeered Oakley. The arena became a powder keg.

On the next play, the refs called a weak foul on Charlie as he was guarding Hardaway up the floor. Charlie calmly, chewing gum, strolled to his spot next to Brown on the foul line while Hardaway got ready for his shots. He hit the first one. As the ball left his hand on the second shot, Charlie got low, used his center of gravity, stuck out his butt and boxed out Brown all the way to the baseline in a reverse bull rush. There was nothing illegal about the box out, but it was aggressive and it ticked off Brown, who snapped and whipped Charlie over his body and out of bounds. A tiny detail lost in the ruckus is that Charlie somehow landed on his feet after being tossed and promptly squared right up to Brown, who was instantaneously taken to the ground by the Knicks' John Wallace. It was chaos.

In seconds, both benches cleared—including the coaches, trainers, players and anyone close enough to run on the floor toward the altercation. It quickly escalated to a mass of suits and bench players trying to separate the fighting athletes. Fans were screeching like they were watching gladiators at the Coliseum.

"Of all the people in that series, of all the antagonists, and tough physical players, Charlie Ward and P.J. Brown were without question two of the tougher, both mentally and physically, players in the league," Breen said. "But they were also two of the kindest—I mean, they were two of the ultimate gentlemen."

When the officials finally got control, they ejected Brown, Starks and, incredibly, Charlie.

After the game, Brown told reporters at his press conference that he thought Charlie was trying to take his knees out. "He went in low like he was playing football or something at Florida State. If he wants to play football he should go back to Florida State."

"I was just trying to protect myself," Charlie said about the fight after the flip. "I'm not going to let anyone treat me like I'm a little kid."

The next morning, the league office announced six player suspensions: Ward, Ewing, Allan Houston, Johnson and Starks for one game each, and Brown for two games.

"I felt like I was robbed," Ewing said.

The Knicks lost the next two games.

• • •

The 1998 off-season was filled with major story lines for the league, the team and for Charlie. Individually, he needed to have surgery for loose cartilage in his right knee that would require four to six weeks of rehab. He was also a free agent for the first time in his career and was weighing offers and options. Team-wise, the Knicks continued to rebuild and evolve, trading away fan favorites Charles Oakley and John Starks for Marcus Camby and Latrell Sprewell in different deals. This was the second major change following the acquisition of Allan Houston the season before. League-wise, the NBA was in a lockout that threatened to cancel the entire 1998-99 season.

The silver lining for Charlie and Tonja was that he'd have plenty of time to rehab and think about where he wanted to play for the next phase of his career. The Toronto Raptors, Detroit Pistons, Orlando Magic and Portland Trail Blazers were all showing interest in him, but his preference was to stay with the Knicks.

Tonja, who used her law degree to co-found a marketing and management company with former NBA player Alex English, had the foresight to set up her career in a way she could do it from anywhere. "If we move, that's fine," she said. "I had career goals when I was a kid and those goals didn't change when I got in a relationship and got married."

During the lockout, the Wards got to spend their first extended amount of time together at home, with Charlie having no road games to keep him away for several weeks at a time and no home games to keep him out until after midnight. The quality time was both new and exciting and it allowed Charlie to "check in on his other life." Even though he slept in most days while Tonja had her normal fifty-minute commute from Stamford to mid-town Manhattan, Charlie made the most of his time at home. He surprised Tonja with dinner, held bible study at his house, and organized three charity events from start to finish on his own. He also devoted himself to the Christian Fellowship movement, traveling twice to meet with fellow Christian and Green Bay Packers star, Reggie White.

The lockout lasted from July 1, 1998 to January 20, 1999. On January 21, the Knicks signed Charlie Ward to a five-year, $30 million deal. His only hesitation was that he wanted assurances he wouldn't be traded. While the Knicks wouldn't include a no-trade clause, they did assure him that he was part of their long-term plans and extended the offer he ultimately signed.

"After it came down to it, my wife and I prayed about it and we came to the revelation that if we were going to get traded, then it was God's will. I'm just very happy and blessed to be here. I have to thank God and then the Knicks for giving me an opportunity when people thought I should be playing football."

The contract was large enough for Charlie to do something he'd been thinking about for a while: buy his parents a new house in Thomasville.

They had been living in the home where he was born for thirty-three years. They raised six children there. With grandchildren on the way and the family expanding, Charlie felt they had earned an upgrade.

"Junior made a statement to us around that time about how we raised all these kids and he never heard either of us complain one time about anything," Charlie's mom said. "I became a member of an organization for mothers of NBA players, and I heard some awful stories involving children and money and contracts. Charlie's dad and I decided we had already been blessed with our children and we didn't need any extra money to be happy. Junior made up his mind to get us a house on his own."

Willard's father had been a contractor and Charlie knew his mother had knowledge of real estate, so he wanted her to have the freedom to lead the land purchase and manage the building project of their dream home. With her real-estate savvy, she chose to buy a large plot of land to sub-divide rather than a single home so that they could offer lots to his siblings. His parents were able to build on the largest lot. Since the Wards were creating the entire subdivision, it fell upon them to name the street all the houses would be on.

"Heisman Way came up in discussion and it was the perfect name to all of us," Charlie Sr. said.

Chapter 27

1999 and Beyond

In 1999, Patrick Ewing was the only starter remaining from the 1993-94 Knicks team that made the NBA Finals. New stars Allan Houston and Latrell Sprewell were leading the way with Kurt Thomas, Marcus Camby, Larry Johnson, Chris Childs and Charlie supporting their efforts.

Houston was a 6'6" shooting guard who grew up in Louisville, Kentucky. His father, Wade Houston, was Denny Crum's assistant at the University of Louisville for thirteen years. In 1989, he was offered the head coaching job at the University of Tennessee, making him the first African-American head coach in the Southeastern Conference. Allan Houston committed to play under his father that year, and though the two wouldn't have much team success in their four years together (60-68 record), Allan finished as the team's all-time leading scorer. The Detroit Pistons selected him eleventh overall in the 1993 NBA Draft and signed him to a three-year deal. In the last year of that deal he averaged 19.7 points per game, giving him leverage as a free agent that he used to sign a monster deal with the Knicks. In his first two years there, he fell short of the scoring, rebounding and assist totals he had with Detroit. As he struggled to acclimate to playing off a scorer like Sprewell and in a city like New York in 1999, he found himself both relying on and continually impressed with Charlie.

"On the court his footwork, his instincts, his hand-eye coordination and his spatial awareness of what everyone was doing was off the charts," Houston said. "He excelled at all the little things. He wasn't bigger than anyone and he wasn't a scorer, but he made it through every pick and disrupted other teams' plans. And you just felt comfortable with him on the floor as a leader. You felt that he'd settle down your unit when he was out there. Even more important, his influence in the locker room and how he carried himself is really what made him special. He honestly inspired me to be a better man."

Even though he wasn't the star, his play inspired others on the court as well. Case in point: Charlie began the '99 season on the bench, with Childs as the starting point guard. Childs eventually requested to come off the bench, saying he felt more comfortable letting Charlie begin the game. The very fact that he felt secure enough to make such a request, and that Charlie could handle it without any ego involved was a tremendous asset for the Knicks.

"That change helped our depth tremendously," Houston said. "Chris came in and was aggressive and confident, knowing that Charlie could start us off."

All that being said, the 1999 New York Knicks were erratic, frustrating and at times completely dysfunctional. They lost the first two games of the lockout-shortened season by close margins, then won the third game by scoring 101 points and pulled out a win in the fourth game despite scoring only seventy-three points. The rest of the league was out of sync as well, but few teams struggled offensively as much as the Knicks, who managed to score fewer than seventy points three times that season. An epically bad 76-63 loss to Chicago (minus Jordan) in the 20th game marked the absolute nadir of basketball in New York. Statistically, it was the worst performance by a Knicks team since the inception of the shot clock.

The book *Just Ballin'*, by reporters Mike Wise and Frank Isola, chronicled the '99 Knicks season and described the scene on the plane after that Bulls game as one of utter indifference by the players and utter contempt for their reaction by Van Gundy. Van Gundy, who was fighting for his job at that point, was nearly apoplectic as the new members of the team were caught laughing on the plane ride home.

"You have to do everything wrong to be as bad as we were," Van Gundy said in the book. "I don't know if it can get worse than this."

The Knicks paid lip service to the loss, holding a player's-only meeting afterward that Van Gundy deemed total BS. He wanted to see action and a sense of team unity, which seemed like it was never coming. Isola and

Wise wrote, "The arrival of Sprewell, Camby, Thomas, [Dennis] Scott and the second-year point guard Rick Brunson changed the dynamics of the locker room. The Knicks were suddenly younger, more single, more hip-hop, and more Generation X.... Those five players quickly formed a bond as newcomers who didn't subscribe to the tired old Knick ways. Their attitude seemed to be brash and straightforward: *Why should we conform to you? We've got just as many rings as you do?*"

Charlie found himself, just as he had in college with Cassell and Sura and Edwards, to be the emotional baseline of the team. On the court, the play was up and down and Van Gundy was often flummoxed about how his team could score sixty-three points one night and lose, then score ninety-four points, 108 points and 113 points during a three-game winning streak. But off the court, Charlie was a steady presence.

"He never had to say much but his presence was so strong," Houston said. "It sounds odd, but it was almost like an aroma he carried. You'd see the biggest and boldest and loudest men soften a bit when they were with him because of the respect they had for him. I used to call it 'The Charlie Ward Effect.'"

Houston explains that Charlie wasn't trying to be anyone's dad, but he simply led by example and it inspired a lot of people. Even Coach Van Gundy.

"Charlie stood for everything a Knick should stand for," he said. "He was a quiet, proud, caring man, but his actions spoke so loudly you'd listen to whatever he said. He was respectful of a lot of different lifestyles, and if you asked him about his Christian beliefs he was direct and straightforward."

It was no secret to anyone who knew Charlie that he was deeply religious and that he openly talked about Christianity. At times, this put him at odds with the reporters covering the team and even with his own teammates. While he had his close-knit group of fellow religious men in Houston, Chris Dudley and Herb Williams, media members remained curious about how the dynamics worked throughout the Knicks organization. Occasionally, when Charlie made comments about topical issues that were unapologetic about his faith, he became the subject of scorn for his beliefs.

"Whenever a person is more righteous than the next he becomes an easy target," Dudley said. "That's what's happening to Charlie now."

The attacks only served to increase Van Gundy's respect for Charlie, even though he didn't quite have the same beliefs.

"Our president, David Checketts, came in one day and he went at Charlie about a number of issues going on with our team at the time," Van Gundy said. "Most guys, when someone is going at them, especially a person in a position of power, shift their weight or look at the ceiling or the floor and dart their eyes. Not Charlie. He looked directly at Mr. Checketts, eye to eye, and he took it. He was respectful and never talked back. That always impressed me, regardless of if I thought what Charlie was saying was right or wrong."

The most famous controversy regarding Charlie and religion would actually come two years later, when Eric Konigsberg wrote a piece for *The New York Times* that excerpted a conversation from a bible study between Charlie and Houston in reference to a biblical quote that alluded to Jews being stubborn. It caused a massive firestorm, though Charlie claimed the quote written about in the piece was actually part of a discussion, not a belief he and his group were espousing.

"I didn't mean to offend any one group because that's not what I'm about," Charlie said in a statement. "I have friends that are Jewish. Actually, my friend is a Jewish guy, his name is Jesus Christ."

The article and the ensuing fallout led to rebukes from NBA Commissioner David Stern, the Anti-Defamation League and other media outlets and religious groups. Charlie, eager to use the situation as a learning experience, agreed to meet with Rabbi Yechiel Eckstein of the International Fellowship of Christians and Jews to learn more about Judaism. In the end, the Anti-Defamation League was satisfied with Charlie's response and the continuing religious education he agreed to. The *New York Post*'s headline on April 24 read: *Ward Apology Applauded*.

To Houston, Charlie's religious nature became something that even teammates who didn't believe as they did or weren't very religious could rally around. He used the beginning of Charlie's pre-game prayer idea as an example.

"One of the traditions that he started was a little pre-game prayer before we'd go out on the court. It wasn't a traditional prayer, it was just guys saying whatever was in their heart or on their mind," he said. "It was daunting for guys to go out on a limb to say something in front of their teammates and be that open and transparent. Initially, very few guys participated, and guys would look around like, 'I hope he doesn't call on me.' And there were guys who you looked at and figured it would never happen. No way they'd ever get involved. But I think at one point everybody did it because it was a way for us to take a moment to get in sync before the game. Guys would come in and say, 'Let us stay healthy and be the best we can be and be good representatives of our families and team and faiths.' That was what most of them were like and it united us."

• • •

From the perspective of a cynical, sarcastic New York Knicks fan in the early spring of 1999, whatever amount of praying the Knicks were doing toward the end of the season wasn't enough. From March 24 to April 19, they were 7-12, but held a .500 record on the season. Rumors of Van Gundy getting fired followed them from city to city as if they were stowed in the luggage. A 6-2 push over the last eight games, including a win on the last night of the season against the Heat, gave them the #8 seed in the playoffs, which meant they had to turn right around to face the #1 seed Miami Heat in the first round.

"It felt like we always had to go through Miami," Charlie said. "And every year the intensity grew stronger."

"We don't like them, they don't like us, so let's get it on," Tim Hardaway said before the series. "I hate the Knicks. Absolutely hate them. That's just the way it is."

The Knicks began the post-season at 25,000 to 1 odds to win the NBA championship—just one reason their twenty-point win against Miami in game one was somewhat shocking. New York jumped out to a ten-point lead in the first quarter and steadily pulled away as the game went on.

Houston scored twenty-two points and Charlie led the team in assists and steals.

Miami came back to win the next game behind twenty-six points from Alonzo Mourning, but when the series went to New York the Heat's momentum seemed to have stayed in South Florida. The Knicks blew out the Heat, 97-73, in game three. Miami then won game four by fifteen points, setting up a winner-take-all game five that nobody expected the Knicks to be in.

The flight to Miami and the circumstances of the game felt eerily similar to the '97 playoffs for Van Gundy, who talked about it in *Just Ballin'*.

"We have to guard against what happened two years ago," he told his players. "We lost a tough game at home in game six, and then we came down here and it carried over into the first quarter of game seven. When you're up eleven in the second half—and you're up four going into the fourth—all you need is twelve minutes of great basketball to close out the series. If you don't get it down, you have the possibility of a hangover.

"We can't be down or frustrated or unhappy that we're back here, or that we're thinking of it as a lost opportunity. We have to look at it as the opportunity to play in a deciding game, where you really find out about people and teams. We have to turn the frustration into anger and do anything it takes to win."

After an early Miami lead in game five was erased by some great guard play by Childs, Ward and Sprewell, the two teams stayed within striking distance of each other the rest of the way. Neither team showed any sign of pulling away until Voshon Lenard and Dan Majerle drained back-to-back three-pointers to give Miami a seven-point lead with ten minutes left.

Ewing, who by this point in the series was running as if he were held together by duct tape and paper clips, came up huge in the final minutes by hitting a jumper, grabbing a rebound and sinking two free throws to keep his team within one point with thirty-nine seconds left.

Sprewell stole the ball from Hardaway and called time out after crossing mid-court. The ensuing play for Sprewell out of the timeout failed when Terry Porter swatted the ball from his hands. Luckily for the Knicks, the ball went out of bounds off Porter, so it was Knicks possession with five seconds left.

Houston executed a perfect curl around Ewing, caught the ball and knocked down the biggest shot of his career. Miami Arena went silent. The Knicks bench went ballistic. The inconsistent team with the coach who was forever on the hot seat had pulled off one of the biggest post-season upsets of all time: an eight seed beating a one seed in a five-game series.

"We got a good roll today," Charlie said. "It sent chills up my spine."

• • •

After winning the DEFCON 1-level series against the Heat, the Knicks maintained a level of defensive intensity the Atlanta Hawks simply could not match in round two. The Knicks systematically swept the Hawks in four straight games, winning by comfortable margins in each. Charlie led the team in assists and three-pointers.

The Eastern Conference Finals pitted the Knicks against the #2 seed Indiana Pacers and one of the most lethal shooters in the game, Reggie Miller. The series presented several intriguing match-ups for the media to discuss leading up: Houston vs. Miller, Ewing vs. Rik Smits, and Mark Jackson and Travis Best matching point guard skills against Ward and Childs. Charlie was familiar with Best from their days playing against each other in the ACC.

Reaching the Eastern Conference Finals brought back memories for Charlie of preparing for a steady stream of pressure-filled games. After a college football career in which the mentality every season was "one loss could ruin our season," and a college hoops career filled with ACC tournaments and NCAA tournaments, things were different in the pros. The lack of playing time in the beginning and lack of reaching a conference finals or NBA Finals had laid dormant the big-game side of Charlie's personality—and he missed it. For his whole competitive life, all the way back to the Thomasville vs. Central high school football rivalry days, he thrived on pressure and wanted the ball in his hands when it mattered.

He was now the starting point guard on a team that was one series away from the NBA Finals. The difference here was that he wasn't an MVP candidate or an all-star or even the focal point of his team's offense.

He was the "glue," as Walter McCarty called him.

He was the "ultimate competitor," as Van Gundy said.

When the Knicks lost Patrick Ewing to injury after the second game of the Eastern Conference Finals, they were forced to reshuffle their lineup to better match up with the Pacers. Dudley, Childs and Sprewell saw their minutes increase, and the pressure shifted to Marcus Camby to produce in Ewing's absence. But in this shuffle, Charlie's minutes dropped to the lowest they had been in a long time, bottoming out at twelve minutes in the Knicks' series-clinching win in game six. He had three steals in those twelve minutes.

"I've always been the kind of guy to do whatever needed to be done to win," Charlie said. "Even if that meant taking a back seat for a while if a better match-up could be on the floor. I always played hard, and when we beat Indiana to go to the NBA Finals it was a team win. We overcame the loss of Patrick and the tough draw of an eighth seed to be one of the last two teams standing. It was like being back in the national championship game at Florida State."

• • •

Forget the 25,000 to 1 odds that Las Vegas was giving the Knicks to win the NBA Finals. What would be the odds of a quarterback of a national championship-winning college football team and/or a Heisman Trophy winner starting a game in the NBA Finals?

A million to 1?

Ten million to 1?

Could Roger Staubach have played shooting guard for the Celtics in the '60s? Could Archie Griffin have gone on to play point guard for the Sonics in the '70s? What about Eddie George as a small forward for the Pistons in the '90s? Imagine Cam Newton as a power forward for the 2017 Warriors team.

Despite the elite athletic ability of each of these Heisman winners, the idea that they could play professional basketball at a high enough level to start on an NBA Finals team still seems laughable.

"That's what people sometimes forget when talking about Charlie," Houston said. "It is so hard to make an NBA roster. Guys play basketball their whole lives just to get a chance. And he played part-time until he was twenty-three and got drafted and played for over a decade. That's hard to comprehend."

Whatever the odds, there were two things for certain:

One, it had never happened before.

And two, Charlie Ward would accomplish the feat in the 1999 NBA Finals against the heavily favored San Antonio Spurs (the Knicks were 9-1 underdogs).

The Spurs, coached by Gregg Popovich, won thirty-seven games in the lockout-shortened season and were the #1 seed in the Western Conference. Their team featured the twin towers of Tim Duncan (another former ACC foe for Charlie) and David Robinson, along with Avery Johnson, Sean Elliott, Mario Elie and Steve Kerr as a sharp shooter off the bench.

After the Knicks' starters were introduced in game one at the Alamodome in San Antonio, the lights went out and the hype music began for the Spurs.

The arena went pitch black.

Flame cannons were wheeled to center court and fired into the air.

Trumpets blared and then the PA system segued to the official, omnipresent soundtrack to all major '90s sporting events: Jock Jams.

Y'all ready for this!!!

Spurs fans rose to their feet and gave their starters a standing ovation. "The Iceman" George Gervin brought out the ceremonial game ball to really ratchet up the crowd. He even performed a mock tip-off to celebrate the Spurs being the first former American Basketball Association team to make it to the NBA Finals. The real tip off between Chris Dudley and David Robinson highlighted the disparity between the two teams in size and in talent—Robinson easily won. As the Spurs moved down the floor, the match-ups were heavily in their favor. The Knicks were called for an illegal defense on the first possession, and then Duncan hit a patented bank jump shot from the wing for the first points of the Finals.

The mismatches only continued from there. With Ewing still in a walking boot and Larry Johnson barely able to walk on his right knee, Van Gundy had few front-court options to turn to. Forget going toe-to-toe, he'd have settled for a big man with two healthy legs.

"At full strength, our margin for error would be small against this team," Van Gundy said. They weren't even close to full strength and lost the game 89-77. Duncan owned them, with thirty-three points and sixteen rebounds.

Charlie had seven points, three assists and two blocks.

Game two was more of the same, except this time the Knicks' offense barely showed up. Houston, Sprewell and Johnson were all forced to play more than forty minutes each, and the Knicks managed only sixty-seven points as a team. The Spurs scored eighty.

"This is only two games, we're not dead," Houston said. "We've been in worse situations."

"We'd been down 0-2 before and this wasn't any different," Charlie said. "We were ailing but it wasn't as if we were going to give up. We'd fought too hard."

The high point of the series, if there was one for the Knicks, was the game-three win at Madison Square Garden. For those sixty minutes, it was essentially the Allan Houston/Latrell Sprewell show. They combined for fifty-eight points in New York's lone win of the Finals.

They lost game four at home, 96-89. Chris Childs suffered a knee injury early in the game and Van Gundy turned to Charlie, who played forty-one minutes. He provided a spark early on and finished the game with eleven points, eight assists and four rebounds. In 1999, the Finals home/away schedule rotation was 2-3-2, so game five was also at Madison Square Garden.

At that time, no team had ever come back from a 3-1 deficit in the NBA Finals, and it didn't appear that a beat-up, beaten-down Knicks team would be the squad to do it. Still, they had faith.

"We can win this series," Van Gundy told his team. "We're only bound by what we think we can accomplish. No eighth seed has ever made it here, either. So history doesn't have to hamper us. All we have to do is win one home game. Then we can go down there and get one road game. And then you're playing the ultimate game."

Despite a Herculean effort from Sprewell, who at one point scored twenty-one of his team's twenty-five points to put the Knicks up 77-75 with three minutes left, New York ran out of luck. Down 78-77 with 2.1 seconds left and possession of the ball, Van Gundy drew up a set play tailor-made for his ex-quarterback to execute. The plan was for Charlie to in-bound the ball and either hit Houston in stride coming off a screen or to thread the needle to Sprewell racing to the basket.

"It was familiar territory," Charlie said. "Just with a different shaped ball."

As he had done during countless fourth-quarter comebacks on the gridiron, Charlie delivered a perfect pass to Sprewell, but his pattern took him too far under the basket. With nowhere to go, Sprewell left the paint and was forced to shoot a fadeaway over Robinson and Duncan. He missed.

"Charlie threw an excellent pass," Sprewell said. "I was just too far under the basket. With their size coming down on me, I didn't have the layup like we planned."

In a way, it was fitting that the Knicks' season ended on a pass from the "best quarterback in New York."

After so much dysfunction and dissention during the year, the teamwork needed for the play to succeed wasn't the problem—the execution just came up a little short.

As for the expectations of them heading into the playoffs?

The Knicks exceeded those beyond anybody's wildest dreams.

"To have the opportunity to play in an NBA Finals was a blessing," Charlie said. "And to watch our team come together to accomplish what we did, that was even more special. That was a tough group of guys."

• • •

Char-lie! Char-lie! Char-lie!

The chants from the Madison Square Garden crowd whirled through the arena like a cyclone. All 19,763 fans in attendance serenaded their longtime point guard with full-throated joy. They'd been waiting for this moment.

It was just under a year since the Knicks had lost the Finals to the Spurs, and they were back in the Eastern Conference Semi-Finals facing their old nemesis, the Miami Heat. The Knicks were down in the series 2-1 after splitting the first two on the road and losing the third game at home.

In game four, Chris Childs got into foul trouble and was forced to sit on the bench for thirty-two minutes of the game. Charlie filled in admirably for most of the game, but in the fourth quarter he took over as if he were back under center for the Seminoles. The heroics began on a drive to the basket to give the Knicks a nine-point lead with four minutes left.

Alonzo Mourning then scored two quick buckets to make the Garden crowd nervous and pull the Heat to within five points. The score was 84-79 when Charlie missed a shot, grabbed his own rebound and put it back. The normally emotionless Charlie smiled and pumped his fist, feeding off the moment and the crowd.

As the game ticked under two minutes, Patrick Ewing fumbled a rebound that appeared to be going out of bounds before Charlie, summoning his elusive days in Bowden's Fast Break Offense, leapt after it and, in Pat Riley's words, "ran down the loose ball, jumped out of bounds, pirouetted in the air and threw a down-and-out pass [to Sprewell]. He is a great athlete and a tough, tough kid."

A moment later he flew back up the court and floated a layup high off the glass, directly over Mourning's outstretched arms, to make it 86-79.

"I got chills just watching, because I was so happy for him," Childs said.

A furious Mourning went down and answered with another basket on his end, but Charlie, absolutely feeling it, wasn't done. He promptly knocked down a jump shot to put the Knicks up 88-81 with 1:09 left. Riley was forced to call a time out. And that's when the crowd went bananas.

Char-lie! Char-lie! Char-lie!

"It was a better feeling than if I had hit the shots," Houston said. "To hear the crowd behind him was a great feeling. We're all so happy to see it, because we know what Charlie means to us. He gives himself so much for the team, not only on the court, but off."

Van Gundy had long called Charlie his best hustle player, and he relied on him over and over to keep his team in the game mentally. That night, however, he was able to rely on him to keep the team in the game on the scoreboard. And it was unforgettable.

"For the first time, I felt like Allan and Latrell," Charlie said. "You know, like you're the go-to guy."

It was the same feeling he had when he was the best football player in the country on the best college team in the country. It was the same feeling he experienced at Thomasville's Central High School. And it was the same feeling he had in Pop Warner and on his driveway and on the streets around Fruit City as a kid. It was the feeling of being unstoppable. He felt it in the biggest games at the Orange Bowl. Now he was feeling it at Madison Square Garden.

No other person on Earth knows what that's like.

Maybe no other person ever will.

Epilogue

Tonja Ward was checking her shopping list as she pushed her cart down an aisle of the grocery store. She had two kids under four years old, so she was stocking up on baby food, finger food, food in pouches, and basically any food that was mashed and minced. She was mostly done with her list, trying to remember if she left anything off when she got the call.

It was Charlie.

He was being traded to the Phoenix Suns.

"After nine years of not really unpacking, we were finally on the move," Tonja said. "It was a paper trade, meaning we wouldn't really end up in Phoenix once the deal shook out. Seven or eight teams had already reached out to Charlie, so we talked about where we wanted to go. The Spurs were one of the teams who made an offer, and if the Spurs call and give you a chance to win a ring, you go."

Prior to calling his wife, Charlie received a call from then Knicks president Isiah Thomas letting him know about the trade the team was making. Thomas was bringing all-star guards Anfernee Hardaway and Stephon Marbury to the Knicks in exchange for Charlie, Howard Eisley, Antonio McDyess, Maciej Lampe, Milos Vujanic and several draft picks.

Although Charlie cherished his career with the Knicks and had grown used to living and working in New York City, he knew it was only a matter of time before a trade like this happened. He felt lucky to be able to land with the defending champions in San Antonio and to get to play for a coach like Gregg Popovich. As an added bonus, he was reunited with his good friend Monty Williams. He was thirty-three years old at the time of the trade and was used sparingly on the bench behind a young Tony Parker during his season with the Spurs. Cruelly, the Spurs lost to the Lakers in the second round of the playoffs that year and then they let Charlie go. They'd win the title again the following year.

"Yes, they sandwiched the championships around our time there," Tonja said, laughing. "But it was wonderful to reconnect with Monty and Ingrid Williams."

After being let go by San Antonio, Jeff Van Gundy, who was then coaching the Houston Rockets, reached out and signed him as a free agent in August.

The Houston Rockets were a team on the rise with a roster that included Tracy McGrady, Jimmy Jackson, Yao Ming, and his old teammate from Florida State, Bob Sura. The team was filled with eclectic personalities, international players, cagey veterans and hungry young guys. Van Gundy envisioned Charlie's role as a leader in the locker room and a stabilizer on the floor. Unfortunately, his body began to break down. He was averaging about twenty-four minutes, five points and three assists through fourteen games when he injured his knee, forcing him to have season-ending surgery on December 4, 2004.

Following a long off-season of rehab and training camp with the Rockets, Van Gundy informed Charlie that he was going to be traded. The Wards had young children in school, they liked living in Houston, and with Charlie at 34 years old they weren't sure moving for a trade was worth uprooting the whole family again. After consulting with Tonja, Charlie reached out to Van Gundy about his options.

"Coach Van Gundy was straightforward with him and told him that he had a choice," Tonja said. "He told Charlie that with his leadership skills and knowledge, he'd always be able to find a job in the league as a strong locker room guy. He said, 'You can always be a journeyman, or you can start coaching.'"

Charlie made the decision to retire as a player, keep his family in Houston, and join Van Gundy's staff. His coaching career started on October 29, 2005. While he enjoyed coaching and working with the players, the time away from his growing family was taking its toll. In 2007, Van Gundy told his staff that he was planning to make a career change in 2008 and wanted to give them a heads up so they could chart their own course.

That's when Charlie decided to go to him and step down. After two years on the Rockets' staff, he informed Van Gundy that he was going to leave the team to coach high school kids.

"He was easily on the path to becoming a head coach in the NBA," Van Gundy said. "Everyone respected him. He had a good base of knowledge about how the NBA worked and how the game itself worked. But he made a family decision and I respect it. You can see that he was meant to teach young people. I can't imagine if you're a high school parent and your son is being coached by a man with the combination of athletic success, personal character and competitive spirit that Charlie has. I say this all the time: We will never see another athlete like Charlie ever again. Heisman Trophy winner as a quarterback. Wins a national championship in college. Starting point guard in the NBA Finals. Long NBA career. Drafted twice in baseball. I still don't think people properly grasp what this guy has done. And now to pass all that knowledge and experience on to high school kids? It's perfect."

• • •

Charlie Ward Jr. is currently the head football coach at Washington High School in Pensacola, Florida.

Acknowledgements

The book you're holding in your hands began with a text message. I had Charlie's number in my phone from a feature I'd written about him previously. At the end of our conversation for that story, I mentioned that I was working on a book with "Mean" Joe Greene. I told Charlie that I had always been fascinated by his unique story and that I might reach out one day about a possible biography about him.

Six months later, I texted him: *Hey Charlie! Do you have time for a phone call in the next few days? Would love to go over some ideas I have for writing your biography.*

He called me back an hour later and there began the process of putting together the book you just read.

First and foremost, I have to thank Charlie for agreeing to work with me on this project. To say you'll participate in a biography about yourself is one thing, but to make yourself available and be completely candid and open in conversations about yourself is another. On all counts, Charlie was beyond gracious with his time, answers and ideas. He also helped secure several key interviews that really helped fill out his life's story.

As you've read, his life's story is also his family's story, and I will be forever grateful for the hospitality and help the Ward family offered me throughout this book. From phone calls with Mr. and Mrs. Ward, Charlie's wife Tonja, and his sister Leta, to my time spent at the Wards' home on Heisman Way in Thomasville, everyone was all in. Their conversations with me were invaluable (and the home-cooked food was incredible).

For the back story on high school football in Thomasville and Charlie's early years as an athlete, Mark Lastinger and Randy Young were my go-to guys and I can't thank them enough. During the early chapters of the book, I leaned on the work of the local paper, the *Thomasville Times-Enterprise* as well as Tommy Rainge and other high school football teammates. For historical information on Florida A&M and Charlie Sr.'s career, Alvin Hollins from FAMU, author Bijan C. Bayne and Samuel G. Freedman's book *Breaking the Line*, were valuable resources.

The excellent reporting by the *Tallahassee Democrat* in the early 1990s was also extremely helpful as I retraced Charlie's ascent with both the football and basketball teams at Florida State. The FSU beat writer at the time, Steve Ellis, proved to be someone whose work I found myself researching on several occasions. His book with Coach Bobby Bowden was also a great resource for me. I would have loved to interview Steve for this project, but was saddened to learn he passed away in 2009. The archives of the local papers in the New York/New Jersey area helped me fill in the gaps of Charlie's time playing at Madison Square Garden. Also, Frank Isola and Mike Wise's book, *Just Ballin'* was a great account of the '99 season and a book I recommend to all Knicks fans.

Coach Mark Richt, Warrick Dunn, William Floyd, Coach Pat Kennedy, Sam Cassell, Allan Houston, Jeff Van Gundy, Tony Dungy and many others were extremely helpful in fleshing out Charlie's time with his various teams across college and the pros. I'd also like to thank Matthew Sign and Steve Hatchell of the National Football Foundation and College Football Hall of Fame for their support as well.

When you undertake a book like this, the story lives in your brain all day, every day for months on end, like a movie that's playing for only you. When that happens, the subject, in this case Charlie Ward, seeps into conversations all the time. So thank you to everyone in my family for listening to stories about Charlie, his teammates and his exploits for the past year. My wife, Steph, attended the University of Miami, as did Charlie's wife, so I often joked that minus the Heisman Trophy, the national championship and NBA career, Charlie and I had a ton in common. Although I commandeered our dining room table with books and research and I let the dog take my place in bed while I wrote late into the night, Steph had my back throughout this project. I also must apologize to the dog for kicking him out of my bed on a nightly basis.

While I'm apologizing, I'll throw one to my brother, who had to endure months of late-night text messages about a variety of topics, including random facts about Charlie, FSU, the Knicks, or my word count, or how much coffee I drank and/or how much coffee I needed. Same to my friends Eddie Coblentz and Sean Carrigan, both die-hard Knicks fans who can arm wrestle for the John Starks biography I now own. The Coblentz family invited me to the Kickoff Classic in 1993, where I got to watch Charlie play quarterback in person against Kansas on his way to a national championship. You could say that the idea for this book started way back then.

Early readers of this manuscript include many members of Charlie's family; my brother Craig; my dad Harvey; longtime friend, colleague and writer, Joe Wuebben; the young Scott Bedgood; and the man who has edited more of my articles, cover stories and books than anyone, the incomparable Jared Evans. Jared helps my words read as they sound in my head, rather than the jumble that sometimes winds up on the page, and for that I will always be grateful. Thank you all for your time, energy, notes and ideas.

And finally, I'd like to thank you, the reader. You could have picked up any book in the world to read and you chose this one. If you're reading this far, then I am forever in your debt. You're the reason all the research and revisions, phone calls and interviews and trips, writing and rewriting is worth it—so that maybe, just maybe, you read this book and it lives in your mind forever as one of your favorites.

—Jon

Bibliography

"1986 Thomas County Central Yellow Jackets Results," Georgia High School Football Historians Association, http://ghsfha.org/w/Special:SchoolHome?view=seasons&season=1986&school=Thomas+-County+Central.

"1998-99 New York Knicks Player Stats – Regular Season," LandOfBasketball.com, http://www.landofbasketball.com/stats_by_team/1998_1999_knicks_rs.htm.

"ACC officials visit Florida St.," Associated Press, Sept. 3, 1990

Almeida, Monica, "U.S. Open '94; Ashe Event: Many Stars, One Cause," *The New York Times*, Aug. 29, 1994.

Anderson, Mark, "Cairo's coach must cope with new faces," *Tallahassee* (FL) *Democrat*, Aug. 24, 1985.

Anderson, Mark, "Could it be a first for Ward?" *Tallahassee* (FL) *Democrat*, June 26, 1994.

Araton, Harvey, "Hindsight, the Knicks and Nelson's Foresight," *The New York Times*, March 2, 2007.

"Area Parks & Recreation," City of Thomasville, https://thomasville.org/parks-and-recreation.

Baab, Kent. "How Heisman Trophy winners have stored their hardware," *The Washington Post*, Dec. 9, 2013.

Baker, Katie, "'It Was Like True, True Disdain for Each Other,'" TheRinger.com, https://www.theringer.com/2017/5/15/16045664/oral-history-nba-playoffs-new-york-knicks-miami-heat-1997-brawl-20-year-anniversary-96b8a5be329f.

Barnes, Craig, "Fast-breaking Ward leads FSU on record romp," (South Florida) *Sun-Sentinel*, Nov. 8, 1992.

Barnes, Craig, "Junior's Act Moves to New Stage/Charlie Ward Has Proved Himself As a Basketball Player, But His Father Always Knew He Was Born To Play Football," (South Florida) *Sun-Sentinel*, Sept. 3, 1992.

Barnes, Craig, "Thomasville Twins," (South Florida) *Sun-Sentinel*, Oct. 16, 1992.

Barnes, Craig, "Ward wakes up, saves FSU," (South Florida) *Sun-Sentinel*, Sept. 13, 1992.

"Basketball Reference (website)," Sports Reference, https://www.basketball-reference.com/

"Beyond the Paint: Charlie Ward (video)," NBA.com, http://www.nba.com/video/2016/12/06/20161206-beyond-paint-ward-feature#/.

Bishop, Brian K., "FSU fans can celebrate a Ward winner," *Tallahassee* (FL) *Democrat*, Dec. 12, 1993.

Bowden, Bobby, *Bobby Bowden's Tales from the Seminole Sideline* (New York: Sports Publishing LLC, 2004).

Bowden, Bobby. *Called to Coach: Reflections on Life, Faith and Football* (New York: Howard Books, 2011).

Brown Clifton, "Pro Basketball: Ward Will Enter Camp With 5-Year Knick Deal," *The New York Times*, Sept. 29, 1994.

Buderi, Robert, "John Elway, a Man for Two Seasons, May Be the Best College Quarterback of All Time," *People*, Nov. 1, 1982.

"Charlie Ward not selected in NFL draft," Associated Press, April 26, 1994.

Cooley, Joshua, "Ward leaves NBA spotlight to coach Christian high school," BPSports, http://www.bpsports.net/bpsports.asp?ID=5736.

Cooper, Barry, "Famu Mourns Loss of Jake Gaither, Its Most Famous Coach, *Orlando Sentinel*, Feb. 19, 1994.

Cooper, Barry, "He can't play, but fans call him – 'Charlie!'" *Orlando Sentinel*, Oct. 27, 1994.

Cooper, Barry, "Knicks, deep at guard, draft Ward at No. 26," *Orlando Sentinel*, June 30, 1994.

Cooper, Barry, "Prop. 48 Has Athletes Hitting The Books Harder," *Orlando Sentinel*, Sept. 6, 1987.

D'Angelo, Tom, "As point guard or QB, Ward leads FSU," *The Palm Beach Post*, Sept. 2, 1992.

D'Angelo, Tom, "Bowden relieved without the burden of No. 1," *The Palm Beach Post*, Aug. 13, 1992.

D'Angelo, Tom, "Seminoles-Tigers: ACC supremacy," *The Palm Beach Post*, Sept. 12, 1992.

Dougherty, Mike, "Knicks Notebook: Practice Not Perfect," *The* (White Plains, NY) *Journal News*, Jan. 22, 1999.

Dulac, Gerry, "Ward's tired arm doesn't worry Bowden," *Pittsburgh Post-*Gazette, Jan. 1, 1994.

Ellis, Steve, "Bowden gives Ward go-ahead for basketball," *Tallahassee* (FL) *Democrat*, Oct. 12, 1990.

Ellis, Steve, "FSU recruit Ward won't enroll in '88," *The Palm Beach Post*, June 28, 1988.

Ellis, Steve, "FSU's last chance to get Metro glory," *Tallahassee* (FL) *Democrat*, March 7, 1991.

Ellis, Steve, "Heisman, hands down," *Tallahassee* (FL) *Democrat*, Dec. 12, 1993.

Ellis, Steve, "'Pass to Dunn was huge, but so many plays were,'" *Tallahassee* (FL) *Democrat*, Dec. 12, 1993.

Ellis, Steve, "Seminole basketball gets strong," *Tallahassee* (FL) *Democrat*, Dec. 14, 1990.

Ellis, Steve, "Seminoles defense falls flat," *The Palm Beach Post*, Sept. 10, 1989.

Ellis, Steve, "Seminoles showed impressive aggression against Eagles," *Tallahassee* (FL) *Democrat*, Sept. 17, 1990.

Ellis, Steve, "Ward's ready to take a shot," *Tallahassee* (FL) *Democrat*, Nov. 27, 1990.

Enriquez, Paul, "Ward debuts with 5 TDs, 5 turnovers as FSU QB," *Florida TODAY*, Sept. 6, 1992.

Ensley, Gerald, "McDuffie's Vision," *Tallahassee* (FL) *Democrat*, Dec. 12, 1993.

"Fans: Ward should stick with career in football," *Pensacola* (FL) *News Journal*, April 24, 1994.

Ferrante, Bob, "FSU hoops continues tradition with Boyd fund-raiser," 247Sports, https://floridastate.247sports.com/Bolt/FSU-hoops-continues-tradition-with-Boyd-fund-raiser-40924996.

Figueroa, Steve, "Versatile Ward may be Georgia squad's best hope," *Orlando Sentinel*, June 12, 1988.

"Fla. State confident despite skid," Associated Press, March 18, 1993.

"Florida State holds off Brazilian national team," *St. Petersburg* (FL) *Times*, Nov. 20, 1990.

"Florida State Men's Basketball – 1990-91 Year In Review," NoleFan.Org, http://www.nolefan.org/summary/b1991.html.

"Fla. St.-Georgia Tech: 'Battle of Thomasville QBs,'" Associated Press, Oct. 17, 1992.

"Florida St.'s Ward set to hit hospital ward," *The Tennessean*, March 28, 1993.

"Florida St. takes shot at Kentucky," *Florida TODAY*, March 27, 1993.

"FOOTBALL: Down the Field, Up the Court: Ward Is a Leader for 2 Teams," *The New York Times*, Nov. 28, 1992.

Freedman, Samuel G. *Breaking the Line: The Season in Black College Football That Transformed the Sport and Changed the Course of Civil Rights* (New York: Simon & Schuster, 2014).

George, Dave, "Ward, Seminoles on ACCelerated program," *The Palm Beach Post*, Sept. 20, 1992.

"Georgia Tech Hall of Fame Class Announced," Georgia Tech Athletics News, Aug. 8, 2003, http://www.ramblinwreck.com/genrel//080503aaa.html.

Goldberg, Jeff, "Knicks Like Sound Of It," *Hartford Courant*, May 15, 2000.

Hambleton, Ken, "Media go gaga for orange peels," *Lincoln* (NB) *Journal Star*, Dec. 30 1993.

Hambrick-Stowe, Thomas, "Jamming the Jews," *Religion in the News*, Summer 2001, http://www.trincoll.edu/depts/csrpl/RINVol4No2/jamming_jews.htm

Harig, Bob, "Buzzer-beaters: Seminoles, Gators prevail," *St. Petersburg* (FL) *Times*, Jan. 10, 1993.

Harig, Bob, "Florida is a lone star state," *St. Petersburg* (FL) *Times*, Nov. 28, 1990.

Harig, Bob, "'I knew I would play one day,'" *St. Petersburg* (FL) *Times*, Aug. 23, 1992.

Harig, Bob, "Ward proves his versatility," *St. Petersburg* (FL) *Times*, Dec. 16, 1991.

Heyman, Brian, "Ward to wear No. 21 for Knicks," *The* (White Plains, NY) *Journal News*, July 8, 1994.

Howard, Johnette, "Sam I Am with Teammates, Foes and Refs/Houston Rocket Point Guard Sam Cassell Likes to Talk the Talk – and He's Happy to Back It Up Come Crunch Times," *Sports Illustrated*, Nov. 13, 1995.

Hyde, Dave, "Performance against UM a Ward winner," (South Florida) *Sun Sentinel*, Oct. 10, 1993.

Isola, Frank, "Knicks' Ward may move for a commitment," (New York) *Daily News*, Jan. 21, 1999.

Isola, Frank, "Ward's the Man about the House," (New York) *Daily News*, Dec. 25, 1998.

"I think Charlie Ward should …" *Tallahassee* (FL) *Democrat*, May 29, 1994.

"It's Charlie Ward's award," (Rochester, NY) *Democrat and Chronicle*, Dec. 10, 1993.

Jacobs, Jeff, "For Once, Crowd On His Side," *Hartford Courant*, May 15, 2000.

"Jake Gaither Loves Violence," Associated Press, Nov. 13, 1969.

Kallestad, Brent, "NFL teams pass on Heisman winner," Associated Press, July 22, 1987.

Kallestad, Brent, "Ward—Man for all seasons," Associated Press, March 7, 1992.

Kennedy, Pat, "Ward can play in NBA, with full commitment," *Orlando Sentinel*, April 24, 1994.

Kilcullen, Matt, "The matchups," *Orlando Sentinel*, March 25, 1993.

"Knicks hire Don Nelson," Associated Press, July 7, 1995.

Lamar, Jim, "Ward's 'Elway drive' gets FSU a victory," *Tallahassee* (FL) *Democrat*, Sept. 13, 1992.

Lamar, Jim, "Ward's presence has stabilizing effect on FSU," *Tallahassee* (FL) *Democrat*, March 20, 1993.

"Land of Basketball (website)," http://www.landofbasketball.com/.

Lane, Woody E., "Coach Nelson calls Ward 'pleasant surprise' of camp," Associated Press, Oct. 15, 1995.

Lawlor, Frank, "The playoffs' focus on brawn may have teams thinking big," *The Philadelphia Inquirer*, June 12, 1994.

Lee, William, "Charlie Ward: The New York Knicks' Heisman Trophy Winner, Daily Knicks, https://dailyknicks.com/2015/02/01/charlie-ward-new-york-knicks-heisman-trophy-winner/.

Markus, Don, "College QBs are majoring in versatility," *The Baltimore Sun*, Oct. 6, 1993.

Markus, Don, "Seminoles' Ward gains an often elusive dream," *The Baltimore Sun*, Jan. 2, 1994.

Markus, Don, "Ward's backup gets lofty passing grade, too," *The Baltimore* Sun, Dec. 31, 1993.

"Memorial Stadium – Death Valley," ClemsonTigers.com, http://www.clemsontigers.com/ViewArticle.dbml?DB_OEM_ID=28500&ATCLID=205504990.

Mizell, Hubert, "Spurrier saves ace for 'Bama," *St. Petersburg* (FL) *Times*, Nov. 29, 1992.

Moffett, Dan, "Ward's only regret: The last play," *The Palm Beach Post*, Nov. 14, 1993.

Moffson, Steven, "Equalization Schools in Georgia's African-American Communities, 1951-1970," Historic Preservation Division/Georgia Department of Natural Resources, Sept. 20, 2010, http://georgiashpo.org/sites/default/files/hpd/pdf/Equalization_Schools_in_Georgia_0.pdf

Murphy, Melissa, "Charlie Ward to Show Tennis Skills to Honor Arthur Ashe," The Associated Press, Aug. 27, 1994.

"NFL History – Super Bowl Winners," ESPN, http://www.espn.com/nfl/superbowl/history/winners.

Nobles, Charlie, "BASKETBALL: That's Just the Way the Ball Bounces," *The New York Times*, June 27, 1994.

Nogowski, John, "Take your improving game to the NBA," *Tallahassee* (FL) *Democrat*, April 10, 1994.

Nogowski, John, "Teams turn out for good look at Mr. Heisman," *Tallahassee* (FL) *Democrat*, April 7, 1994.

"'Noles pulverize Clemson, 57-0," Associated Press, Sept. 12, 1993.

"Orange Bowl: Nebraska vs. Florida State," (South Florida) *Sun-Sentinel*, Jan. 1, 1994.

Page, Rodney, "FSU falls in exhibition minus Douglas, Dobard," *Orlando Sentinel*, Nov. 15, 1990.

Pearlman, Jeff. *Gunslinger: The Remarkable, Improbable, Iconic Life of Brett Favre* (Boston: Houghton Mifflin Harcourt), 2016.

Plaschke, Bill, "Sorry Charlie: NFL Snubs Ward," *Los Angeles Times* (Washington Edition), April 26, 1994.

"PRO BASKETBALL: Ward and Williams Get Their Rookie Due," *The New York Times*, July 14, 1994.

Pruneda, Maria, "Charlie's Angles," *The Jackson* (TN) *Sun*, April 11, 1994.

Pucin, Diane, "Ward, Florida St. Thinking Touchdowns, Not Turnovers," *The Philadelphia Inquirer*, Oct. 3, 1992.

"Reserve duo leads victory," Associated Press, Nov. 4, 1995.

Roberts, Jeannie, "No. 2 Thomasville beats No. 1 Central," *Tallahassee* (FL) *Democrat*, Oct. 17, 1987.

Roberts, Selena, "Magic like what Ward can offer," *Orlando Sentinel*, June 25, 1994.

Romano, John, "Ward proves too much for UF," *St. Petersburg* (FL) *Times*, Nov. 29, 1992.

Schmadtke, Alan, "As usual, FSU plans to humble a legend," *Orlando Sentinel*, Nov. 13, 1993.

Schmadtke, Alan, "Title gone, pride left," *Orlando Sentinel*, Jan. 1, 1993.

Schmadtke, Alan, "Ward wows scouts," *Orlando Sentinel*, April 7, 1994.

Schmitz, Brian, "Ward surprises Aces, ignites 'Noles with 3s," *Orlando Sentinel*, March 19, 1993.

"Seminoles leave Metro in style," Associated Press, March 10, 1991.

"Seminoles shock No. 5 North Carolina 86-74," Associated Press, Dec. 16, 1991.

Simmons, David Lee, "Charlie and His Big Decision," *Tallahassee* (FL) *Democrat*, April 10, 1994.

Simmons, David Lee, "FSU basketball hoping Ward is answer to its ills," *Tallahasse*e (FL) *Democrat*, Jan. 16, 1994.

Simmons, David Lee, "Kennedy hopes Seminoles get a boost from Ward's return," *Tallahassee* (FL) *Democrat*, Jan. 10, 1994.

"Sinkola Plantation Quail Hunting," Sinkola Plantation, Thomasville, Georgia, http://sinkola.com/Welcome.html.

Smith, Timothy W., "On Pro Football: Ward Gets the Big Snub But Not Without Issue," *The New York* Times, May 2, 1994.

Snook, Jeff, "Hurricanes-Seminoles: Just another classic," *The Palm Beach Post*, Oct. 28, 1989.

Snook, Jeff, "Improved defense key for Seminoles success," *The Palm Beach Post*, Sept. 10, 1990.

Talbott, Chris, "Boyd fills void in FSU's backcourt; Kennedy guard against inexperience," *The Palm Beach Post*, Nov. 22, 1990.

Tatum, Kevin, and Tim Panaccio, "As a QB, Can Charlie Ward be courted?" *The Philadelphia Inquirer*, June 16, 1996.

Temkin, Barry, and Linda Young, "Prop 48 Gets Mixed Reviews/Athletes Paying More Attention," *Chicago Tribune*, Oct. 19, 1990.

"The Buzz: Heisman news and views," Heisman Trust, http://heisman.com/index.aspx.

Thompson, Clint, "Central Football Heroes," *Thomasville* (NC) *Times-Enterprise*, Dec. 9, 2005.

Thompson, Clint, "Rainge keeps scaling major hurdles," *Thomasville* (NC) *Times-Enterprise*, Dec. 9, 2005.

Tolley, Scott, "Big win should keep FSU No. 2," *The Palm Beach Post*, Nov. 20, 1993.

Tolley, Scott, "Bowden's nightmare: FSU a 14-point favorite over UM," *The Palm Beach Post*, Oct. 4, 1993.

Tolley, Scott, "Florida State QB still elusive on plans," *The Palm Beach Post*, Dec. 12 1993.

"Turral's career at FSU over; UM loses starter for season," *St. Petersburg* (FL) *Times*, Aug. 20, 1991.

Vilona, Bill, "Basketball should be Ward's sport," *Pensacola* (FL) *News Journal*, April 24, 1994.

Vilona, Bill, "Bowden: FSU has arrived," *Pensacola* (FL) *News Journal*, Jan. 2, 1993.

Vilona, Bill, "Bowden shows offense not set in its old ways," *Florida TODAY*, Sept. 13, 1992.

Vilona, Bill, "Draft day no big deal for Heisman winner Ward," *Pensacola* (FL) *News Journal*, April 24, 1994.

Vilona Bill, "Florida State tips W. Kentucky," *Pensacol*a (FL) *News Journal*, March 26, 1993.

Vilona, Bill, "FSU deposes Duke 89-88," *Florida TODAY*, Jan. 25, 1993.

Vilona, Bill, "FSU earns victory despite sloppy play," *Florida TODAY*, Sept. 13, 1992.

Vilona, Bill, "Kannell comes on strong at FSU," *Pensacola* (FL) *News Journal*, Sept. 6, 1992.

Vilona, Bill, "QB Ward survives Nebraska's big hits," *Pensacola* (FL) *News Journal*, Jan. 2, 1993.

Vilona, Bill, "Seminoles gain confidence as Duke stumbles," *Pensacola* (FL) *News Journal*, Jan. 24, 1993.

Vilona, Bill, "Seminoles wants to leave Metro as tourney champs," *Pensacola* (FL) *News Journal*, March 7, 1991.

Vilona, Bill, "Talk of Thomasville," *Pensacola* (FL) *News Journal*, Dec. 8, 1993.

Vilona, Bill, "Virginia wards off FSU 80-76," *Florida TODAY*, Jan. 7, 1993.

Vilona, Bill, "Ward not phased by 2-sport stardom," *Pensacola* (FL) *News Journal*, Aug. 16, 1992.

Vilona, Bill, "Ward part of FSU's quarterback corps," *Florida TODAY*, Sept. 2, 1990.

Vilona, Bill, "Youth rivals find bigger playground," *Florida TODAY*, Oct. 17, 1992.

"Ward ready to play hoops," Associated Press, Jan. 14, 1994.

Watz, Don, "Thomasville Central extracts its revenge on Thomasville," *Tallahassee* (FL) *Democrat*, Nov. 28, 1987.

"Wayne McDuffie Bio," Florida State University, http://seminoles.com/wayne-mcduffie-bio/.

"Weather History for KTLH – August, 1990," Weather Underground, https://www.wunderground.com/history/airport/KTLH/1990/8/29/WeeklyHistory.html?req_city=&req_state=&req_statename=&reqdb.zip=&reqdb.magic=&reqdb.wmo=.

"WEDDINGS: Tonja F. Harding, Charlie Ward Jr.," *The New York Times*, Aug. 27, 1995.

"Wells' 3-pointer lifts Seminoles over Duke," Associated Press, Jan. 25, 1993.

"Where Are They Now? – Charlie Ward," NBA.com, http://www.nba.com/knicks/history/watnward.html.

White, Brian, "Florida State shows mettle under pressure," *Florida TODAY*, Sept. 13, 1992.

Wise, Mike. *Just Ballin': The Chaotic Rise of the New York Knicks* (New York: Simon & Schuster, 1999).

Wojciechowski, Gene, "His Empire Is Crumbling: Suddenly, Louisville's Coach Can't Win at Anything, Including Basketball Games," *Los Angeles Times*, Feb. 5, 1991.

Young, Bob, "Rudy T just a little superstitious for title game," *The Arizona Republic*, June 22, 1994.

Young, Randy, "Offering heart felt feelings," *Thomasville* (NC) *Times-Enterprise*, June 29, 2016. http://www.ramblinwreck.com/genrel//080503aaa.html

Thomasville – Thomas County Sports Hall of Fame Bio for Charlie Ward Jr.

Affectionately known to many in Thomas County as "Junior", he could be unequivocally the finest, most multi-talented athlete to ever have participated in sports activities in Thomas County. His list of them: At FSU in his senior year he set 19 school and 7 ACC records, won the Heisman Trophy (largest margin ever), All ACC, All American and the Davey O'Brien Award. He was undrafted by the NFL and became a 1st round draft pick of the New York Knicks of the NBA. He helped the Knicks reach the playoffs 6 straight years from 1996 to 2001. He played 11 seasons in the NBA with New York, San Antonio, and Houston. Then served 2 years as assistant coach of the Houston Rockets. In 2006, he was elected to the College Football Hall of Fame. In 2009, he was inducted in to the Orange Bowl Hall of Fame. In 2011, he was selected as the John Wooden Keys to Life Award Winner.

Through the years, "Junior" has underwritten countless Christian basketball camps, enlisted guest speakers at Bible studies, and has spoken at numerous Christian centered events in many areas of the country. Athletically and spiritually there has never been a finer role model to come from Thomas County, Georgia.

College Football Hall of Fame Member Bio for Charlie Ward Jr.

A truly amazing athlete, Charlie Ward is one of the finest all-around performers in the Hall of Fame roster. In his freshman season, Ward played little quarterback, as he was the Florida State punter. He then sat out the 1990 season while he became the starting point guard on the FSU basketball team. As a sophomore, he was still experiencing more success on the basketball court. As a quarterback he only attempted nine passes and his athletic skills were even used at wide receiver.

In 1992, Ward finally received an opportunity at quarterback. He led the Seminoles to an ACC title, Orange Bowl win and was named as the Conference Player of the Year. He became a second team All-America, was a finalist for the O'Brien Award, and finished sixth in the Heisman voting. His senior year saw Ward lead FSU to its first national championship as he captured the Heisman Trophy and the Maxwell, Camp and O'Brien awards. At the time, his victory margin in the Heisman vote was the largest ever.

In that 1993 season he threw 27 scoring passes with only four being intercepted. While highly desired by the pros, he cast his lot with basketball enjoying an 11season career in the National Basketball Association. Ward was such a complete athlete that he was also drafted in the major league baseball draft even though he did not play college baseball. While at FSU he served as student body vice president.

Charlie Ward Career Statistics

Florida State Football

Position: Punter and Quarterback

Passing

						Passing Categories					
Year	University	Conf	Pos	G	Cmp	Att	Pct	Yds	TD	Int	Rate
1989	Florida State	In.	P	11	0	5	0.0	0	0	1	-40.0
1991	Florida State	In.	QB	12	5	9	55.6	68	0	0	119.0
1992	Florida State	ACC	QB	11	204	365	55.9	2647	22	17	127.4
1993	Florida State	ACC	QB	11	264	380	69.5	3032	27	4	157.8
Career	Florida State				473	759	62.3	5747	49	22	141.4

Rushing and Receiving

					Rushing				Receiving				Scrimmage			
Year	University	Conf	Pos	G	Att	Yds	Avg	TD	Rec	Yds	Avg	TD	Plays	Yds	Avg	TD
1989	Florida State	In.	P	11	2	21	10.5	0					2	21	10.5	0
1991	Florida State	In.	QB	12	5	25	5.0	0					5	25	5.0	0
1992	Florida State	ACC	QB	11	100	504	5.0	6					100	504	5.0	6
1993	Florida State	ACC	QB	11	65	339	5.2	4	1	10	10.0	0	66	349	5.3	4
Career	Florida State				172	889	5.2	10	1	10	10.0	0	173	899	5.2	10

Punting

						Punting		
Year	University	Conf	Class	Pos	G	Punts	Yds	Avg
1989	Florida State	In.		P	11	35	1297	37.1
1991	Florida State	In.		QB	12			
1992	Florida State	ACC		QB	11			
1993	Florida State	ACC		QB	11			
Career	Florida State					35	1297	37.1

Heisman Year Statistics

Charlie Ward's Heisman Year Statistics

Date	Opponent	Result	Att	Comp	Pct.	Yards	YPA	TD	Int	Rating	Rushes	Yards	YPC	TD	Plays	Total Off	YPP	Total TDs
8/28/93	+Kansas	W 42-0	26	16	61.5	194	7.46	0	0	124.22	4	0	0.00	0	30	194	6.46	0
9/4/93	at Duke	W 45-7	31	22	70.9	272	8.77	2	0	165.96	5	41	8.20	1	36	313	8.69	3
9/11/93	#23 Clemson	W 57-0	33	25	75.7	317	9.60	4	0	196.45	4	32	8.00	0	37	349	9.43	4
9/18/93	at #19 N. Carolina	W 33-7	41	27	65.8	303	7.39	2	1	139.15	5	69	13.80	0	46	372	8.08	2
10/2/93	Georgia Tech	W 51-0	28	21	75.0	222	7.92	4	0	188.74	8	36	4.50	0	36	258	7.16	4
10/9/93	#15 Miami (Fla.)	W 28-10	31	21	67.7	256	8.25	1	0	147.75	8	17	2.10	1	39	273	7.00	2
10/16/93	Virginia	W 40-14	31	23	74.1	322	10.38	3	0	193.38	5	38	7.60	1	36	360	10.00	4
10/30/93	Wake Forest	W 54-0	20	13	65.0	125	6.25	0	0	117.50	4	9	2.50	0	24	134	5.58	0
11/6/93	at Maryland (DNP)	W 49-20	--	--	--	--	--	--	--	--	--	--	--	--	--	--	--	--
11/13/93	at #2 Notre Dame	L 24-31	50	31	62.0	297	5.94	3	1	127.70	11	38	3.50	0	61	335	5.48	3^
11/20/93	North Carolina St.	W 62-3	36	27	75.0	278	7.72	4	0	176.53	5	30	6.00	1	41	308	7.51	5
11/27/93	at #5 Florida	W 33-21	53	38	71.6	446	8.41	4	2	159.74	6	29	4.83	0	59	475	8.05	4
Heisman Stats	**AP #1, Coaches #3**	**11-1**	**380**	**264**	**69.4**	**3032**	**7.97**	**27**	**4**	**157.84**	**65**	**339**	**5.20**	**4**	**445**	**3371**	**7.57**	**31**
01/01/94	+ #3 Nebraska	W 18-16	43	24	55.8	286	6.65	0	0	111.68	8	-3	-3.75	0	51	283	5.54	0
Totals	**12-1 (#1 in both polls)**		**423**	**288**	**68.0**	**3318**	**7.84**	**27**	**4**	**153.15**	**73**	**336**	**4.60**	**4**	**496**	**3654**	**7.36**	**31**

+ - Neutral Site

* -- Ward was injured late in the first half against Wake Forest and sat out the next week at Maryland.

^ -- Ward caught 1 pass for 10 yards against Notre Dame.

Florida State Basketball
Per Game Statistics

Season	School	Conf	G	MP	FG%	3P%	FT%	TRB	AST	STL	BLK	PTS
1990-91	FSU	Metro	30	23.8	.455	.313	.713	3.0	3.4	2.4	0.3	8.0
1991-92	FSU	ACC	28	30.0	.497	.458	.530	3.2	4.4	2.7	0.2	7.2
1992-93	FSU	ACC	17	32.8	.462	.320	.667	2.6	5.5	2.8	0.3	7.8
1993-94	FSU	ACC	16	35.9	.365	.253	.625	3.9	4.9	2.8	0.1	10.5
Career	FSU		91	29.5	.441	.323	.636	3.1	4.4	2.6	0.2	8.1

NBA Career Per Game Statistics

Season	Team	Games	Rebounds	Assists	Steals	Blocks	Points
1994-95	Knicks	10	0.6	0.4	0.2	0.0	1.6
1995-96	Knicks	62	1.6	2.1	0.9	0.1	3.9
1996-97	Knicks	79	2.8	4.1	1.1	0.2	5.2
1997-98	Knicks	82	3.3	5.7	1.8	0.5	7.8
1998-99	Knicks	50	3.4	5.4	2.1	0.2	7.6
1999-00	Knicks	72	3.2	4.2	1.3	0.2	7.3
2000-01	Knicks	61	2.6	4.5	1.1	0.2	7.1
2001-02	Knicks	63	2.0	3.2	1.1	0.2	5.2
2002-03	Knicks	66	2.7	4.6	1.2	0.2	7.2
2003-04	Total	71	2.0	3.0	0.9	0.2	6.0
2003-04	Knicks	35	2.7	4.9	1.3	0.2	8.7
2003-04	Spurs	36	1.3	1.3	0.5	0.1	3.3
2004-05	Rockets	14	2.8	3.1	1.1	0.0	5.4
	Career:	630	2.6	4.0	1.2	0.2	6.3

NBA Playoffs Per Game Statistics

Playoffs	Team	Games	Rebounds	Assists	Steals	Points
1996	Knicks	7	1.3	2.4	1.6	4.6
1997	Knicks	9	2.8	4.3	1.4	2.2
1998	Knicks	10	2.8	6.0	2.0	6.6
1999	Knicks	20	2.3	3.8	1.8	4.6
2000	Knicks	16	4.3	4.1	1.4	9.4
2001	Knicks	5	1.4	1.4	0.4	5.0
2004	Spurs	5	0.0	0.2	0.4	2.2
	Career:	72	2.5	3.7	1.5	5.5

Other Books By Jon Finkel

"Mean" Joe Greene: Built By Football
w/ 4x Super Bowl Champion and Hall of Famer "Mean" Joe Greene

Forces of Character: Conversations About Building a Life of Impact
w/ 3x Super Bowl Champion and Fighter Pilot Chad Hennings

Jocks-in-Chief
From Football Stars and Brawlers, to Feats of Strength and Iron Butt, A Complete Ranking of the Most Athletic Presidents of the United States

The Dadvantage
Stay in Shape on No Sleep, with No Time and No Equipment

Heart Over Height
w/ 3x NBA Slam Dunk Champion Nate Robinson

The Three Dollar Scholar
Awesome Advice for Acing Life's Major Decisions and Mindless Debates

For author information and speaking availability, visit:

www.jonfinkel.com

CPSIA information can be obtained
at www.ICGtesting.com
Printed in the USA
LVOW07*2158261217
560848LV00002B/8/P

9 780998 627328